ANNALS

OF

Witchcraft in New England,

AND ELSEWHERE IN

THE UNITED STATES,

FROM THEIR FIRST SETTLEMENT.

DRAWN UP FROM UNPUBLISHED AND OTHER WELL AUTHENTICATED
RECORDS OF THE ALLEGED OPERATIONS OF WITCHES AND
THEIR INSTIGATOR, THE DEVIL.

By SAMUEL G. DRAKE.

Benjamin Blom
New York

First Published Boston 1869
Reissued 1967 by
Benjamin Blom, Inc. N.Y. 10452
Library of Congress Catalogue Card No. 67-13327

Woodward's
Historical Series.
No. VIII.

John Wentworth

TO THE

HON. JOHN WENTWORTH, LL. D.,

OF CHICAGO,

ONE OF THE VICE-PRESIDENTS OF THE NEW ENGLAND HISTORIC-
GENEALOGICAL SOCIETY,

This Book is Dedicated

AS AN ACKNOWLEDGMENT OF HIS VALUABLE SERVICES
IN THE CAUSE OF RESCUING MATERIALS FOR
THE HISTORY OF THE FOUNDERS
OF NEW ENGLAND,

BY THE

AUTHOR.

PREFACE.

THIS is the first Attempt, so far as is known to the Writer, to collect together the Annals of Witchcraft in this Country. Like all first Attempts in an untrodden Path of History, this may fall short of Expectation in several respects. Those who look for a Succession of Tales of Horrour of the most terrible Kind may be disappointed, while others will rejoice that there are no more of them, and may be satisfied that the Tragedies are interspersed here and there by Comedies.

It has doubtless been a Question with all Readers of Accounts of the Witchcraft Cases which have occurred in this Country, how it happened that they were so similar to those which took place in England. The Question is easily answered; in other Words the Similarity is easily accounted for. Witchcraft was itself imported by those who first practised it here, and was perpetuated by the Importers and their immediate Descendants.

Books on Magick, Sorcery and Witchcraft were brought to this Country by the early Settlers. These were studied, and their Contents enlarged upon according to the Powers of the Imagination of those who were ambitious to appear wiser than their Neighbours.

So much Prominence has been given to what is called the *Salem Witchcraft,* that what had occurred in the Country before and since 1692 is, and has been, overlooked or almost entirely lost sight of. It will be seen by the following Work that it was a Part of the social Life of the People, and to them of the greatest Importance through all the earlier Periods of their History from the Promulgation of their Laws to the year 1700. The Question arises naturally, Why has the Subject of Witchcraft been passed over so lightly by the general, and almost entirely by the local Historian? It can hardly be supposed that they purposely omit those Details with a Belief that they will be forgotten, and the Reproach they occasion with them.

Preface.

This would be a short sighted Decision indeed. But the Affair at Salem has not been omitted. That has been a Peg on which to hang Reproaches against New England, early and late; as though it were the Corner-stone of all the Troubles of the Kind which ever happened in the Land. No Attempt will be made in Defence of that terrible Delusion, nor of those concerned in it; as that would be to defend a debasing Ignorance, the Progenitor of the more debasing Superstition.

It cannot but be acknowledged that those in Authority at that Day were men "fearing God," conscientious to the last Degree, and therefore felt themselves compelled to obey the solemn Injunction "not to suffer a Witch to live." Their Consciences would allow them no Alternative but to obey that Command; not entirely upon the Evidence of their own Senses but always with the Decision of twelve of the best Citizens of the Community where the Cases occurred.

If those who are so free with their Denunciations of the Proceedings of 1692 will reflect, they will find themselves in a Dilemma of this Sort: with Believers in the Injunctions of the Bible, or Disbelievers in them. The former obeyed those Injunctions, the latter evaded or disbelieved them.

The Inference is too apparent to need further Attention.

The following Annals have been derived from Materials widely scattered. I have thought for a long Period that such a Work should be composed, because there is, and doubtless always will be, a Desire to know what could be found upon the Subject, that might be relied upon as authentick. As to this latter Particular, it may be proper to state, that I have admitted Nothing into these Pages not well authenticated by Documents, and generally of the Time of the Occurrences.

It was my Fortune many Years ago, to come into Possession of a great Amount of original Papers, on a large Number of historical Subjects. Among them were many upon the Subject of Witchcraft, and Witch Trials. From these a very important and considerable Portion of the ensuing Volume has been composed.

It would seem from many Circumstances that the early Emigrants to New England were familiar with Books on Witchcraft, and doubtless some of them brought Works on that Subject with them; yet the Scarcity of all Kinds of Books and their high Prices at that Period in England would seem hardly to allow of their being common. A Catalogue of such Works as were extant at that Time would be one of very great Interest, but it would be too extensive for this Preface. References to many will be found in the Introduction to the *Witchcraft Delusion* published in 1866. The Work of the Rev. William Perkins, entitled the *Damned Art of Witchcraft*, Dr. Cotton Mather's *Memorable Providences relating to Witchcraft* (1689), Dr. Increase Mather's *Remarkable Providences* (1684), Mr. Richard Baxter's *Certainty of the World of Spirits* (1691), and a *Trial of Witches*, before Sir Matthew Hale (1661), were perhaps the Works the best known to the People of New England at the Time of the Salem Tragedies. As the Work of Hale (written in March, 1661), was of the first Authority in England, and referred to here with unbounded Confidence, a brief Extract from it may be of Interest in this Connection: He says, "That there are such evil Angels [as Witches] it is without all Question. The Old Testament assures us of it, as it easily appears upon the Consideration of the Temptation of our first Parents; the History of Abimeleck and the men of Shechem; the History of Saul and the Witch of Endor; the History of Micaiah and the false Prophets; the History of Job; the Prophecy of the Defolation of Babylon, wherein the Satyrs were to inhabit. The New Teftament more explicitly and more abundantly clears it, by the Hiftory of the Temptation of our Lord; the Demoniacks of feveral Symptoms cured by our Lord and his Apoftles; the Proceffion of the Evil Spirit, and his Return with feven other Spirits; the Vifion of the Fall of Satan from Heaven like Lightning by our Saviour; the feveral Affertings of it in the Gofpel and Apoftolical Epiftles; the Prince of the Power of the Air. It is alfo confirmed to us by daily Experience of the Power and Energy of thefe Evil Spirits in Witches, and by them." This, and a great Deal more was written by the Lord Chief Juftice after he had prefided at certain Witch Trials, in Purfuance of which Divers had fuffered Death. The Subftance of thofe Trials may be seen in *The Wonders of the Invifible World* as introductory to and Authority for thofe at Salem.[1] And as a further Bulwark againft the Sadducees of that Generation, the Doctor adds: "The Venerable Baxter very truly fays, Judge Hale was a Perfon, than whom, no Man was more backward to condemn a Witch, without full Evidence."

---

[1] See *The Witchcraft Delufion in New England*, I, 141-151.

Preface. xiii

The Work of Judge Hale above referred to would make a very suitable Chapter in the *Magnalia;* for his Relations of bewitched Persons are as astonishing as any contained in that wonderful Book; and their Reporter as implicitly believed them as did Dr. Mather those which he recorded. That Judge was more regarded in New England than any other as Authority, because of his great Piety and Purity of Character; and while these Qualities are not denied him in this Age, his Weakness, Credulity and Stupidity are quite as apparent.

I will notice a few other Works in this Place upon the Subject of Witchcraft.

As late as 1715, a Work in two handsome Volumes was published by well known Booksellers in London, entitled *A Compleat History of Magick, Sorcery and Witchcraft*. These Volumes were in the duodecimo Form, and contained above five hundred Pages, close Print. From the Contents one would hardly be led to suppose that the Reality of Witchcraft had to that Time ever been questioned by Anybody, except Infidels. It embraces all of those numerous Trials and Executions in England with the same Complacency and Satisfaction as Dr. Cotton Mather detailed those of New England in his *Wonders of the Invisible World.* In fact, it embraces an Abstract of that Work also. These Volumes were printed for E. Curll, at the Sign of the Dial and Bible, J. Pemberton, at the Sign of the Buck and Sun, opposite St. Dunstan's Church in Fleet Street; and W. Taylor, at the Ship in Pater-Noster-Row; and whoever has recently visited Fleet Street might have seen the beautifully symmetrical old Dunstan, founded some 760 Years ago, upon which Curll and Pemberton daily looked, and which is likely long to remain for others to look upon, there being no Back-Bay in London into which to send the Churches of that ancient City.[1]

There were not many Works written, or if written were not published, exposing the Belief in Witchcraft, until a comparatively late Period of the Delusion. There were two Reasons for this. One was there were comparatively few who did not believe in it, and the other was the Daner of losing their Standing in Society, and being exposed to Persecutions of every Kind.

---

[1] The Writer has no Objection to urge against the People of Boston for wishing to have all their Churches on the lately filled Quagmire. If they desire to remove their Churches there, and to go and live there themselves to get away from their less opulent Neighbours we recommend those Neighbours to allow them to enjoy their Solitude.

Preface. xv

I have shown in the Introduction to *The Witch-craft Delusion* that there was one Man in England who successfully battled against it, while at the same Time he believed in it, or pretended to believe in it, as the only Course then safe to be taken. This was Sir Robert Filmer. He preceded Mr. Calef, but Mr. Calef does not seem to have been aware that such a Champion was in the field. Cotemporary with Filmer was JOHN BRINLEY, GENT, who published a Work with this Title, *A Discovery of the Impostures of Witches and Astrologers*, London, Printed for John Wright, at the Crown on Ludgate-Hill, and sold by Edward Milward, Bookseller, in Leitchfield, 1680. This is a small 16mo of 127 Pages, dedicated to Sir Brian Broughton of Broughton, Baronet, dated Brockton in the County of Stafford, Nov. 7th, 1679.[1] Like Filmer, Brinley believed or pretended to believe in Witchcraft. His first Chapter opens thus: "An Owl, an Hare, and an Old-woman, was anciently the Emblem of Superstition; and truly if we shall diligently search into the Causes of this Error, we shall find that Ignorance, and Dotage, vain Hopes, and foolish Fears, ground-

---

[1] The only Copy of this curious Book known to me belongs to my Friend GEORGE BRINLEY, ESQ., of Hartford.

less Expectations, and casual Events have been the Springs from whence this Folly proceeds, which is the Mother of all these Omens and Prognostications."

This is a good Common Sense Opening to his Work. I will in the next and last Place give an Example of the opposite Sort. His fourth Chapter is thus headed: "That Devils may do Mischief to Man or Beast, without any Association with Witch or Wizard." He then goes on: "Though we do not deny, but shall hereafter prove, that there are Witches, and Necromancers, and such Persons as make wicked Contracts with the Devil, to the Ruin of their own Souls, and the Prejudice of others; yet it is most certain, that the Devil often does much Evil of himself (by God's Permission) without any Association with any of his forementioned Instruments." It is unnecessary to extract further from this Author, for his Attributes of the Devil do not differ materially from what is laid down by Dr. Mather; both of which it may be said have "whipped the Devil round the Stump," quite sufficiently.

A

PRELIMINARY DISSERTATION

UPON

Matters connected with Witchcraft.

As the Mifts clear up from the Mountains, fo is Ignorance, the Parent of Superftition, forced from its benighted Places. In the one Cafe the Mifts of the Valleys loofe their Hold as Cultivation advances; hence they efcape to the neighbouring Elevations, and even there are forced gradually to recede, and fo by Degrees finally difappear. But the Mifts of Superftition, hanging over the human Family, have not yet been entirely difperfed by the Sun of Education and the unerring Teachings of fcientifick Difcoveries.

That Superftition oppreffes the World at large, even to this Day, cannot be difputed, and the Profpect appears fmall that it will ever be otherwife. While it is true that, in remote and thinly fettled Regions its Reign is more fupreme than in compact and cultivated Communities, it is equally true that it has a Hold here, not a little furprifing to those accustomed to contemplate, and allow themselves to view Mankind as they are. There is Antagonism between Reason and Superstition; a Warfare which has continued for Ages. And it must be conceded that, upon the whole, the Victory is still with the latter. Science and its true Votaries repose with their Armour on, have gained the Victory for themselves, thrown up their limited Breastworks, and said to their Enemy on the mountain Slopes, "We have no Intention to dislodge you. We know you are numerous and a great Power in the World. We will uphold your Supremacy, allow your Flag to be flaunted over us and in our Faces even; but we have the Satisfaction of knowing your Pretensions are false, and that your Empire must come to an End."

It is thus that an Empire founded in Intolerance, is submitted to by its less powerful Neighbour, under the false Conclusion that its Assumptions and Superstitions are necessary Evils; and therefore while knowing their Rights dare not maintain them; because those Rights are declared unpopular, and subversive of established Customs—Customs founded in, what now must appear to all who think without Prejudice, a most transparent System of Deception.

The unexampled Efforts to hold the World in Ignorance, and the vast Amounts of Treasure expended to propagate and maintain false Opinions, may safely be said, to be sufficient to have, ere this, educated the enslaved Millions past and present, in Truths of the first Importance to the Stability of Nations, and the Peace and Happiness of all People.

But whoever hopes or expects to abolish or annihilate Antagonism, may hope and expect to the End of Time. It is a Principle in Nature, and can no more be annihilated or obliterated than any Principle in the material Universe. There is Nothing without it, because Nothing can exist without it. And when it is fully understood, Nations and Communities may work together for the general Good of all; as it keeps the Planets in their Course, and all Things in their Places upon and around them. The same Principles exist in the animate as in the inanimate World. Their Operation or Action in animal Life may be termed *Spirit*, and the two antagonistick Principles here, being as essential as in inanimate Nature, and being as little understood, are denominated *good* and *bad;* which attributes depend entirely on their Management as respects their Agency. Thus, Fire and Water are, in certain Conditions, terrible Agencies, and being strikingly antagonistick, serve to illustrate the Theory. They may be said to be the Origin of every Good and every Evil. They largely enter into the Composition of all Bodies. It is the antagonistick Principle that keeps them there, and they fall asunder by the Action of other antagonistick Agencies, as incomprehensible as those we have just mentioned. Whoever pretends to comprehend or explain them is either deficient in mental Endowment, or is a Pretender and Deceiver.

A Power actuates Humanity, or Powers, if we please, but of which we know no more than of that which causes the Sun to rise. This Power is Life, and into this enters the antagonistick Principles. This we know, because, we at the same Time are conscious of two Motives in our Mind at the same Time; one urging the Performance of an Action and the other resisting it. The Minds of intelligent Beings thus circumstanced gave rise to the Idea among primitive People, that these two Motives were caused by a good and an evil Spirit. If, in following the one, the Result was to all Appearances, to the Injury of no one, but on the Contrary, resulted in Benefits to some, it went to the Credit of the *good* Spirit; while, if the Result was injurious, it was pronounced Evil, and the Performer a *Do-evil* or *Devil*.[1]

Another View may be taken of the Powers of Actions: What may appear as an Evil under some Circumstances, may, under others, be pronounced Benefits. Hence arises the Saying that what is good for one Person may be bad for another; or, according to the Proverb, "It is an ill Wind that blows good to no one." Sailors once thought, that, when Winds kept them long from their Course, they were caused by some evil Spirit; and they sometimes charged one or more of their Number as the Authors of such adverse Wind, laid violent Hands upon them and cast them into the Sea. His Executioners did not reflect, that the Wind against which they were contending, was carrying those bound in the opposite Direction to their desired Haven. Neither did they reflect, that if a Mortal could control one of the Elements, it would be singular indeed if he could not control others, and thereby render their Efforts of no Avail.

At the Time New England began to be settled the Belief in Leagues with the Powers of Darkness by frail human Beings was nearly universal. The

[1] This may not be according to the Lexicographers, but it suits our Purpose.

Power or Principle before spoken of seems to have found no Place in the human Intellect. Education was controlled and shaped according to the Dogmas of the dark Ages. It is still in a great Measure under the Pressure of that Incubus. So wedded do Men become to Absurdities, because they are sanctioned and believed by their Predecessors, that they seemingly become a Part of their Natures. And, Deceptions practiced in an Age of almost heathen Darkness, which would not gain a Moment's Credence in this Age, are clung to with as much Faith as they were by the weakest Minds in the Age of their Creation.

As the all-pervading Principle of the Universe could not be understood, its Mystery was pretended to be solved to a certain Degree by dividing it into a good and a bad controlling Power. There was, and is to this Day, among unenlightened People, opposite Opinions held, as to the controlling of those Powers. Some believe that natural Phenomena, as Earthquakes, Thunder, and all other threatening Disturbances of the Elements are the Work of evil Spirits. Hence that Cause was to be worshipped, and Sacrifices made to it to propitiate it; hoping thereby to avert the Evil from themselves.

Plagues, Tempests, Inundations, and indeed all Occurrences unexplainable by human Sagacity are Miracles. Science, however, has diminished their Number, and rendered many natural Results, formerly viewed as Miracles no Miracles at all. When a Town or City was swallowed up by the Opening of the Earth under it, and all its People cut off by it, those of other Places tried to persuade themselves that it was not their Lot to meet such a Doom, because they were a better Community! Such Events were in the Mind of the great poetical Philosopher when he wrote the following transcendently beautiful Lines:

> "But errs not Nature from its gracious End,
> From burning Suns when livid Deaths descend;
> When Earthquakes swallow, or when Tempests sweep
> Towns to one Grave, whole Nations to the Deep?"

Another has beautifully expressed himself thus:

> "Think ye that they on whom the Ruin fell,
> Were worse than those who lived their Fate to tell?"

Thus, in all Ages and in all Countries Superstition held Mankind in those dismal Fetters, until Science by Degrees has partially relieved them. It had not made such slow Progress but for the inherent Love of Mystery so firmly enthroned in the human Mind. Nor is it strange that it is thus, becaufe the Birth of all Things is a Myftery — a Miracle if you will — to every one. Our Being and the Being of all Things are equally fo. No primeval Forefts of a new World are neceffary, by their gloomy Silence to engender indefcribable Forms, in the Imagination. The Countries whence our Anceftors came had few of thefe. Lonely ivied Ruins and Solitary Depofitories of the Dead they had indeed, if fuch were neceffary to the Propagation and Production of Witches, and their kindred Ghofts and Apparitions.

Strange and contradictory Notions have always prevailed regarding the Being, Powers and Agencies of Witches; and in the Attempts of "Believers" to explain them, they have by their Contradictions, and Affumptions of Things as Facts which had no Exiftence except in their difordered or confufed Brains, confounded the Underftandings of thofe whom they pretended to enlighten.

Such a Clafs of Inftructors has written numerous Works on the *Origin of Evil*, and *Original Sin*. If by fuch Books they have advanced Knowledge a Hair's Breadth in the Direction intended, it may perhaps be found exhibited in the more modern Effays of a tranfcendental Character. If thefe or thofe Writers have made the World better, they have certainly taken a round-about Way for it; and with the same Kind of Teachings it is quite certain that much Time will elapse before the People "of the most enlightened Country on the Globe" will be sufficiently enlightened to distinguish whether a Man will make a good or bad chief Magistrate of a Town or of the Nation; yet, with such Light as is supposed to surround a Centre of Intelligence, a most contemptible Demagogue may succeed in obtaining what had hitherto been deemed a high Position, but by him so degraded that it may be a Question whether the Position will confer Honor on a Successor.

It is evident that when our Ancestors left the Shores of England, they did not leave behind them the Superstitions of their Progenitors. From the remotest period Stories of the most marvellous Character had been transmitted from those of one Generation to the succeeding one, and there does not appear to have been any Time when the World was free from the Visitations of what was termed Witchcraft. There was indeed a short Period after the Settlement of this Country that little seems to have been heard about it. This Paucity was doubtless owing to the Circumstance that Everyone had too much to do to provide xxvi *Dissertation.*

himself with the Necessaries of Life, to allow his Mind to dwell on Matters, which, if closely followed up, could lead to Nothing but Poverty, Starvation and Ruin.

Yet all through those few Years between the coming over and the first Outbreak of Witchcraft, it was smouldering among the People, like the internal Fires of the Earth preparatory to a volcanic Eruption.

It appears that the People of the New Haven Colony were the first to be disturbed by "the Powers of the Invisible World," but the Records of the early Affairs are very deficient, and afford but an imperfect Insight into them. The early Enactments of Laws against Witches were occasioned by Accusations of Persons believed or pretended to be such. Of this there can be no Doubt. But no Records of Accusations appear previous to the Laws, notwithstanding they were the Occasion of such Laws.

As early as 1642,[1] the Laws defined eleven Crimes punishable by Death. The Second in

---

[1] It is scarcely necessary to state that all the Proceedings against Witches in England and this Country, were in Pursuance of the Act passed by the British Parliament, in Compliment, (as De Foe says) to the King's Opinion of Devils and Witches, and to the Book he wrote, entitled Demonology, reprinted in London the same Year (1603.) See *Witchcraft Delusion in New England*, I, xliii.

the Series reads, "Yf any Man or Woman be a Witch, that is, hath or confulteth with a familiar Spirit, they fhall be put to Death." This is agreeable to the thirteenth and fixth, feventeenth and fecond of Deuteronomy, and Exodus the twenty-fecond and twentieth. No Perfon, therefore, could have the Hardihood to open his Mouth to queftion fuch a Law. To define what was meant by Witchcraft and what were the Attributes of a Witch, Refort was probably had to Books on Witchcraft, as there does not appear to have been any generally fettled Idea or acknowledged Standard for Definitions of any Kind, though it is true that Dictionaries of the Englifh Language, or rather of many (for there was no Completenefs to them) Englifh Words had been publifhed a few Years before the great and final Outbreak of 1692–3. Hence we are told, that People had different Opinions about Trials, and Statutes on the Subject. We are told too, that many faw the Danger of Proceeding in Trials of the accufed, but that none had the moral Courage to oppofe such Proceedings; for the Few in Authority were viewed as infallible by the great Body of the People. To deny the Authority of Rulers was next to a capital Offence. The Courts did not

xxviii   *Dissertation.*

have the Sanction of Lord Chief Justice Hale, for his *Matters of Fact concerning Witches and Witchcraft* was not printed till 1693, and its Licence is dated May 18th of the same Year.

It is a pitiful Extenuation of the Acts under Consideration, that they were those of pious and good People, but there seems to be nothing better to offer. That such Men as Robert Burton, Lord Bacon, and Joseph Addison believed in Witchcraft; and that Sir William Blackstone "quite frowned" on Disbelievers in it,[1] and that Dr. Samuel Johnson "more than inclined to the same Side," only proves, that however great (in common Estimation) and learned a Man may be, these are no Guaranty that his Intellect may not be too shallow at some Points to afford a Footing for common Sense. Even the great Sir Isaac Newton, although he may not have come in Contact with Witchcraft, was as superstitiously inclined as many other great Minds of the Time in which he lived. Perhaps he might safely be classed with the learned Cudworth, with his

---

[1] Judge Blackstone's Opinion, as given in his Commentaries (iv, 60, ed. 1775), on the Laws of England amounts to about as much as did that of Gen. Jackson, as to the Genuineness of a Bank Note, as related by Major Downing. The Major states that having a Bill, the Genuineness of which he was unable to determine, took it to the General to get his Opinion. After considerable Scrutiny, the Sage replied, that he thought *it was about middling!*

Dissertation.

three kinds of Fatalism, who maintained that those that did not believe in the Existence of Witchcraft were Atheists. But they lived in Times when the absurd Opinion prevailed, that Beliefs were subject to the Bidding of those in Authority; and to this Day, wherever the Minds of the People are under these Shackles, human Progress is kept in Abeyance.

The Delusion was not confined to any particular Sect in Religion, but it prevailed about equally among Catholicks, Protestants, and the Aborigines of all Countries. It is probable, however, as is elsewhere remarked, that it flourished most where Ignorance prevailed, to the greatest Degree.

It is said, that after the famous Bull of Pope Innocent the VIII, in 1484, dooming Witches to Death, the Numbers that suffered surpasses all rational Belief. It became a Reign of Terror in every Land. None were safe, but every Moment of their Lives were liable to be seized and hurried before Judges, and the vilest Fictions given in and received for Evidence; all of which, by calm and rational Investigation, would generally be found to have had its Origin in some private and childish Quarrels among Neighbours, or in the Brain of some Individuals whose Reason had been wrecked by Caufes beyond the Power of thofe profeffing "Chirurgery" to underftand.

But whoever has attended at all to the Hiftory of the Progrefs of human Intelligence, knows that no Section of Country can claim an Exemption from having been, at fome Time, under the humiliating and combined Powers of Ignorance and Superftition. Yet, as Communities advanced into the dim Light of Knowledge, fome came accidentally in Advance of others. If this Advance happened to be owing to Circumftances not controlled by fuperior intellectual Endowments, it would fhow a Want of Civility for the more fortunate to taunt the lefs fo by Flings to remind them of a former degraded Condition, from which themfelves had juft emerged. We remark this, becaufe many Writers and Speakers refer to the Delufions of 1692, and 1693 as though they were the firft, laft and only ones ever known in all the World. Hence many imagine that Salem was worfe than Sodom; while the Truth is, the mournful Calamity of Witchcraft neither began nor ended at Salem.

Some of the fame Clafs of Writers of the prefent Day, if not infidioufly, ignorantly fpeak of "Witchcraft among the Puritans," as though it was Something peculiar to that Sect; although they may not intend to give that Impreffion, it will neverthelefs be inferred by cafual and fuperficial Readers. It fhould be expreffly ftated that the Delufion came to an End only by the Light fent forth by that much abufed Denomination.

It is not a Cuftom among the moft enlightened to harp and ring Changes upon Puritans and Witchcraft. It favors of the Times fucceeding the Reftoration of the Stuarts, in the Perfon of Charles the Second. Writers then pointed to the Cromwellian Period as that in which Witchcraft flourifhed more than ever before, which only betrayed their Ignorance of its previous Hiftory.[1]

The amiable and excellent Dwight remarks to fuch as are here fpoken of, "the early Settlers of New England have been accufed of Superftition. In fome Degree juftly. To what Nation is it not applicable? Their Defcendants hung the Witches at Salem, and for this Conduct merited the fevereft Cenfure. Still the New England People were as little ftained with this Guilt, as thofe who with as little Indecency exult over their Faults and Errors."[2] It might be well to inquire what Clafs of

---

[1] Sycophantick and bigoted Lloyd, gives Currency to a Story about the Declaration of a Witch, in Favour of the Proceedings of the Republicans.— *State Worthies*, Page 209 *edition* 1668.

[2] *Travels in New England*, I, 135.

People it was who "indecently" exulted over the Faults and Errors of the Puritans of New England? That Queſtion has been anſwered ſo triumphantly, and handled ſo maſterly by the accompliſhed Dr. Bacon, that if the Revilers of the Puritans will read it with Candour, it would ſeal their Mouths forever.[1]

Elaborate "Chronicles" and "Hiſtories of New England" have been written without noticing the Troubles of the People occaſioned by their Superſtition and Belief in an Agency of the Devil. As well might a Hiſtory of the Country be written leaving out what a Belief in Chriſtianity has done.[2] And yet, from Intimations like the following, we ſee what Terrors our Anceſtors lived in, and by which their Advance in all intellectual Improvement muſt have been greatly impeded: "I could with *unqueſtionable* Evidence relate the tragical Deaths of ſeveral good Men in this Land attended with ſuch *præternatural Circumſtances*,"[3] as that of Mr. Philip Smith.

To thoſe who wonder that People ever believed

---

[1] *Thirteen Hiſtorical Diſcourſes*, 33, &c.

[2] Neither Young nor Palfrey has taken any Notice of Witchcraft, if we judge by the Abſence of any Reference to the Subject in their Indexes.

[3] Mather, *Magnalia*.

Dissertation.

in, and prosecuted supposed Witches in New England, we recommend them to inquire if there be not yet those labouring under a Superstition themselves, equally reprehensible for the Times in which they live.

By many it has been urged in Extenuation of what was done in New England in Respect to Witchcraft, that it was much worse in every Country of Europe at the same Time and long after. Let that Consideration excuse us as far as it may; while the Consolation thus afforded is the same as in a Case of Loss to a Man who had learned that his Neighbour had been equally unfortunate; or, to console ourselves we had found out that Ignorance and Superstition prevailed to as great, if not in a greater Degree, in Europe, than in New England. Thus Dr. Cotton Mather brings forward several Cases of European Witchcraft as a Sort of Palliative for those in this Country. Certainly if European Examples are any Excuse we have enough of them. For the Remark of Hutchinson will, on Examination be found to be true, namely, that "more had been put to Death in a single County in England, in a short Space of Time, than have suffered in all

New England from the firſt Settlement to his Time."

No Matter what has been done elſewhere. It excuſes us in the ſame Way as we are excuſed for having Progenitors, born in a Country where it was Infidelity not to believe in Witchcraft. Viewing the Matter in this Light, we find a weſtern Biſhop indulging in Sentiments like theſe: "We can ſcarcely even gueſs, why it was that the Witches took ſo remarkable a Fancy to the early Yankees. Whether it was that there was ſome ſecret Congeniality of Feeling between the two, or that the Devil envied, and ſought to mar by his diabolical Incantations, the extraordinary *Sanctity* of the Pilgrim Fathers, we know not." Then, after copious Extracts from that Part of Dr. Mather's *Magnalia* devoted to Witchcraft, this model Biſhop flippantly, and doubtleſs ſatisfactorily to himſelf, proceeds: "Verily, if all theſe Things be true, we muſt admit that the Demons were particularly intimate with the early Puritans of New England; rather more, in Fact, than was at all comfortable for the Latter. Shrewd and calculating as were the early Yankees, the Imps who played ſuch fantaſtick Tricks among them, were much ſhrewder. The inviſible Spirits knew their Trade much better than to try wooden Hams or Nutmegs, or to attempt the impoffible Tafk of overreaching their Friends in a Bargain."

When fuch are the Inculcations of a fouth-weftern Head of the Church, we ought not to expect Anything but ruffianly Treatment when any of us of New England happen to travel into that Region. We are forry to obferve that this Bifhop bears a New England Surname, yet he may never have feen the Country of which he fo fneeringly fpeaks, while he may know by this Time, that to fuch *Apoftles* as he, is mainly attributable the bloody Scenes of a four years' Rebellion.

It is not fo ftrange that ignorant People fhould be found even in great Cities wallowing in Superftition, and believing in the Reality of Witchcraft; but that Men accuftomed to literary Society fhould be the Dupes of fuch Abfurdities amidft the Means of daily Improvement, is not fo eafily comprehended.

In all Periods of Hiftory have appeared Prophets, or Pretenders to the Ability to foretell future Events. As Witches were fuppofed to be able to do this they too were Prophets; but to the Apprehenfion of fenfible People of this Age, there are few more contemptible Beings than thofe who are going about prating of an approaching Millennium, pretending to fix the Date when Chrift is to make his Appearance. Illiterate People, like the late William Miller, who have fcarcely read Anything except the Bible, may claim fome Excufe for not knowing how many have, from *actual* Calculations, fixed upon the precife Day and even Hour of that Event. It would feem, that if thefe millennium Quacks fhould once fee a Catalogue of thofe Prophecies, and learn the Confidence with which they were put forth, and that their Calculations were as well grounded as any that can in Reafon be made, from the Premifes made Ufe of, the World might in Future be relieved from the Infliction of Floods of *ill*-literature upon this Subject. But, as though Mankind had learned Nothing from the Paft in this Refpect, we fee the Prefs teeming with millennium humbug Pamphlets even to our own Times. And however this may be viewed, it is only a Branch of that Superftition, out of which Witchcraft is another and perhaps earlier Branch.

Great Pains have been taken to explain away the Devil out of the New Teftament, by Attempts to prove that the plaineft Language is, and always has been mifunderftood. When to Perfons of ordinary common Senfe it is perfectly clear, that if what is written and received as the Word of God means Anything it means what it fays. Neverthelefs we meet with fome moft ingenious and learned Arguments, turning all Paffages where the Devil figures into Allegories, while they do not meddle with Witches.[1]

The eminent Dr. Lardner has proved to the Satisfaction of Thoufands that the New Teftament is full of Facts fuftaining the Words of thofe Books as they ftand, literally.[2] Befides, every good Lutheran believes in the perfonal Encounter the old Saint of Erfurth had with the Devil on a certain Occafion. And one much nearer the Time of the Event than we are fays:

> "Did not the Devil appear to Martin
> Luther in Germany, for certain?
> And would have gull'd him with a Trick,
> But Mart. was too, too politick?"

Thus verifying to his early Friends, (the Catholicks), their old Proverb, "that a young Saint will prove an old Devil." Yet, one of our early New England Divines believed with Erafmus, who faid "the Devil was the Author of that Proverb."[3]

---

[1] The Rev. M. C. Conway's *Natural Hiftory of the Devil.*

[2] *Cafe of the Demoniacs.* 1758.

[3] See Dr. I. Mather's *Election Sermon,* 1677, P. 101.

The Undertaking would be by no Means inconsiderable, to collect even the Titles of Works on the Subject of Witchcraft, without including those of our own Times. For the last half Century they have been issued generally as Novels, but some of them so artfully that many have doubtless taken them for Realities. Here is a Specimen: *The Phantom World, translated from the French of Calmet, with a Preface and Notes by [the] Rev. Henry Christmas; giving a general Survey of the History and Philosophy of Spirits, Ghosts, Elves, Fairies, Spooks, Bogles, Bugaboos, and Hobgoblins.* Upon this Title one, a Writer in a popular Work, remarked: "It will probably meet with an extensive Circulation, in these Days when Connecticut Divines are haunted by infernal Visits, and the Rochester Sibyls are on Exhibition in New York."

When the above Announcement was made, about eighteen Years ago, the Farce of Spirit-rappings and Table-turnings was at its Height; and it was reported, with what of Truth we cannot say, that a Number of Believers in these "spiritual Manifestations" had formed a Settlement at a Place called Mountain Cave, in Fayette County in Virginia, having purchased fourteen thousand

Dollars' Worth of farming Lands thereabouts, and that Families were being added to the firſt Adventurers which had previouſly reſided at Auburn in New York. They carried on the Iſſue of Newſpapers, the Writings in which were "the Dictation of the Spirits." Whether this Community was in Exiſtence in the Time of the late Rebellion, we have not heard. This is introduced as another Illuſtration of what has been often aſſerted, that there is Nothing too abſurd or ridiculous, where Myſtery lies at the Bottom, to obtain devoted Followers. About the Time this Colony of Spiritual Rappers was formed, ſome waggiſh Editor remarked: "Somewhere in Virginia, is a Place called Mountain Cave, where Spiritual Rappers have colonized in large Numbers and ſtarted a Paper. The Covies, ſays the New York Dutchman, have bored a Hole down through this poor contemptible Hemiſphere and can ſee clean into the next World."

Having become tired of the old Notions of Revelation taught them by their Anceſtors, new Theories are invented. Thoſe find Followers for a Time, and are then ſucceeded by others; which, though equally ſhallow and abſurd, have their Followers; and thus it will probably always be, because all People are born in Ignorance and have Everything to learn.

The Thousands, if not Millions of Volumes which have been written and circulated for the Enlightenment of the ignorant World regarding a future State and Things appertaining thereto cannot but be immeasurably bewildering to all those who are inclined to consult them for the kind of Information most interesting, and in their Opinion, most important to them. Nor will it ever be otherwise so long as the Writers of such Works as we refer to base all their crude Arguments on false Foundations, or rather on no Foundation at all. With this Class of Writers it makes no Difference how often their Foundations have been shown to be false, they have no Will to desert them. They begin and end their Labours on Assumption. To explain away Witches from the Bible has occupied Pens which should have been better employed. The same may be said of those who have attempted to argue the Devil out of the New Testament. The elegant Style of Lardner has effected Nothing but an Exhibition of fine Writing. His latest Imitators will soon be forgotten, though some of them may have been read on Account of the Singularity of their Subject.

One who wrote anonymously, and published his "Essay" in 1833, among some sensible Remarks has this: "Those who think that Demoniacks were actually tortured by the Devil—that he brought Disorders upon them—threw them down—prevented them from speaking, hearing, and seeing, generally say it was Something peculiar to that Age," &c. To which this Essayist very significantly inquires, why it was that the Devil always threw his Victims *down*, and never threw them *up?* There was published the previous Year an *Essay on the Demoniacs of the New Testament*, accompanied by the well known Initials of E. S. G. In this there is such a nice balancing of syllogistick Ideas, that a common Mind may find itself bewildered and in serious Doubt whether the Writer does really mean Anything.

In an Attempt to controvert the Theories of modern Spiritualists, a Preacher tells us that "what was Falsehood and Imposture in the Days of the Hebrew Commonwealth, has not become by the mere Lapse of Time, a great and beneficent Discovery, opening new Fountains of Knowledge." At the same Time he tells us that Spiritualism "is a Branch of the Art of Divination practised in the Old World from Time Immemorial."

But it is better to give Things their real Names. It is not eafy to diftinguifh between a *Branch* of this Kind and the Tree itfelf. The Truth feems to be, that the Witchcraft of former Days had become fo unpopular, that it could not be made any longer to fubferve the Interefts of thofe who practifed it. Hence it is given a new Name, and yet retains the fame Myftery of Development.

Fortune-telling is as much a Branch of Witchcraft as Spirit-rapping, Table-turning, or any other of the "occult Sciences." Thefe are the legitimate Progenitors of Ghofts or Apparitions. It would not require a very dark Night to produce thefe Spectres in the Imagination of thofe returning from a Vifit to a Fortune-teller, or by paffing the filent and lonely Church-yard. How woefully did our Quaker Poet err, when he fancied he was finging a Requiem over the laft Witch of his native Land in thefe Lines: —

> "How has New England's Romance fled,
>   Even as a Vifion of the Morning!
> Its Rites foregone — its Guardians dead —
> Its Altar-fires extinguifhed —
> Its Prieftefses, bereft of Dread,
>   Waking the verieft Urchins fcorning!
> No more along the fhadowy Glen,
> Glide the dim Ghofts of murdered Men, —

Dissertation. xliii

No more the Unquiet Church-yard Dead,
Glimpse upward from their turfy Bed,
  Startling the Traveller, late and loane;
As, on some Night of cloudy Weather,
They commune silently together,
  Each sitting on his own Head-stone!
The rooflefs House, decayed, deserted,
Its living Tenants all departed,
No longer rings with Midnight Revel,
Of Witch, or Ghost, or Goblin evil;
No hellish Flame sends out its Flashes
Through creviced Roof and shattered Sashes!—
The Witch-grass round the Hazel spring,
May sharply to the night Air sing,
But there no more shall withered Hags
Refresh at Ease their Broomstick Nags;
Or taste those hazel-shadowed Waters
As Beverage meet for Satan's Daughters;
No more their mimick Tones be heard—
The Mew of Cat—the Chirp of Bird,
Shrill blending with the hoarser Laughter
Of the fell Demon following after."

We say how egregiously he erred in supposing that "New England Romance had fled!" thirty-seven Years ago, because he must have known that haunted Houses existed and Ghosts flitted about as they lifted in the very Borders of the great Metropolis near the present Time; that within a Year, many, perhaps several thousands, went out of this City of Boston to see a haunted

Houfe in the Vicinity. Whether, as they approached the Place, the Hairs of their Heads ftood erect, their Teeth chattered, and their Knees fmote together, we cannot fay, but fome of them returned with myfterious Countenances, and it was many Days before they were willing to give up the Idea that they did not come very near feeing a Nonentity. About the fame Time, Ghofts were having a brave Time at Fort Warren down in the Harbour, according to Reports current in the City. Many Perfons, it is faid, went down towards the Ifland on which the Fort is fituated, but probably had not the Courage to land, as they made no Report afterwards.

The Reader fhould now be informed that the poetical Extract foregoing is from a Poem commemorative of as great and notorious a Witch as any that can be found defcribed in the ANNALS OF WITCHCRAFT; and that we are indebted to the Bard of Lynn for a graphic Outline of her real Hiftory. But the Reader fhould be reminded that the amiable and excellent Author of that Work was himfelf a Poet, and that it is poffible that his Account may have a Tinge of Poetry, or be a little bordering on Romance. With this Premonition it fhall follow in his own Words:

Dissertation.

"The celebrated Mary Pitcher, a profeſſed Fortune-teller, died April 9th, 1813, aged 75. Her Grandfather, John Dimond, lived at Marblehead, and for many Years exerciſed the ſame Pretenſions. Her Father, Capt. John Dimond, was Maſter of a Veſſel from that Place, and was living in 1770. Mary Dimond was born in the Year 1738. She was connected with ſome of the beſt Families in Eſſex County, and with the Exception of her extraordinary Pretenſions, there was Nothing diſreputable in her Life or Character. She was of the medium Height and Size for a Woman, with a good Form and agreeable Manners. Her Head, phrenologically conſidered, was ſomewhat capacious; her Forehead broad and full, her Hair dark Brown, her Noſe inclining to long, and her Face pale and thin. There was nothing groſs or ſenſual in her Appearance — her Countenance was rather Intellectual; and ſhe had that Contour of Face and Expreſſion which, without being poſitively beautiful is, neverthelefs, decidedly intereſting — a thoughtful, penſive, and ſometimes downcaſt Look, almoſt approaching to Melancholy — an Eye, when it looked at you, of calm and keen Penetration — and an Expreſſion of intelligent Diſcernment, half mingled with a Glance of Shrewdnefs. She took a poor Man for a Hufband, and then adopted what fhe Doubtlefs thought the harmlefs Employment of Fortune-telling, in Order to fupport her Children. In this fhe was probably more fuccefsful than fhe herfelf had anticipated; and fhe became celebrated, not only throughout America, but throughout the World, for her Skill. There was no Port on either Continent, where floated the Flag of an American Ship, that had not heard of the Fame of MOLL PITCHER. To her came the Rich and the Poor — the Wife and the Ignorant — the Accomplifhed and the Vulgar — the Timid and the Brave. The ignorant Sailor, who believed in the Omens and Dreams of Superftition, and the intelligent Merchant, whofe Ships were freighted for diftant Lands, alike fought her Dwelling; and many a Veffel has been deferted by its Crew, and waited idly at the Wharves, for Weeks, in Confequence of her unlucky Predictions. Many Perfons came from Places far remote, to confult her on Affairs of Love or Lofs of Property; or to obtain her Surmifes refpecting the Viciffitudes of their future Fortune. Every Youth, who was not affured of the reciprocal Affection of his fair one, and every Maid who was desirous of anticipating the Hour of her highest Felicity, repaired at Evening to her humble Dwelling, which stood on what was then a lonely Road, near the Foot of High Rock, with the single Dwelling of Dr. Henry Burchard nearly opposite; over whose Gateway were the two Bones of a great Whale, disposed in the Form of a Gothic Arch. There for more than fifty Years, in her unpretending Mansion, did she answer the Inquiries of the simple Rustic from the Wilds of New Hampshire, and the wealthy Noble from Europe; and, doubtless her Predictions have had an Influence in shaping the Fortunes of Thousands."

This is a Sketch drawn from Life. Mr. Lewis remembered Mary Pitcher well, for he lived near her, and was eighteen Years of Age when she died. " Her Husband was a Shoemaker named Robert Pitcher, to whom she was married October 2d, 1760, of Course at the Age of twenty-two. She had one Son, John, and three Daughters, Rebecca, Ruth, and Lydia, who married respectably, and some of her Descendants are among the prettiest young Ladies of Lynn."[1]

[1] Mr. NEWHALL in his valuable Additions to the History of Lynn has given a Fac Simile of the Autograph of MARY PITCHER, and an Engraving of the House in which she lived.

Another, one of New England's elegant Writers, who alſo knew the celebrated Mary Pitcher, has left the following Note upon her: "She was ſo well known to moſt Perſons, that their Recollections will be better than any Deſcription. She had thin Lips, the arched Eyebrows, the chappy Finger, and that Shrewdneſs which have ſo often been the Characteriſtics of thoſe who have deceived the World by pretending to tell Fortunes, or to find loſt Goods. It can do no Harm to amuſe ourſelves by the Hiſtory of any Deluſion when it has paſſed. The Age of Reaſon has come, and Superſtition is now ſhaking from her Raven Wings the laſt Dewdrops ſwept from the Fens of Ignorance, and the Light of Knowledge has broken the Enchanter's Wand and the Sorcerer's Cup."[1]

Had this excellent Writer lived thirty Years later he would have found that Something of the Wand Kind has been more active than ever, and that the Wand of the Spirit-Rapper is far in advance of that of the Conjuror of his Time. They hold Communion with the Dead and lead captive the ſtrong minded living of our Day. Alas for the Age of Reaſon! It is in Proſpect

[1] Samuel L. Knapp in 1825.

Dissertation. xlix

like that glorious funny Point called the West, which when reached is no longer there, but becomes the opposite — the East.

Notwithstanding the great Fame of Moll Pitcher, there was another Female quite as notorious and contemporary with her, residing in Newburyport, and therefore better known perhaps to Mr. Knapp than the Former. This Woman would probably have rivalled Mary in Fame, had she resided as near Boston. Of that, however, the Reader can judge, after the Perusal of what Mr. Knapp has left us. He says: "The Writer remembers, in his short Life, three Persons, not only reputed, as many more have been, but absolutely believed by a great Portion of the Credulous, to have practised the Arts of Witchcraft. The first lived in Newburyport. She was a Woman of extraordinary Appearance — she was short, but stout; had a strongly marked Face, large greenish Eyes, prominent Nose, and a large Mouth, with a perfect Set of double Teeth all around. Her Voice was stentorian. She came to Newburyport in 1759 or 60, and was probably the Appendage of a Scotch Officer in Amherst's Army. Her Acquirements and her Address were such that she at once obtained a

School, and received the honourable Appellation of Dame Hooper, and afterwards that of Madam Hooper. Her Temper was excessively irascible, and being rather restive under such Confinement, she gave up her School, after she had formed a thorough Acquaintance with the People. Her Guesses were often so shrewd that some began to stare, and at length, as the Wonders of her Skill increased, pronounced her a Witch. This Character being once fixed, she availed herself of the Belief, to live upon the Credulity of the Publick. The best informed felt no Desire to quarrel with her, and others often propitiated her good Will with Presents. She had Access to every House, and made frequent Visits to numerous Families. The Children bowed to her *Divinity* as she entered the House of their Parents, and she being well informed, astonished them with sage Remarks. She was the most acute Physiognomist I ever saw, and read the Character even of a Child at a Glance. Her Speeches were short, striking, and, like those of the Sybil, generally equivocal. An hundred of them are fresh in my Memory at this Moment, and are quite equal to those left us from the ancient Oracles. She told Fortunes, found lost Goods, and was consulted on other Subjects with Gravity, by the sober part of the Community. In her latter Days she degenerated from her high Standing, and became not only a Fortune-Teller, but something lower, in the Estimation of many; yet, such was the Fear of this Woman, that the grave Fathers of the Town, quick scented, and unequalled in their Exertions to exterminate Vice, did not dare interfere with her. The Orgies of Bacchus and Venus were celebrated in her Den, without the slightest Fear of Detection or Punishment. It is true her Habitation was on the farthest Verge of the Town, and where her Bacchantes could not disturb many. Boys ran past her House, if obliged to go that Way in the Evening, without looking about them. Old Age at length came upon her, and her shrewd Guesses no longer passed for Foreknowledge. Many who had often consulted her, and believed in her Power, now thought her League with the Devil had run out—that she was a miserable Wretch, polluted by infernal Associates, without retaining a Particle of their accursed Knowledge. None but Hags came near her, and she expired on a Bed of filthy Straw. The Wardrobe she possessed on her Arrival, was so abundant as to have lasted during her Life."

Our Author extracts Edmund Spenser's Description of the Abode of a Witch,[1] in speaking of another Woman, who in her Time passed current for a Witch. This was one "*Mother* Danforth." But where the "gloomy, hollow Glen" was containing her Cottage he does not inform us; but says, "This harmless old Woman was often charged with afflicting Men, Women and Children, and playing off her Pranks upon Horses, Cattle, Sheep, and above all on Cats. The best authenticated Stories were told of her being seen in the Air on a Broomstick, and holding a *Sabbath*, with others of her Race, in a desolate Island. *Mother* Danforth was the Leader of the frightful Band. None of those Experiments which often sent less careful Witches to their long Account, ever reached her — she was Proof against every witch-killing Process; she had been shot at in the Form of a Cat, with silver Bullets, but all to no Effect."

But the Author of this Extract does not tell what became of Mother Danforth. She no doubt died a natural Death, as thousands of other aged Females have in various Parts of the Coun-

---

[1] See *The Witchcraft Delusion in N. Eng.*, I, xlix.

try. The Writer is not as old as he from whom the above Extracts are made, but it was his Fortune in Youth to be acquainted in many Towns, in nearly all of which there was a reputed Witch. In one in particular, a Daughter-in-law sustained the Belief of her Neighbours that her Mother-in-law was a Witch, that she was known to have been absent at Nights attending Witch-Meetings; that she had been rid by her and exhibited her worn Hands, though when rid she was turned into a Horse. At the same Time it was well known that the old Mother-in-law had been bed-rid many Years, and had not for a long Time left her Bed without Assistance!

ANNALS OF
Witchcraft in New England.

LAWS againſt Witchcraft naturally grew out of a Demand by the People for a Remedy for that particular Evil. That it was a fancied or imaginary Evil made no Difference. Theſe Laws gradually dropped out of the Statute Books, as the People became enlightened; and ſo it was with many other Laws, enacted in about as much Darkneſs as were thoſe againſt Witchcraft. But with theſe — ſome of which diſgrace the Statute Books of the preſent Day — we now have Nothing to do.

1636.

The People of Plymouth had been disturbed by Witches doubtless before the Year 1636, or they would not have, in that Year, included in their Summary of Offences "lyable to Death," one in these words:—"Solemn Compaction or conversing with the Divell by way of Witchcraft, Conjuration or the like." Ten Years later it was reenacted, yet no Intimation is found in the Records that any new Cause had transpired.

1642.

There does not appear to have been any particular Cause for including Witchcraft among the capital Offences at this Period in the Colony of Connecticut; but as they drew their Capital Code from the Bible, it was necessarily included, and in these words:— "Yf any Man or Woman be a Witch, that is, hath or consulteth with a Familiar Spirit, they shall be put to death." The Colony of Massachusetts had the previous Year adopted the Body of Liberties, which contains the same Clause concerning Witches and Witchcraft.

1646.

The Law against Witchcraft, enacted in 1642, is reenacted, and we do not find any Alteration or Reenactment until October, 1692. Up to this Time Proceedings in Cases of Witchcraft were "according to the Directions given in the Laws of God and the wholesome Statutes of the English Nation." But upon the Opening of the Tragedy in Salem Village, in the Beginning of 1692, the old Enactments were thought insufficient, and a new and more verbose one was drawn up and passed [1] by the General Court, the Governour and Council having in the mean Time requested the Opinion of several of the principal Ministers upon the State of Things as they then stood, according to the Practice under the old Charter. Their Opinion was given in Writing, and consisted of eight Articles, which may be read in the *History of Massachusetts*.[2]

A Person of Windsor was put to Death on the Charge of Witchcraft at Hartford. No Circumstances have been found, nor the Name of the Sufferer.[3]

1647.

What had influenced the People of Rhode Island to cause the General Court of that Colony to make the following Enactment, does not appear. In the Acts of May of the Year 1647, we find "Witchcraft is forbidden by this present Assembly to be used in this Colonie; and the Penaltie imposed by the Authoritie that we are subject

---

[1] See Dane's *Charters and Laws*, 735.

[2] *Hutchinson*, II, 50, 51, who does not appear to have known that it was composed by Dr. Cotton Mather. But Mather, in his *War* with Calef, says, ' it was *my* poor Hand which drew up that Advice."—*Some Few Remarks*, 39.

[3] Winthrop, *Journal*, II, 307.

to, is Felonie of Death." It is probable that Somebody had been "uſing" it, or their Intentions to do ſo were ſtrongly ſuſpected.

1648.

The firſt Execution for Witchcraft in the Colony of Maſſachuſetts Bay, was at Boſton on the 15th of June, 1648. Accuſations were probably common long before this, but now came a tangible Caſe, and it was carried through with as much Satisfaction to the Authorities, apparently, as ever the Indians burnt a Priſoner at the Stake.

The Victim was a Female named Margaret Jones, the Wife of Thomas Jones of Charleſtown, who periſhed on the Gallows, as much for her good Offices, as for the evil Influences imputed to her. She had been, like many other Mothers among the early Settlers, a Phyſician; but being once ſuſpected of Witchcraft, "was found to have ſuch a malignant Touch, as many Perſons were taken with Deafneſs, or Vomiting, or other violent Pains or Sickneſs." Her Medicines, though harmleſs in themſelves, "yet had extraordinary violent Effects;" that ſuch as refuſed her Medicines, "ſhe would tell that they would never be healed, and accordingly their Diſeaſes and Hurts continued, with Relapſe againſt the ordinary Courſe, and beyond the Apprehenſion of all Phyſicians and Surgeons." And, as ſhe lay in Priſon, "a little Child was ſeen to run from her into another Room, and being followed by an Officer, it was vanished." There was other Testimony against her more ridiculous than this, but not necessary to be recited. To make her Case as bad as possible, the Recorder of it says "her Behaviour at her Trial was intemperate, lying notoriously, and railing upon the Jury and Witnesses," and that "in like Distemper she died." It is not unlikely that this poor forsaken Woman was distracted with Indignation at the Utterances of the false Witnesses, when she saw her Life was sworn away by them. The deluded Court denounced her frantick Denial of the Charges as "lying notoriously." And in the probably honest Belief in Witchcraft, the same Recorder[1] says, in the most complacent Credulity, that "the same Day and Hour she was executed, there was a very great Tempest at Connecticut, which blew down many Trees, &c." Another equally credulous Gentleman, writing a Letter to a Friend, dated at Boston on the 13th of the same Month, says: "The Witche is condemned, and to be hanged Tomorrow, being Lecture Day."

Whether there were any other suspected Persons at the time Margaret Jones was prosecuted, we have no Means of ascertaining, yet it is more than probable that a supposed Spirit of Darkness had been whispering in the Ears of the Men in Authority in Boston; for about a Month before the Execution of Margaret, they passed this Order:

---

[1] John Winthrop.

"The Courte defire the Courfe which hath been taken in England for Difcovery of Witches, by watching them a certain Time. It is ordered, that the beft and fureft Way may forthwith be put in Practice; to begin this Night, if it may be, being the 18th of the third Month, and that the Hufband may be confined to a private Roome, and be alfo then watched."

That the Court was ftirred up to ferret out Witches, by the late Succeffes in that Bufinefs in England,— feveral Perfons having been tried, condemned and executed in Feverfham about two Years before — is not improbable. By "the Courfe which hath been taken in England for the Difcovery of Witches," the Court had Reference to the Employment of Witch-Finders, one Matthew Hopkins having had great Succefs. By his infernal Pretenfions "fome fcores" of innocent bewildered People met violent Deaths at the Hands of the Executioner, all along from 1634 to 1646. But to return to the Cafe of Margaret Jones. She having gone down to an ignominious Grave, leaving her Hufband to fuffer the Taunts and Jeers of the ignorant Multitude, efcaped further Profecution. Thefe were fo infufferable that his Means of Living were cut off, and he was compelled to try to feek another Afylum. A Ship was lying in the Harbor bound for Barbadoes. In this he took Paffage. But he was not thus to efcape Perfecution. On this "Ship of 300 Tons" were eighty Horfes. Thefe caufed the Veffel to roll confiderably, perhaps heavily, which to Persons of any Sea Experience would have been no Miracle. But Mr. Jones was a Witch, a Warrant was sued out for his Apprehension, and he was hurried thence to Prison,[1] and there left by the Recorder of the Account, who has left his Readers in Ignorance of what became of him. Whether he were the Thomas *Joanes* of Elzing, who in 1637 took Passage at Yarmouth for New England, cannot be positively stated, although he is probably the same Person. If so, his Age at that Time was 25 Years, and he married subsequently.[2]

To whom is referred in the following Passage, written about 1693, is not clear: "We have been advised by some credible Christians yet alive, that a Malefactor, accused of Witchcraft, as well as Murder, and executed in this Place more than forty Years ago, did then give Notice of an horrible PLOT against the Country by WITCHCRAFT, and a Foundation of WITCHCRAFT then laid, which, if it were not seasonably discovered, would probably blow up and pull down all the Churches in the Country. And we have with Horror seen the Discovery of such a Witchcraft. An Army of Devils is horribly broke in upon the Place, which is the Centre, and after a Sort, the First-born of our English Settlements."[3]

---

[1] See *Hist. and Antiq's Boston*, 49 and Authorities, 308-9.

[2] See *Founders of New England,*

[3] *Wonders of the Invisible World.*

Mary Johnson was executed at Hartford for Witchcraft. Neither her Trial nor Execution appear in the publifhed Records of the General Court of Connecticut. She was the fame Perfon, it is fuppofed, who at the Auguft Term, 1646, the General Court ordered, "for Theuery, is to be prefently whipped, and to be brought forth a Month hence at Wethersfield, and there whipped."

About two Years later, namely, December 7th, 1648, is found the following brief Entry refpecting Mary *Jonfon*, doubtlefs the fame who had been ordered to be whipped, as juft mentioned: "The Jury finds the Bill of Inditement againft Mary Jonfon, that, by her owne Confeffion, fhee is guilty of Familiarity with the Deuill."

Concerning this Cafe, as in many others, we have a good deal in Amount, and yet but few Facts; are told that "her Confeffion was attended with fuch convictive Circumftances, that it could not be flighted." But unfortunately none of the *convictive* Circumftances are given, that the Readers might have the Satisfaction of exercifing their own Judgement, as to their *convictivenefs*. We muft therefore take the only Account we have as we find it, feeling that the original Narrator implicitly believed every Word of it. He fays, "very many material Paffages relating to this Matter are now loft; but fo much as is well known, and can ftill be proved, fhall be inferted.

"She faid her firft Familiarity with the Devil came through Difcontent, and wifhing the Devil to take this and that, and the Devil to do that and t'other Thing. Whereupon a Devil appeared unto her, tendring her what Services might beft content her. A Devil accordingly did for her many Services. Her Mafter blamed her for not carrying out the Afhes, and a Devil afterwards would clear the Hearth of Afhes for her. Her Mafter fending her to drive out the Hogs, that fometimes broke into their Field, a Devil would fcowre the Hogs away, and make her laugh to fee how he fcared them. She confeffed that fhe had murdered a Child, and committed Uncleannes both with Men and with Devils. In the Time of her Imprifonment, the famous Mr. [Samuel] Stone was at great Pains to promote her Converfion from the Devil to God." The fame Author tells us fhe went out of the World with comfortable Hopes, having been by the "beft Obfervers judged very Penitent before her Execution and at it."

Thus we are left in utter Ignorance as to what was produced againft Mary Johnfon at her Trial, if fhe had any. But at the Term of Court before mentioned, we find a Lift of the Jury, compofed of the following Names: "Mr. Phelps, John Tailecoate, Will. Wadfworth, Andr. Bacon, Sam. Smith, Nath Dickerfon, Thomas Coleman, John Demyn, Mr. Clarke, Mr. Allyn, Will. Gibbens, John More." Edward Hopkins, Efq., was Governour. "Mr. Wells, Mr. Woollcott, Mr. Webfter, and Mr. Cullick," were Magiftrates."

1650.

It is incidentally mentioned by Hutchinson, that no Person was convicted for Witchcraft in New England, before the Year 1650, "when, a poor Wretch, Mary Oliver, probably weary of her Life from the general Reputation of being a Witch, after long Examination, was brought to Confession of her Guilt, but I do not find that she was executed." It would seem from this Passage of the Historian, that he did not consider Mary Johnson to have been convicted, or probably he had no Knowledge of her Case.

1651.

We come now to a Case quite as deplorable as that of the Year 1648, already considered. It occurred in the Town of Springfield, on the Connecticut River, and has been several Times noticed by local and other Writers, none of whom, however, have given a satisfactory Account of it, because the Materials were unknown to them. It is referred to by Capt. Edward Johnson, in his loose way, in his *Wonder Working Providence*, &c., which brings down his *History of New England* to 1651, and was printed in 1654. In speaking of the Settlement of Springfield he says: "There hath of late been more than one or two in this Town, greatly suspected of Witchcraft, yet have they used much Diligence, both for the finding them out, and for the Lord's assisting them against their Witchery; yet have they, as is supposed, bewitched not a few Persons, among whom two of the Reverend Elder's Children." The Reverend Elder was Mr. George Moxon, the first Minister of the Place.[1] The Author just mentioned is the only one remembered among the early New England Writers who notices the Witchcraft Troubles at Springfield. Some of our own Times relate them, or what they happen to know of them, with the same Feeling, apparently, as they would relate a nursery Tale to their Children; seeming not to be sensible of the Horrors and Privations suffered by the Fathers and Mothers of the Land, in that dark Period of its History.

It is quite Evident from Capt. Johnson's Account, that Witchcraft in Springfield was about coeval with the first Settlement of the Place, which was in 1636. The Company which made the Settlement there was led by Mr. William Pynchon, a Gentleman of Learning and Enterprise, and afterwards a Magistrate.

According to Captain Johnson, Witches were disturbing the Peace of the People of Springfield ten Years before legal Steps were taken to put a Stop to them. On whom or how many Suspicions were fixed before Mr. Pynchon felt com-

---

[1] It is reported that Mary Parson was tried, about the End of February (1661) for, as the Indictment runs, that being seduced by the Devil, at Springfield, she consulted with a familiar Spirit, making a Covenant with him, and had used divers devilish Practices by Witchcraft, to the Hurt of Martha and Rebeca Moxon, against the Word of God, &c. She pleaded not Guilty, and the Court finally discharged her.— See Judd's *History Hadley*, 234.

pelled to set up his Inquisition, we shall probably never know. Perhaps they were at first among a Class of Denizens of too high social Standing to admit an Interference. But in the latter Part of the Year 1650, Suspicions fell on a Man named Hugh Parsons. This Man appears to have been one of the first Settlers of the Town, probably went there in Mr. Pynchon's Company. He was an honest, sensible laboring Man, a Sawyer by Occupation, and it may be well to remark that, before Mills were built, the Business of a Sawyer was not inconsiderable, in the then Wilderness of New England. After a few Years' Residence at Springfield, Mr. Parsons married a young Woman named Mary Lewis. The Marriage took place October 27th, 1645. Their first Child, at least the first we find recorded, was born on the 4th of October, 1649. This Child was named Samuel, and it died at the Age of one Year. The following Year, on the 26th of October, they had another, a Son, which they named Joshua. It was soon after the Birth of this Child that the Charge of Witchcraft was made against the Father. The Mother's Sickness, consequent, perhaps, upon the Privations and Hardships of a Wilderness, deprived her of Reason, and the Course pursued after she was thus afflicted, rendered her permanently insane. This Condition was declared to be produced by Witchcraft, and the Testimony of this sick and insane Woman was taken as legal Evidence against her Husband, and afterwards against herself. Her Illness immediately after the Birth of her Child, was, as before remarked, doubtless caused by prematurely expoſing herſelf, which ſo affected the Health of the Child, that it fell into a Languiſhment, and being deprived of the Care it required, its Death followed on the 1ſt of March, 1651. Whereupon the Clamour againſt the Father increaſed, and he was denounced as a Witch on all Sides.

Mrs. Parſons was ſent to Boſton and here impriſoned, about the 1ſt of May. At length, on the 7th of May, 1651, her Caſe was brought before the General Court, and the following Record is the Reſult of their Deliberation: "Mary Parſons of Springfield having two Bills of Indictment framed againſt her, the one for having Familiarity with the Devill as a Witch, to which ſhe pleaded not Guilty, and not ſufficient Euidence appearing to proue the ſame, ſhe was aquited of Witchcraft. The ſecond Indictment was for wilfully and moſt wickedly murdering her owne Child, to which ſhee pleaded guilty, confeſt the Fact, and according to her Deſerts was condemned to Dy."

A Jury had previouſly convicted Hugh, the Huſband of Mary Parſons, of the Crime of Witchcraft, by the Practice of which as charged, he had cauſed his Child's Death; but in the mean Time the poor, diſtreſſed and wretched Wife had confeſſed herſelf a Witch, and that ſhe had killed the Child. This Confeſſion cauſed the Court to come to the Decſion juſt recorded; and on the 27th of the ſame Month they came to the following Decifion in the Hufband's Cafe: "The Magiftrates not confenting to the Verdict of the Jury in Parfons's Cafe, the Caufe coming legally to the General Court for Iffue, the Court on Perufal of the Euidence brought in againft him for Witchcraft, doe judge that he is not legally Guilty of Witchcraft; fo not to Dy by our Law."

Hence in the Law-Logic of that Time one was confidered Guilty till another for the fame Crime was found fo; reminding us of the vicarious Punifhment (though not exactly a Parallel Cafe) fo ludicroufly paraded by Butler, as being in Ufe in New England, in its early Settlement.

Thus, after a long and tedious Profecution at Springfield, he was fent to Bofton to be finally difpofed of; and here a Bill of Indictment was "framed" againft him, of which this is a Copy: "The Grand Jurie for this Comanwelth prefent Hugh Parfons of Springfield, not haueing ye Feare of God before his Eyes, in or abought March laft, and diuers Times before and fince, at Springfield aforefaid (as they conceued) had familier and wiced Conuerfe with ye Deuil, and did ufe diuers duelifh Practifes and Witchcrafte to ye Hurte of diuers Perfons, as by feueral Witneffes and Sercumftanfes doth apr. and doe leaue him to ye Corte for his further tryal for his Life."

The Verdict of the Trial Jury was rendered in Writing and is in thefe Words:

"The Jurie of Life and Death findes againft Hugh Parfons, by ye Teftemony of fuch as apearde in Corte, foe much as giues them Grounde not to cleare him, but cofidered with yᵉ Teftimonys of diuers yᵗ are at Springfield, whofe Teftimonys were onely fent in Writeinge, as alfo yᵉ Confeffion of Mary Parfons, and yᵉ Impeachment of fome of yᵉ bewitched Perfons of yᵉ faid Hew Parfons, which, if yᵉ General Corte make yᵉ Confeffion of Mary Parfons and yᵉ impechment of yᵉ bewitched Perfons or other of them, and yᵉ Teftemonys yᵗ are in Writeinge, but appeared not in Perfon authentike Teftimonys acordinge to Law, then yᵉ Jurie findes yᵉ faide Hugh Parfons Giltie of yᵉ fin of Wichcrafte.

EDWARD HUTCHINSON,[1] *Foreman,*"
with yᵉ Confent of yᵉ reft of yᵉ Jurie.

It is Plain that the Jury intended to throw the Refponfibility on the General Court, which was a fafe and eafy Way to difpofe of the Cafe, the Murder of the Child having been affumed by its poor demented Mother. It is Evident, however, that there was a lingering Belief in the Minds of the Jury, that Hugh had been practifing Witchcraft on his Neighbours at Springfield; but as it was chiefly in cutting boiled Puddings longitudinally, filing of Saws in the Night Time, and fome few other equally innocent (though invifible-handed) Amufements, they thought it Beft to fhuffle over them, as fet forth in the above Verdict.

---

[1] The Great-Grand-Father of Gov. Thomas Hutchinfon, the Hiftorian of *Maffachufetts Bay.* He died Aug. 19th, 1675, of Wounds received in an Attack by the Indians at Wickabang Pond, a few Days previous. The Governour does not mention this Circumftance in his Hiftory.

What became of the friendlefs Man, after his Trial, does not clearly appear. He did not probably remain long in Bofton, and never returned to Springfield, as fome of his Effects were not long after fold for him by Mr. John Pynchon, and the Proceeds remitted to him in Bofton. It is believed that he went to Narraganfet, and thence to Long Ifland, which are all the Traces we have of him.

It appears from the Teftimonies (which will be found in the Appendix) that there was Something like Confpiracy againft Parfons, for as late as the 7th of April, when Jonathan Taylor gave in his Teftimony at the Court, he faid that Hugh Parfons came to him and defired to know who were his Accufers; and on Taylor's refufing to tell him, Hugh replied, "I know you can tell. Was it ever known that a Man fhould be accufed and not know his Accufers?" It will be found that whenever Anything is recorded of what Parfons faid, on any Occafion, it fhows a good Underftanding and Common Senfe. Some Allowance will of Neceffity be made, as it all comes from his Accufers.

There no doubt was Something of an extenfive Enmity againft Parfons, as is inferred from the general Tenour of the Teftimonies againft him, and his Examinations. The Teftimonies amount to Nothing, being a Collection of as childifh Nonfenfe as ever was got together; and how a Man of Senfe, as Mr. Pynchon is fuppofed to have been, could have fat, day after day and liftened to it, is as aſtoniſhing as the Matter itſelf is puerile, abſurd and ridiculous.

As has been noticed in other Proſecutions, ſo in this, it is very obſervable that the accuſed Party had many Enemies. He was ſhrewd in making Bargains, and perhaps might have taken advantage Sometimes, when he thought he had made a hard one, or been overreached, of attempting to "throw it up." But there is no Evidence of Diſhoneſty on his Part. He was a Brickmaker as well as a Sawyer, or he carried on the latter Buſineſs. He had a Difficulty with Mr. Moxon, the Miniſter, reſpecting the Bricks for the Chimney of his Houſe. Hence Mr. Moxon was among his Accuſers. It is inferred that the Miniſter had ſome Advantage by the Contract, and that Parſons thought he ought not to be held to perform it, but he did not refuſe to perform his Part, only, was wont to remark as on ſimilar Occaſions, that if Mr. Moxon exacted its Performance "it would do him no good," or that he "would be Even with him." Theſe were very common Expreſſions with him, and ſeem to have had great Weight with his Accuſers, as Evidence that he practiſed Witchcraft.

Parſons was proſecuted ſome Time before this (1649) Witchcraft Affair, by "the Widow Marſhfield," for a Libel, by Words uttered by his Wife. We learn this incidentally, and by Inference alſo, that the Libel conſiſted in Mrs. Parſons ſaying that Goodwife Marſhfield had bewitched Mr. Moxon's Children. The Caſe went againſt him and he was condemned to pay the heavy Amount of twenty-four Bufhels of Indian Corn, and twenty Shillings in Money. Both Parfons and his Wife declared that this was owing to falfe Swearing. Hence, the Records of that Cafe would doubtlefs difclofe the Names of thofe who fwore againft him, and that the fame Individuals came forward on the fame Side to prove him a Witch.

From what can be gathered in examining the Teftimonies, it is Evident that Parfons's Wife was a turbulent Woman, and by her unbridled Tongue had been the Means of the Profecution for Slander before mentioned. This may have been the Caufe of some Neglect of her on his Part. This Neglect may alfo have been a Caufe of inconfiderate Complaints and harfh Speeches to Others by her againft her Hufband; and he appears to have been a Man of ftrong Refentments, and it was very Natural that he fhould exhibit them on fuch Occafions, and that Altercations arofe, and were continued until an entire Eftrangement and Hatred put an End to all Affection. At length ill Health, and a naturally bad Temper threw her into a State of Infanity, fo plainly exhibited at the Examination of her Hufband.

Some Time previous to the 15th of May of this Year the People of Stratford, in Connecticut were in great Commotion by Witchcraft breaking out there. Records, fo far as can be learned, are nearly Silent refpecting it. From fuch Intimations and incidental Notices as have been gathered, it is Evident that one Goodwife Baffett was tried, condemned for a Witch, and executed in that Town. Her Trial took place fubfequently to the 15th of May, as will appear from the following Entry in the Court Records of Connecticut, in thefe Words: "The Gouernour, Mr. Cullick and Mr. Clarke are defired to goe downe to Stratford to keepe Courte vppon the Tryall of Goody Baffett for her Life; and if the Gouernour cannott goe, then Mr. Wells is to goe in his Roome." It may be worth Attention to remark that John Haynes, Efq., was Governour, Mr. John Cullick, Mr. Daniel Clarke, and Mr. John Wells were Magiftrates.

As to who Goodwife Baffett was there appears no prefent Means of knowing, and it may hardly be worth While to venture Conjectures on the Queftion. Prefident Dwight Somewhere mentions her Execution, and Profeffor Kingfley adverts to it in his *Centennial* of 1838 at Newhaven. She was moft likely an elderly Woman, who came to New England as a Member of fome Family, and perhaps without any near Relative; and having become old, and none to take an Intereft in her Welfare, it was eafy, in thofe Days, and under fuch Circumftances, when the Cry of "Witch" was once fet up, to hunt down and ruin the decrepit and friendlefs.

Some Writers, with a greater Defire to make their Neighbourhood appear free from Blemifhes than to relate Facts, have denied that there is any

Proof that Executions for Witchcraft took place within their Jurisdiction. But in the Case of Goodwife Bassett, Doubts appear to be gratuitous. Three Places were known in Stratford where *Gallows* had stood, before 1680.[1] Persons of the Name of *Bassett* were early quite numerous in Connecticut.

1652.

No accurate Opinion can be formed as to the Extent of a Disturbance occasioned by Agents from the Invisible World, by a single Instance that happens to be recorded. It is reasonable to suppose that Accusations went on in a Village or Town many Months, and perhaps Years, before the Courts felt obliged to take Cognizance of them. Thus in the Town of Ipswich, in a Court held there in 1652, we are assured on the best Authority, that a Man was sentenced to be whipt, or to pay twenty Shillings "for having Familiarity with the Devil;"[2] while we are not told the name of the Man, or what Evidence he was convicted on. How such a Sentence could have been rendered under the Laws even then in force, it is not Easy to see.

On recurring to a late elaborate Work[3] the Name of the Accused was found to be John Bradstreet of Rowley, and that his Crime pro-

---

[1] Hinman, *Genealogy of the Puritans*, 160.

[2] Felt, *Hist. Ipswich, from Quarterly Court Files*, 207.

[3] By the Rev. Mr. C. W. Upham.

bably was for telling his Dreams. Francis Parat and his Wife, of Rowley; and William Bartholomew of Ipfwich, evidenced that Bradftreet told them that he read in a Book of Magick, and that he heard a Voice afking him what Work he had for him. He [the Voice] anfwered, "Go make a Bridge of Sand over the Sea; go make a Ladder of Sand up to Heaven, and go to God and come down no more." For this idle and nonfenfical Talk, and "telling a Lie," he was condemned to pay twenty Shillings or be whipped. He had been convicted before of lying.

1653.

The Affairs at Springfield were fcarcely over before the "Devill" was "difcovered" among the Women of New Haven Colony, and indirectly among the fober and ftrong minded Men of that Place. It is told, by way of prefatory Matter,[1] that "Moleftations from Evil Spirits, in more fenfible and furprifing Operations than thofe finer Methods wherein they commonly work upon the Minds of all Men, but efpecially of *Ill Men*, have fo abounded in this Countrey, that I queftion whether any one Town has been free from *fad Examples* of them. The Neighbours have not been careful enough to *Record* and Atteft the prodigious Occurrences of this Importance, which have been among us. Many *true* and *ftrange* Occurrences from the Invifible World, in thefe

[1] By Dr. C. Mather, Magnalia, B. VI, 66.

Parts of the World, are faultily buried in Oblivion.[1] But some of these very stupendious Things have had their Memory preserved in the written Memorials of honest, prudent, and faithful Men; for every one of which we have had such a sufficient Evidence, that no *Reasonable* Man in this whole Countrie ever did question them." Whence it follows, that all who did question them were *un*-reasonable Persons.

The second Person who suffered Death in the New Haven Colony, so far as Researches up to this Time have discovered, was a Woman, named Knapp. It is remarked by a modern Hand, that "she suffered terribly by Witchcraft, if the trifling Story in the *Magnalia* is good for Anything."[2] But if the Accounts contained in the original Records are reliable, of which there can be no Doubt, the "trifling" lies at the Door of our Cotemporary. In following that Account, however, he has placed the Case of "terrible Suffering" about twenty Years later than its actual Occurrence; unless there were two Persons of the Name of Knapp who suffered for Witch-

---

[1] Was the "prodigious Occurrence" at Springfield unknown to the Drs. Mather, or did they purposely omit it? I see no Reason for their omitting it, unless it were to obliviate Mr. Pynchon and Mr. Moxon. The former being in Advance of the Age on the Question of Religious Liberty, and the latter because he was of the same Opinion.

[2] The "Story" is copied by Dr. C. Mather from the *Remarkable Providences* of his Father. Mr. Savage probably knew this, but it afforded him more Pleasure to hurl a Missile at the Son than at the real Author. See *N. Eng. Gen. Dict. Art.* KNAPP.

craft, one in 1653, and the other in 1671. This Point we muſt leave for him or others to reconcile, and ſpeak from the Record before us.

Of the Trial and Execution of Goodwife Knapp. What Facts we poſſeſs regarding her Caſe came out at an Arraignment of Mr. Roger Ludlow, at the May Term of the "Court of Magiſtrates" at New Haven, for defaming the Character of the Wife of Thomas Staplies, "in reporting to Mr. Dauenport and Mrs. Dauenport, that ſhe had laid herſelfe vnder a new Suſpition of being a Witch; that ſhe had cauſed Knapp's Wife to be new ſearched after ſhe was hanged, and when ſhe ſaw the Teates, ſaid, if they were the Markes of a Witch, then ſhe was one, or ſhe had ſuch Markes; ſecondly, Mr. Ludlow ſaid Knapps Wife told him that Goodwife Staplies was a Witch; thirdly, that Mr. Ludlow hath ſlandered Goodwife Staplies in ſaying that ſhe made a Trade of lying, &c."

On the Trial, Mr. Ludlow failed to convince the Court that he did not thus charge Mrs. Staplies with being a Witch, or to make it appear that ſhe was a Witch. Whereupon the Court ordered that Mr. Ludlow "pay to Thomas Staplies, by way of Fine, for Reparation of his Wiues Name Ten Pounds, and for his Trouble and Charge in following the Suit Five Pounds more." He was fined at the next Term Ten Pounds additional for accuſing her of lying.

It would ſeem that Mr. Ludlow had been instrumental in causing Mrs. Knapp[1] to be put to Death; and that Mrs. Staplies's chief Sin was in not believing that she, Goodwife Knapp, was Guilty, and in reporting agreeably to her Belief. Lawyers were employed on both Sides; Ensign Alexander Bryan on the Part of Mr. Ludlow, and Mr. John Banks for Mr. Staplies. Specimens of the Testimony, so far as they bear on the Case of Mrs Knapp, follow:

Mr. Davenport[2] testified, "that, Mr. Ludlow, sitting with him and his Wife alone, and discoursing of the Passages concerning Knapp's Wife the Witch, and her Execution, said that she came down from the Ladder, (as he [Davenport] understood it,) and desired to speak with him [Ludlow] alone, and told him who was the Witch spoken of; and so farr as he remembers, he, or his Wife asked him who it was; he said she named Goodwife Staplies. Mr. Dauenport replyed, that he beleeued it was vtterly vntrue, and spoken [by Knapp] out of Malice. Mr. Ludlow answered that he hoped better of her [Staplies] but said she was a foolish Woman; and then told them a further Storey — how she tumbled the Corpse of the Witch vp and downe after her Death, before sundrie Women, and

---

[1] I have not followed the Record in respect to the Prefixes or Titles of some Persons, but have used Mrs., Mr., Goodwife and Goodman indiscriminately, the Records themselves having little of Uniformity in this Particular.

[2] The Rev. John Davenport, afterwards of the First Church, Boston.

fpoke to this Effect,— If thefe be the Markes of a Witch, I am one, or I have fuch Markes."

Mrs. Davenport corroborated the Evidence given by her Hufband. "Goodwif Sherwood of Fairfield affirmeth vpon Oath, that vpon fome Debate betwixt Mr. Ludlow and Goodwife Staplies, fhe heard Mr. Ludlow charge Goodwif Staplies with a Tract of lying, and that in Difcourfe fhe heard him fo charge her feuerall Times."

Hefter, Wife of Andrew Ward, teftified, "that aboute a Day after that Goodwife Knapp was condemned for a Witch, fhe goeing to the Prifon Houfe where faid Knapp was kept, fhe, the faid Knapp, voluntarily, without any Occafion giuen her, faid that Goodwife Staplyes, told her that an Indian brought vnto her, the faid Staplyes, two little Things brighter than the Light of the Day, and told the faid Goodwife Staplyes they were Indian Gods, as the Indian called them, and the Indian withall told her, the faid Staplyes, if fhe would keepe them, fhe fhould be fo big Rich, all one God; and that the faid Staplyes told the faid Knapp fhe gaue them again to the faid Indian, but fhe could not tell whether fhe did fo or no."

Lucy, the Wife of Thomas Pell fwore, "that aboute a Day after Goodwife Knapp was condemned for a Witch, Miftris Jones earneftly intreated her to goe to the faid Kapp, who had fent for her; that fhe called the faid Hefter Ward, and they went together;" that the faid Knapp fpoke "Word for Word as Hefter Ward had testified. Further, Mistris Pell testified, "that she being one of ye Women that was required to search the said Knapp before she was condemned; and then Mistris Jones pressed the said Knapp to confess whether ther were any other that were Witches; because Goodwife Bassett, when she was condemned, said there was another Witch in Fairfield, that held her Head full high; and then the said Goodwife Knapp stepped a little aside, and told her, this deponent, Goodwife Bassett meant not her. She asked her whom she meant, and she named Goodwife Staplyes, and then uttered the same Speeches as formerly concerning the Indian Gods."

Elizabeth Brewster swore, "that after Goodwife Knap was executed, as soone as she was cut downe, she, the said Knapp, being carried to the Graue Side, Goodwife Staplyes with some other Women went to search the said Knapp, concerning findeing out Teates; and Goodwife Staplyes handled her very much, and called to Goodwife Lockwood, and said, those were no Witches Teats, but such as she herself had, and other Women might have the same; and wringing her Hands and takeing ye Lords Name in her Mouth, and said,—Will you say these were Witches Teates, they were not, and called upon Goodwife Lockwood to come and see them. Then she called on Goodwife Odell to come and examine the Teats, for she had been one of the Searchers before the Execution, but she would not. Then she [Staplies] called Goodwife Lockwood to come forward and examine the Teats, and faid to her,—Will you fay thefe are Witch Teats? I have fuch myfelf, and fo have you. Goodwife Lockwood replyed, if I had fuch I would be hanged, and deferve it too. Then Goodwife Odell came neare, and told Goodwife Staplies that no honeſt Woman had fuch Teats. And then all the Women rebuking her [Staplies] and faid they were Witches Teates; then the faid Staplies yielded it." Her yielding doubtlefs amounted to this, that finding fhe could not convince the others, ceafed to fay Anything further at that Time, as fenfible People do now-a-days.

Mary Brewfter teſtified that fhe was "at the Grave-Side" after the Execution, and faw Goodwife Staplies make the Examination of the Teats, but "went away, as having no Defire to look vpon them."

Sufan, Wife of Robert Lockwood, fwore that fhe was at the Execution of Goodwife Knapp, "that was hanged for a Witch," and after fhe was cut down and brought to the Grave was prefent with other Women to fearch for Teats; that Goodwife Staplies was handling the dead Woman "where the Teates were;" that Goodwife Staplies "ſtood vp and called three or four Times, and bid me come looke of them." When fhe had done fo Mrs. Staplies afked her Opinion, as to whether they were Witch Teats? She anfwered, "No Matter. She had Teates, and confeffed fhe was a Witch. That was fufficient." Whereupon Mrs. Staplies faid: "If thefe be

Teates, here are no more than I myself have, or any other Woman, or you either if you would search your Body." Susan Lockwood replied that she did not know what Mrs. Staplies had, but for herself, "if any finde any such Things aboute me, I deserued to be hanged as she was."

"Thomas Sheruington and Christopher Combstocke and Goodwife Baldwine were altogether at the Prison House where Goodwife Knapp was, and the said Goodwife Baldwin asked her the said Knapp whether she knew of any other [Witch]. She said there were some, or one, that had received Indian Gods that were very bright. Baldwin asked her how she could tell if she were not a Witch herself. She said the party told her so, and her Husband was Witness to it."

Rebecka, Wife of Cornelius Hall, swore that when Mrs. Knapp was on her way to be executed, Mr. Ludlow and her Father (Mr. Jones) pressing the said Knapp to confess that she was a Witch, Mrs. Staplies said, "Why should she confess that which she was not? She made no Doubt if she were one she would confess it."

Deborah Lockwood, aged about Seventeen, swore, that she was present when Mrs. Knapp was going to Execution, "beteene Tryes and the Mill, she heard Goodwife Staplyes say to Goodwife Gould, she was perswaded Goodwife Knapp was no Witch. Goodwife Gould said, Sister Staplyes, she is a Witch, and hath confessed having had Familiarity with the Deuill. Staplies replied, I was with her Yefterday or laft Night, and fhe faid no fuch Thing as I heard."

Bethia Brundifh, aged about Sixteen, faid as fhe was "goeing to Execution of Goodwife Knapp, who was condemned for a Witch by the Court and Jury at Fairfield, there being prefent herfelfe and Deborah Lockwood and Sarah Cabel, fhe heard Goodwife Staplyes fay, that fhe thought Goodwife Knapp was no Witch, and Goodwife Gould prefently reproved her for it."

Goodwife Whitlocke of Fairfield was the next Witnefs. She teftified before Mr. William Fowler of Milford, May 27th, 1654, was prefent at the Execution of Mrs. Knapp, "and nex to Goody Stapleys when they were goeing to put the dead Corpes into the Grave, feuerall Women were looking for the Markes of a Witch vpon the dead Body, and feuerall of them faid they could find none, and this Deponent faid, nor I; and fhe heard Goodwife Staplyes fay, nor I; then came one that had fearched the faid Witch, and fhewed them the Markes that were vpon her; then Goodwife Staplyes faid fhe never faw·fuch in all her Life; and that fhe was perfwaded that no honeft Woman had fuch Things as thofe were."

Goodwife Barlow of Fairfield fimilarly teftified. She with one of her Neighbours defired to fee the Marks of a Witch when Mrs. Knapp was ready to be buried, and they looked but found none. Then Goodwife Staplyes came and one or two more. "Goodwife Staplleyes kneeled downe by them, and they all looked but found them not, and said they saw Nothing but what is common to other Women; but after they found them they all wondered, and Goodwife Staplyes in Particular, and said they never saw such Things in their Life before, so they went away."

The Wife of John Thompson of Fairfield went to the Grave also with the others, and "desired to see the Marks of the Witch," but found none at first; "then the Midwife came and shewed them," and Goodwife Staplyes exclaimed as stated by the other Witnesses. The Wife of Richard Lyon, and Goodwife Squire of Fairfield swore also to the same purport.

Goodwife Sherwood of Fairfield swore that on the Day Mrs. Knapp was condemned, "she was there to see her, all being gone forth but Goodwife Odill and herself, then there came in Mistris Pell and her two daughters, Elizabeth and Mary, Goody Lockwood and Goodwife Purdy." Mistris Pell told Mrs. Kapp she was sent to her "to have her confess," and that if she knew any other Witches to discover them, that now she was condemned, and must die, her Confession could not prejudice her Case. As to herself and Family, Mistris Pell said they had not testified against her; that "the Jury and Godly Magistrates had found her Guilty, and that the last Evidence cast the Cause."[1] The next day Mistris

---

[1] This has Reference probably to the Person who testified last before the Jury, on Mrs Knapp's Trial at Fairfield; and from the Testimony of Goodwife Sherwood it is inferred that Goodwife Staplies was the last Witness.

Pell went "to the Witch again," with Mr. Jones, Elizabeth and Mary Pell, Miſtris Ward and Goodwife Lockwood. Miſtris Pell deſired Mrs. Knap "to lay open herſelf, and make Way for the Miniſter to do her Good." Elizabeth Pell "bid her doe as the other Witch at the other Towne did,[1] and diſcover all ſhe knew to be Witches." Mrs. Knapp meekly replied that ſhe muſt not ſay what was not true, and muſt not wrong Anybody; that when ſhe came to the Ladder, if ſhe had Anything to ſay ſhe would ſay it to Mr. Ludlow and the Miniſter. Elizabeth Brewſter then preſent ſaid to her, "If you keepe it till you come to the Ladder, the Diuill will have you quick." Mrs. Knapp replied, "you would have me ſay that Goodwife Staplyes is a Witch, but I have Sins enough to anſwer for already, and I hope I ſhall not add to my Condemnation." She denied ever having ſaid ſhe knew of a Witch in the Town.

The poor Woman was evidently cruſhed by a Swarm of deluded Wretches, all endeavouring to convince her that ſhe was going into Eternity with a Lie on her Tongue, and knowing of other Witches, would not name them; warning her to "take heede that the Deuill perſwaded her not to ſow malicious Seed to doe hurt when ſhe was dead." At this, and much other ſimilar Stuff, Goodwife Knapp "burſt forth into weeping,"

---

[1] The "other Witch" was probably a Woman named Baſſett, who it would ſeem had been executed in 1651.— See ante, *ſub ano idem*.

and defired her Tormentor to pray for her. Whether Mr. Buckley was prefent does not appear, but he was at the Execution, and among thofe who faw the Grave clofe over her. This was Mr. Gerfhom Buckley the Minifter of Fairfield, and no Voice of his was raifed againft the Execution, fo far as appears anywhere.

With all the Details here related, and acceffible to a Hiftorian of Connecticut, it is ftrange he fhould fay, "From a careful Examination of the Records of New Haven Colony, it does not appear that there ever was even a Conviction for the Crime of Witchcraft, within that Jurifdiction, much lefs was there ever an Execution"![1]

Not long after Mr. Ludlow was fined twenty-five Pounds for defaming the Character of Mrs. Staplies, he left the Jurifdiction, is faid to have gone to Virginia, and nothing was heard of him afterwards. It would feem that he had rendered himfelf very unpopular by the Part he had taken in bringing Mrs. Knapp to the Gallows. That Unpopularity may have had an earlier Date, perhaps Mrs. Baffett's Profecution and Execution may have been under his Direction. It is evident that the People were divided into bitter Parties, and that one Party oppofed the other, not on the Ground that either difbelieved in Witchcraft, but becaufe of Quarrels which had Nothing to do with that Phantom.

There is a little Uncertainty as to the precife

---

[1] Hollifter's *Hift. Connecticut*, II, 533.

Year in which the grim Messenger of Darkness first appeared in the Disguise of a Bird to a Family in Andover. The following Copy from the original Deposition in the Writer's Possession will display all the Facts for the Reader's Deliberation. It was made before the venerable Governor Bradstreet in 1659, from which it appears that the Visit of the Witch took place about five or six Years previous, namely, in 1653 or 1654. Bradstreet found himself circumstanced similarly to Mr. Pynchon, not long before, as has been related. These Gentlemen probably would never have taken away the Life of an Individual, although Believers in the Reality of Witchcraft; but if left to themselves would have found ample Excuse for not proceeding to Extremities, from honest Doubts as to the Fact being fully proved.

"The Deposicons of Job Tylar aged about 40 Years, Mary his Wife, Moses Tyl^r his Son aged betwixt 17 and 18 Years, and Mary Tylar about 15 Yeares old.

"These Deponents witnesse that they saw a Thing like a Bird to come in at the Dore of there House with John Godfery in the Night about the Bignes of a Black Bird or rather bigger, to wit as big as a Pigion, and did fly about; John Godfery labouring to catch it and the Bird vanished, as they conceived, through the Chinck of a ioynted Bord, and being asked by the Man of the House wherfore it came, he answered, It came to fuck your Wife. This was (as they remember) about 5 or 6 Yeares fince.

"Taken vpon Oath of the 4 aboue menconed pties, this 27. 4. 59. before mee
"Simon Bradftreete.

"Ouned in Court 7 M^rch, 1665, by Job Tylar and Mofes Tylar.   E. R. Sec.

"Ouned in Court 13 March 65 by Mary Tyler on her former Oath.   E. R. S^c."

1653–5.

The Commotion of 1653, in the Town of New Haven, alleged to have been caufed by Witchcraft, muft have been long and fadly remembered. At this Period there was living there, a reftlefs inquifitive old Woman, named Elizabeth Godman. She was probably one of the moft intenfe Believers in Witchcraft, being always ready when Anything tranfpired, which fhe, in her very limited Knowledge, could not fee the remote or even the immediate Caufe, tò charge it to the Work of the "Diuell," or his Agents, fuppofed then by Everybody to be hovering in the Air juft above them, ready to take advantage of all human Frailties.

How long before the Seffion of the "Court of Magiftrates" of New Haven, which commenced on the 4th of Auguft of this Year, the firft Trouble from the "Invifible World" began, cannot be ftated; but there was living at New Haven at that Time a Mrs. Godman, as juft mentioned, in the Family of Thomas Johnſon. She appears to have previouſly reſided in the "Bay," at or near Boſton, at the Time of ſome Witch Troubles in that Colony, and may have left there in Conſequence of thoſe Troubles, but how that may have been cannot be definitely ſtated. At all Events, many of the firſt People of New Haven ſaw, or thought they ſaw Cauſe to accuſe Mrs. Godman of Witchcraft; but the Proſecutions which followed in Conſequence were inſtituted by Mrs. Godman herſelf. She went before the Court for Redreſs, becauſe of, as ſhe alleged, falſe Accuſations; but as the Parties accuſed were of the higheſt Standing the Tables were at once turned, becauſe the Court believed her Accuſers inſtead of her. Among theſe were Goodwife Larremore, Goodman Jeremy Whitnels, Mr. Stephen Goodyeare, and Mrs. Goodyeare, Mr. William Hooke, and Mrs. Hooke, Mrs. Atwater, Hannah and Elizabeth Lamberton, Goodwife Thorpe, Mrs. Biſhop, Mary Miles, "&c."

The Court conſiſted of Theophilus Eaton, Eſq., the Governour, Mr. Stephen Goodyeare, Dept. Governour, Francis Newman, Capt. John Aſtwood and Mr. William Leete, Magiſtrates.

The firſt who gave her Reaſons for what ſhe had ſaid of Mrs. Godman, was Goodwife Larremore. She ſaid that as ſoon as "ſhe ſaw her come in at Goodman Whitnels ſhe thought of a Witch; once ſhe ſpoke to that Purpoſe at Mr. Hookes; and her Ground was becauſe Mr. Dauenport, about that Time, had occaſion in his

Miniftry to fpeak of Witches; and fhowed that a froward difcontented Frame of Spirit was a Subject fitt for yᵉ Devill to worke vpon in that way, and fhe looked vpon Mrs. Godman to be of fuch a Frame of Spirit, but for faying fo at Goodman Whitnels fhe denies it." Mrs. Godman anfwered that Mr. Whitnel's Maid confirmed what fhe faid; but when the Maid came fhe faid fhe thought fhe heard Goodwife Larremore fay "fhe thought of a Witch in the Bay when fhe fee Mrs. Godman." The Governor afked Mrs. Larremore if fhe thought Mrs. Godman a Witch, and fhe faid fhe did not. The Court then told Mrs. Godman that fhe had warned divers Perfons to appear, and demanded of her what her Charges were againft them. She faid they had given out Speeches that made Folks think fhe was a Witch; "and firft fhe charged Mrs. Atwater to be yᵉ Caufe of all;" who had faid fhe was a Witch, and that Hobbamock (the Divil of the Indians) was her Hufband. The Court informed her that fhe could prove Nothing, although fhe had been notified to have her Witneffes ready.

Then "fundrie Paffages in yᵉ Wrighting were read." As "yᵉ Wrighting" is not given in the Record, it is conjectured that it was Notes taken before a previous Court, and confifted of Charges and Evidence going to prove that Mrs. Godman was a Witch; for when the Writing was read the Court inquired of her "if thefe Thinges did not giue juft Ground of Sufpition to all that heard them, that fhe was a Witch?" She confeſſed they did; "but ſaid if ſhe ſpake ſuch Things as is in Mr. Hookes Relation, ſhe was not herſelfe; but Mrs. Hooke teſtifyed that ſhe was in a ſober Frame, and ſpake in a deliberate Way, as ordinarily ſhe is at other Times."

Beſides what was evidenced in the "Wrighting," Mrs. Godman was reminded of what was ſaid at the Governour's, where the Writing was made, "aboute Mr. Goodyeares falling into a ſwonding Fitt, after he had ſpoken Something one Night in the Expoſition of a Chapter, which ſhe, being preſent, liked not; but ſaid it was againſt her, and as ſoon as Mr. Goodyeare had done Duties, ſhe flung out of the Roome in a diſcontented Way, and caſt a fierce Looke vpon Mr. Goodyeare as ſhe went out; and immediately Mr. Goodyeare, though well before, fell into a Swond. And beſide her notorious lying in this Buſineſs, for being aſked how ſhe came to know this, ſhe ſaid ſhe was preſent, yet Mr. Goodyeare, Mrs. Goodyeare, Hannah and Elizabeth Lamberton all affirm ſhe was not in ye Roome, but gone vp into the Chamber."

The Court, having acted the Part of an Attorney for the Perſons accuſed, now ſummed up their Judgment in theſe Words: That "Mrs. Godman hath vnjuſtly called heither the ſeuerall Perſons before named, being ſhe can proue Nothing againſt them, and that her Cariage doth juſtly render her ſuſpitious of Witchcraft, which ſhe herſelfe in ſo many Words confeſſeth, therefore the Court wiſheth her to looke to her Carriage, for if further Proofe come, thefe Paffages will not be forgotten, and therefore gaue her Charge not to goe in an offenfive Way to Folkes Houfes in a rayling Manner, as it feemeth fhe hath done, but that fhe keepe her Place, and meddle with her owne Bufinefs."

On the previous Examination of Mrs. Godwin, fhe was afked what fhe had againft Mr. and Mrs. Hooke? It feems they had intimated that fhe had caufed the Sicknefs of their Son. Now "Mr. Hooke faid hee was not without Feares, and hee had Reafons for it, becaufe fhee was fhut out at Mr. Atwaters vpon Sufpition, and he was troubled in his Sleepe aboute Witches when his Boye was ficke, which was in a verey ftrang Manner; and he looked vpon her as a mallitious one, prepared to that Mifchief; and fhe would often fpeak aboute Witches and rather juftifye them, and faid, Why doe they provoake them? Why do they not let them come into the Church? Another Time fhe faid fhe had fome Thoughts, what if the Devill fhould come to fucke her and fhe refolued he fhould not."

Another of Mr. Hooke's Accufations was that Mrs. Godwin would know what was faid and done at Church Meetings, before the Meetings were over, "as aboute Delaware Bay, aboute Mr. Cheever, and aboute Goodman Lawfon, and fome other Things." An Indian Squaw Servant named Time, figuered alfo as a Witnefs againft her. When Time afked Mrs. Godman how fhe knew Things? She anfwered fhe would not tell.

To which Time said "Did not yͤ Devill tell you?" Quite as senseless was the Testimony of one Henry Boutle; to the Effect that Mrs. Godwin talked and muttered to herself. Mr. Hooke testified further, that he had heard that Witches, that is, Persons afflicted "that way, would hardly be kept away from yͤ Houses where they doe Mischief; and so it was with her when his Boy was sicke, she would not be kept away from him, nor gett away when she was there; and one Time Mrs. Hooke bid her goe away, and thrust her from yͤ Boy, but she turned againe, and said she would looke on him." On one Occasion Mrs. Goodyeare and Mrs. Godwin had a Talk as to the Occasion of the Illness of the Child. The last named asked the other if she thought it was bewitched? Her answer implied the Affirmative. And when Mr. Goodyeare asked Mrs. Godwin if she was not the Cause of the Boy's Sickness? "She denyed it, but in such a Way as if she could scarce denye it."[1] In being importuned to give a Reason for the Boy's Sickness, she said it might be "that he had turned his Braines with sliding;" yet she doubted not he would recover, "though he was handled in such a strange Manner as the Doctor said he had not met with the Like."

Mr. Hooke appears as the leading Accuser. In the Course of his Evidence he said that when

---

[1] For Shallowness of Understanding it would be difficult to find a Parallel to this. Believe a Person bad enough to be a Witch, and yet the same Person hesitate to tell a Lie!

Mr. James Bishop was married, Mrs. Godwin came to him in much Trouble, "so as he thought it might be from some Affection" she had for Mr. Bishop; so he asked her if that were not the Case, and she said it was. Mr. Hooke further adds, that as soon as Mr. and Mrs. Bishop were "contracted," Mrs. Bishop fell into "very strang Fitts, which hath continewed, at Times ever since; and much Suspition there is that she hath bine the Cause of the Loss of Mrs. Byshop's Children, for she could tell when Mrs. Bishop was to be brought to bedd." When Mrs. Godman was asked why Mrs. Bishop's Children died, she said she supposed it was because of the Mother's "longing," or something to that Effect; and Jane Hooke said that Mrs. Godman told her that Mrs. Bishop was much "given to longing, and that was the Reason she lost her Children."

Another very remarkable Circumstance was, and it was a "suspitious" one, that on a certain Time she knew that Mrs. Atwater had Figs in her Pocket. She knew she had because she smelt them, but Jane Hooke was present at the Time and could not smell Figs; therefore Mrs. Godman came under additional "Suspition" of Witchcraft. And Mrs. Atwater said Mrs. Godman "could tell that they at one time had Pease Porridge, when they could none of them tell how she came to know" it. Further, Mrs. Atwater said that on the night the Figs were smelt, they had Strangers to Supper, and Mrs. Godman was there; "she cutt a Sopp and put in Pann;

Betty Brewſter called the Maide to tell her, and ſaid ſhe [Godman] was aboute her Workes of Darkneſs, and was ſuſpitious of her, and that Night Betty Brewſter was in a moſt miſerable Caſe, hearing a moſt dreadfull Noiſe, which put her in great Feare and Trembling, which put her into ſuch a Sweate as ſhe was all on a Water when Mary Miles came to go to Bed, who had fallen a ſleepe by the Fire, which ſhe vſed not to doe, and in ye Morning ſhe looked as one y^t had bine almoſt Dead." Mrs. Atwater now told Mrs. Godwin ſhe was ſuſpicious of her, and "forwarned her of her Houſe;" at which " ſhe ſaid ſhe would haue her before ye Court; yet the next Night ſhe came againe for Beare."

With ſuch trifling Details was much Time conſumed by the Court, occupying ſeveral Days and many Pages of its Records. So much only was intended to be given here as would enable future Inquirers into the Condition of Society and its Laws at this Period in the Life of New England, to form a correct Opinion. No Deciſion of the Court is recorded, reſpecting the Diſpoſal of Mrs. Godman. But about two Years later, namely, on the 17th of October, 1655, ſhe was called before the Court of Magiſtrates, conſiſting of Theophilus Eaton, Eſq., Governour, Francis Newman, Mr. Benjamin Fenn, and Mr. William Leete, Magiſtrates. Being " called before this Court and told that vpon Grounds formerly declared, which ſtand vpon Record, ſhe by her owne Confeſſion remains vnder Suſpition for Witchcraft, and one more is now added, and that is, that one time this laſt Summer, comeing to Mr. Hookes to beg ſome Beare, was at firſt denyed; but after, ſhe was offered ſome by his Daughter which ſtood ready drawne, but ſhe refuſed it and would haue ſome newly drawne, which ſhe had, yet went away in a muttering diſcontented Manner; and after this, that Night, though the Beare was good and freſh, yet the next Morning was hott, ſoure and ill taſted; yea ſo hott as the Barrell was warme without Side; and when they opened the Bung it ſteamed forth. They brewed againe and it was ſo alſo, and ſo continewed foure or fiue Times, one after another." Such were the principal Charges againſt her; at leaſt theſe thus vaguely ſet forth appear in the Records of the Supreme Court of the Colony, then denominated the "Court of Magiſtrates."

The Records contain none of the Evidence which ſhe brought forward on her Part, but ſay "ſhe brought diuers to the Court that they might ſay ſomething to cleare her, and much Time was ſpent in hearing them, but to little purpoſe; the Grounds of Suſpition remaining full as ſtrong as before, and ſhe found full of lying; wherefore the Court declared vnto her, that though the Euidence is not ſufficient as yet to take away her Life, yet the Suſpitions are cleere and many, which ſhe cannot by all the Meanes ſhe hath vſed, free herſelf from; therefore ſhe muſt forbeare from goeing from Houſe to Houſe to give

Offence, and carry it orderly in the Family where fhe is; which, if fhe doe not, fhe will caufe the Court to committ her to Prifon again; and that fhe doe now prefently, vpon her Freedom giue Securitie for her good Behauiour: and fhe did now, before the Court, ingage fifty Pound of her Eftate, that is in Mr. Goodyeers Hand, for her good Behauiuor, which is further to be cleered next Court, when Mr. Goodyeare is at Home."

As no notice appears in the Records of the "next Court," no further Proceedings, were probably had againft her; and from the New Haven Records we learn that Mrs. Godman lived in the Family of Thomas Johnfon, and that fhe died on the 9th of October, 1660.[1]

1655.

An Abftract of the Laws of New England, as prepared by the Rev. Mr. John Cotton was publifhed in London. In this, among the Capital Crimes is Witchcraft, "which is Fellowfhip by Covenant with a familiare Spirit, to be punifhed with Death." It futher enacts, that, Confulters with Witches not to be tolerated, but either to be cut off by Death or Banifhment, or other fuitable Punifhment."[2]

It was thought an appropriate Time to re-enact and promulgate Laws againft Familiarity with the Devil, the Fathers of that Day being weak

---

[1] See *Colonial Records of New Haven*, I, 29, 151.

[2] Hutchinson's *Collection of Original Papers*, 172.

enough to suppose they could prevent it; and we are told — what it is easy to believe — that Accusations at this Period were common in all Parts of New England.[1] One certainly was executed in Boston in 1656, but her Prosecution and Condemnation took place the Year before. This was Mrs. Anne Hibbins, Wife of Mr. William Hibbins.[2] It is said that several Persons were executed in the Vicinity and certainly one in Boston, in 1655[1] but no Names or other Facts appear.

1656.

Respecting the Execution of Mrs. Hibbins, that those who consummated it may bear their Share of the Transaction, their Names are here subjoined: John Endicott and Richard Bellingham were Governour and Deputy Governour; Simon Bradstreet, Samuel Symonds, Robert Bridges, Thomas Wiggin, Daniel Gookin, Daniel Denison, Simon Willard, and Humphrey Atherton were Assistants; Edward Rawson was Secretary.

The Case is abruptly brought up on the 14th of May in the General Court, and thus disposed of; the Jury having failed to bring her in guilty: "The Magistrates not receaving the Verdict of the Jury in Mrs. Hibbens hir Case, having binn on Triall for Witchcraft, it came, and fell of

---

[1] Dr. William Bentley, the excellent Historian of Salem.

[2] For further Particulars, see *Hist. and Antiqs. Boston*, 346.

Courfe to the Generall Court. Mrs. Ann Hibbins was called forth, appeared at the Barr. The Indictment againft her was read, to which fhe anfwered, Not guilty, and was willing to be trjed by God and this Court. The Evidences againft hir was read, the Partjes wittneffing being prefent, hir Anfwers confidered on and the whole Court being mett together, by theire Vote, determined that Mrs. Anne Hibbens is guilty of Witchcraft, according to the Bill of Indictment found againft hir by the Jury of Life and Death. The Governour, in open Court, pronounct Sentence accordingly; declaring fhe was to goe from the Barr to the Place from whence fhe came, and from thence to the Place of Execution, and there to hang till fhe was dead." Then follows: " Itt is ordered, that Warrant fhall iffue out from the Secretary to the Marfhall General for the Execution of Mrs. Hibbens, on the 5th Day next come Fortnight, prefently after the Lecture at Bofton, being the 19th of June next; the Marfhall Generall taking with him a fufficient Guard."

The Evidence which fent this poor Woman to an ignominious Grave, was doubtlefs fimilar to that given at other Trials; but if preferved it has not been met with. According to Hutchinfon, this was the fecond Execution for Witchcraft in New England, of which there is any Record.

In Hampton, New Hampfhire, a Profecution commenced againft a fuppofed Witch in the Year

1656; and although Everybody in the Town, or nearly Everybody "and his Relations" believed the Accufed a Witch, fhe *was* "fuffered to live." Her Name was Eunice Cole, Wife of William Cole who died in 1662. From his Will made a few Days before his Death, the Inference is drawn that he was much younger than his Wife; but if fo it is a fomewhat of an anomalous Cafe, as Eunice was old enough for a Witch fix Years earlier, and as a general Thing, only aged Females were Witches in thofe Days.

According to the unvarying Traditions in the Town, Unice was a terrible Character, who, in the Imaginations of moft of the People, could do fuperhuman Things. The very Mention of her Name would hufh crying Children, and hurry truant Boys to School. The Hiftorian of the Town was difpofed to give her no enviable Character, averring that "fhe was a fruitful Source of Vexation for a long Series of Years; hated and defpifed for her ugly and malicious Difpofition, and feared on account of her fuppofed Alliance with the Devil."[1] But the diligent Hiftorian did not meet with her earlieft Profecution. He informs us that foon after the Death of her Hufband, the Deputy from the Town to the General Court was charged with a Petition to allow the Town to detain "Unice Coule att the Houfe of Correction according to the Court Order." About three Years later,

---

[1] *Manufcript Hiftory of Hampton*, by the late E. W. Toppan.

namely, October, 1665, William Salter acknowledged the receipt of eight Pounds, "on Account of the Town of Hampton, being due unto me for the Maintainance of Eunice Cole, Prifoner." And, on the 8th of June, 1668, Mr. Salter acknowledged the Receipt of another eight Pounds, "in hogfhead Staves, for keeping Goodwife Cole this Yeare."

Eunice feems to have been alternately at large and in Prifon; and although reprefented as being a Terror to the Town, owing to her fuppofed League with the Devil, fhe does not feem to have prevented mifchievous Youngfters from exercifing their diabolical or fome other Propenfity of playing all Kinds of malicious Tricks upon her. Hence fhe became a poor Outcaft, defpifed by the Ignorant, and but faintly pitied, if at all, by the better Part of the People. Hence the Cry of Witch! Witch! was eafily ftarted at any Time, and as late as September, 1680, fhe was up before a "Quarter Court" in Hampton, Maj. Richard Waldron prefiding, "being by Authoritie committed to Prifon on Sufpition of being a Witch; and from Examination of Teftimonys the Court vehemently fufpects her fo to be." But the Court decided that "no full Proof" appearing, ordered her to be imprifoned, and "a Lock kept on her Leg," at the Pleafure of the Court, and the Select Men "to take Care to provide for her as formerly." She muft now have been very old, as it was twenty-four Years after her Profecution in 1656. For fome Years, how many is not stated, she lived alone in a little Hut which stood on a Spot in the Rear of that on which the Academy now stands. In that she died, with none to assuage her last Sufferings. Some Days having elapsed before her Death was known, and then, according to the current Tradition, it required no little Bravery on the Part of the Inhabitants, to muster Courage enough to break into her Cabin; this was at length effected, and the Remains dragged out, a Hole dug near by, and the Body tumbled in, and thus she was there buried; and then a Stake was driven through the Body agreeably to the Superstition of the Times.

So far as is known, the following Depositions are the first Acts in the Tragedy of Eunice Cole. Thomas Colman or Coleman, on whose Account an Action was commenced, settled in Hampton before 1650. He came there from Newbury, in which Place he is found as early as 1635. His Children, born in Hampton, were Benjamin, 1640; Joseph, 1642; and Isaac, 1647. Abraham Drake was Son of Robert, at whose House the Meeting of the "Celekte" Men was held, as mentioned in the Deposition. Robert Drake and his Family came from Colchester, in Essex, England. Coleman, if the same mentioned in the *Founders of New England*, came from Marlborough in Wiltshire, in 1635.

"The Depoceshon of Thomas Coleman and Abraham Drake. Theafe Deponents faith, aboute a Yeare and halfe agon, thay being at Robart Drakes Houce at a Metinge with the

Celekte Men, Eunes Cooles cam in two the ſaid Houce and demand Help of the Celkt Men for Wood or other Thinges, and the Celekt Men tould hur ſhee had an Eſtate of hur oune, and neded noe Help of the Toune; whar vppon Eunes ancered, they cold help Good man Robe, being a luſte Man, and ſhee coolde hau none, but Eunes ſaid all ould not, or *ſhould not doe*, and about two or thre Dayes after this, ſaid Robe loſt a Kowe and a Sheepe yerry ſtrangly, and one of the Men then preſant tould Yunes Cooles ſhee ſhold looke at a Hand of God in it, for with-drauing the Pepell Hartes from helping of hur. Eunes Cooles ancered, noe, twas the Deuill did it. Depoſed in Court, 5 September, 56.

"EDW. RAWSON, *Secret*.

"Thomas Coleman and John Redman, de-poſed to yᵉ Evidence, and pticularly to yᵉ Words *ſhould not doe*. 5th September, 56.

"EDW. RAWSON, *Secrety*."

[The laſt Sentence in the firſt Paragraph, and all of the laſt Paragraph are in the Autograph of Secretary Rawſon.]

One Caſe of Witchcraft is recorded this Year at Portſmouth in New Hampſhire. Jane, the Wife of Thomas Walford, fell under as ſtrong Suſpicions as could well be imagined; and pro-bably as much to the Point as any ever indulged in elſewhere; but fortunately the Authorities could not be inſtigated by the Clamours of the Multitude to proceed to Extremities.

The Evidence againſt Goodwife Walford being,

in some Respects a little peculiar, a Specimen of it follows, She was brought before the Court of Assistants on the Complaint of Susannah Trimmings, who testified: "As I was going Home on Sunday Night, the 30th of March, I heard a rustling in the Woods, which I supposed to be occasioned by Swine; and presently there appeared a Woman whom I apprehended to be old Goodwife Walford. She asked me where my Consort was. I answered I had none. She said, thy Consort is at Home by this Time. Lend me a Pound of Cotton. I told her I had but two Pounds in the House, and I would not spare any to my Mother. She said I had better have done it, that my Sorrow was very great already, and it should be greater, for I was going a great Journey, but should never come there. She then left me, and I was struck, *as with a Clap of Fire* on the Back, and she vanished toward the Water Side, in my Apprehension, in the *Shape of a Cat*. She had on her Head a white linnen Hood, tied under her Chin, and her Waistcoat and Petticoat were red, with an old green Apron, and a black Hat upon her Head.

"Taken upon Oath, 18 April, 1656, before Bryan Pendleton, Henry Sherburn, and Renald Fernald."

If this Testimony did not serve to convict Mrs. Walford of Witchcraft, it will serve some future Artist as an excellent Description of the Costume of an old Woman of this Period; for there may be no Question but that the Witness described the common Drefs of the Party againft whom fhe was witneffing, which no Doubt was the nearly univerfal Coftume at the Time.

Oliver Trimmings, Hufband of this Witnefs, teftified: "My Wife came Home in a fad Condition. She paffed by me with her Child in her Arms, laid the Child on the Bed, fat down upon the Cheft, and leaned upon her Elbow. Three Times I afked her how fhe did. She could not fpeak. I took her in my Arms and held her up, and repeated the Queftion. She forced Breath, and Something ftopped in her Throat, as if it would have ftopped her Breath. I unlaced her Clothes, and foon fhe fpake, and faid, Lord have Mercy upon me, this wicked Woman will kill me. I afked her what Woman. She faid Goodwife Walford. I tried to perfuad her it was only her Weaknefs. She told me no, and related as above, that her Back was as a Flame of Fire, and her lower Parts were, as it were, numb, and without Feeling. I pinched her, and fhe felt not. She continued that Night, and the Day and Night following, very ill, and is ftill bad of her Limbs, and complains ftill daily of it." *Sworn as above.*

Nicholas Rowe teftified: "That Jane Walford, fhortly after fhe was accufed, came to the Deponent in Bed, in the Evening, and put her Hand upon his Breaft, fo that he could not fpeak and was in great Pain till the next Day. By the Light of the Fire in the next Room, it appeared to be Goody Walford, but fhe did not fpeak. She repeated her Visit about a Week after, and did as before, but said Nothing."

Elisa Barton deposed, that "she saw Susannah Trimmings at the Time she was ill, and her Face was coloured and spotted with several Colours. She told me the Story, who replied, that it was Nothing but her Fantasy. Her Eyes looked as if they had been scalded."

John Puddington said, that "three Years ago, Goodwife Walford came to his Mothers. She said that her own Husband called her an old Witch; and when she came to her Cattle, her Husband would bid her begone; for she did overlook the Cattle, which is as much as to say in our Country bewitching."

Agnes Puddington said, that "on the 11th of April the Wife of Mr. Evans came to her House, and lay there all Night; that a little after Sunset she saw a yellowish Cat; and Mrs. Evans said she was followed by a Cat wherever she went. John came and saw a Cat in the Garden, took down his Gun to shoot her. The Cat got upon a Tree, and the Gun would not take Fire, and afterward the Cock would not stand. She afterwards saw three Cats. The yellow one vanished away on the plain Ground, and she could not tell which Way they went."[1]

Three others deposed that they heard Elizabeth, the Wife of Nicholas Rowe, say there were three Men Witches at Strawberry Bank. One

---

[1] Adams's *Annals Portsmouth*, 38-49, with Additions and Corrections from the *New Hampshire Provincial Papers*.

was Thomas Turpin, who was drowned; Another was "old Ham. The other fhould be Namelefs, becaufe he fhould be Blamelefs."

Upon thefe Teftimonies Goodwife Walton was bound over to the next Court, which fat in June following, when fhe was again "bound over." When the Action was finally dropped does not appear, but about thirteen Years after, namely, in 1669, Jane profecuted one Robert Coutch or Couch, for Slander, in that faid Couch had reported that fhe was a Witch. She got her Cafe, but not her Claim entirely. The Court feem to have thought, that to be called a Witch, at that Time, was not very damaging to the Character of an old Woman, who probably, or poffibly had a high Character as a Termagant. They therefore ordered Couch to pay her five Pounds, and the Court the Cofts of the Profecution.

The following is given from fpicy George Bifhop,[1] who not very unaptly fpeaks of the "Bloody Laws and Proceedings" in Maffachufetts during the Adminiftration of Lieutenant Governour Bellingham as "Draconica." He fays, and it is believed truly, that fome of the Quakers who came to Bofton this Year were treated as Witches, and accufed by Perfons in Authority as being fuch.

Ann Auftin and Mary Fifher, were, for dif-

---

[1] *New England Judged, by the Spirit of the Lord*, &c. But for a more full Detail refpecting the Treatment of thofe mifguided Women, the Reader is referred to Beffe's *Sufferings of the Quakers*, II, 177, &c. A Work of the higheft Authority in Quaker Hiftory.

tributing certain Books to make Proselytes to the Principles of their Sect, sent to Prison by the Governor, declaring them Witches, "and appointing Women to search them, who took Men to help them, in Case they had refused, who stripped them stark naked, not missing Head or Feet, searching betwixt their Toes, and amongst their Hair, turning and abusing their Bodies in such a Manner, as Modesty will not admit to mention."

Their Books were taken from them, and "the Executioners appointed to destroy them." Although these Females were denounced as Witches, and although the Law existed that Witches should be put to Death, the Authorities either set the Law at Defiance, or they did not believe their own Charges. No Escape from this Dilemma could be pretended. But they undertook to cheat the Devil by transporting them beyond Seas.

We do not hear that Cassandra Southwick was accused of being a Witch, and yet if any Quaker ever was a Witch she must have been one, as the Authorities treated her in the same Manner as they did the two Females just noticed. Whittier, however, has given the worst Phase of the Proceedings in Cassandra's Case, relying, it seems, entirely upon George Bishop, while Besse is more reliable.

She is thus poetically painted in Prison, the Night before she was to be shipped away to be sold for Prison Fees:

" All Night I sat unsleeping, for I knew that on the Morrow
The Ruler and the cruel Priest would mock me in my Sorrow,
Dragged to their Place of Market, and bargained for and sold,
Like a Lamb before the Shambles, like a Heifer from the Fold!

" Slow broke the gray cold Morning; again the Sunshine fell,
Flecked with the Shade of Bar and Grate within my lonely Cell;
At length the heavy Bolts fell back, my Door was open cast,
And slowly at the Sheriff's Side, up the long Street I passed;
I heard the Murmur round me, and felt, but dared not see,
How, from every Door and Window, the People gazed on me.
And Doubt and Fear fell on me, Shame burned upon my Cheek,
Swam Earth and Sky around me, my trembling Limbs grew weak."

Having arrived at the Place of Embarcation, Cassandra is made to say:

" And there were ancient Citizens, cloak-wrapped and grave and cold,
And grim and stout Sea-captains with Faces bronzed and old,
And on his Horse, with Rawson, his cruel Clerk at hand,
Sat dark and haughty Endicott, the Ruler of the Land.

" Dark lowered the Brows of Endicott, and with a deeper Red
O'er Rawson's wine-empurpled Cheek the Flush of Anger spread;
'Good People,' quoth the white-lipped Priest, 'heed not her Words so wild,
Her Master speaks within her,—the Devil owns his Child!'

" Then to the stout Sea-captains, the Sheriff, turning, said,—
' Which of ye, worthy Seamen, will take this Quaker Maid?
In the Isle of fair Barbadoes, or on Virginia's Shore,
You may hold her at a higher Price than Indian Girl or Moor.'"

And so on, with full poetic License, the Poet

tells us that no one would undertake the Transportation of the "Quaker Maid," and that she thus triumphantly and scornfully added:

"I looked on haughty Endicott; with Weapon half-way drawn,
   Swept round the Throng his Lion Glare of bitter Hate and
      Scorn;
Fiercely he drew his Bridle-rein, and turned in Silence back,
And sneering Priest and baffled Clerk rode murmuring in his
      Track."

1657.

A Case of the supposed black Art of Diabolism disturbed the People of Easthampton on Long Island in 1657. A Mrs. Garlicke was brought before the Town Court on Suspicion of Witchcraft, and a Number of Witnesses were examined in Support of the Charge. The Magistrates after hearing the Testimony,[1] and not being skilled in the Science of Demonology,[2] concluded to send the Accused to the General Court of Connecticut, in which the occult Doctrine would probably be more safely applied.

Goodwife Garlicke was accordingly sent to Hartford, and the General Court took the following Action upon her Case[2] at the May Term, 1658. Easthampton was then within the Jurisdiction of the Colony of Connecticut, having been formally "annexed" at this Court. The Court returned the Woman, and in a Letter signified to the Town Authorities, that they had

---

[1] Wood, *Hist. L. Island*, 24.   [2] Prime, *Hist. L. Island*, 89.

duly confidered the Cafe of Goodwife Garlicke, having "paffed a legall tryall therevpon; wherevpon, tho there did not appeare fufficient Evidence to proue her guilty, yet we cannot but well approue and commend the Chriftian Care and Prudence of thofe in Authority with you, in fearching into y^t Cafe. Alfo we thinke good to certify, that it is defired and expected, by this Court, that you fhould carry neighbourly and peaceably, without juft Offence to Jos. Garlicke[1] and his Wife, and that they fhould doe the like to you. And ye Charge, we conceive and advife, may be juftly borne as followeth: That Jos. Garlick fhould beare ye Charge of his Wives Dyet and Ward at Home, with ye Charge of her Tranceportation Hither and returne Home; that your Towne fhould beare all theire owne Charges at Home, and the Charge of theire Meffengers and Witneffes in bringinge the Cafe to Tryall here and theire returne Home. The Court being content to put ye Charge of the Tryall here, vpon ye Countrys Account."[2]

It is creditably reported by a local Authority, that Mrs. Garlick had been employed in the Family of Capt. Lyon Gardiner, and that another Woman in the fame Employ had accufed Mrs.

---

[1] His Chriftian Name may be very uncertain, from what is here or elfewhere given of it. Thompfon, *Hift. Long Ifland*, I, 302, fays it was *Jofhua*, Prime has it *John*. Thompfon is probably Right. Savage (upon what Authority we do not know) takes the Abbreviation in *Ct. Col. Records*, as printed by Trumbull, to be *Jofeph* Jofiah would have anfwered his Purpofe as well.

[2] *Col. Records Connecticut*, I, 572·3.

Garlick of caufing the Death of her Child; while, according to Capt. Gardiner, the Woman who had been a Witnefs againft Mrs. Garlick, had taken an Indian Child to nurfe, and ftarved her own Child to Death for the Sake of the Pay fhe was to receive for fupporting the Indian Child.[1]

1659.

To what Extent "Witchery" was practifed in Say Brook in Connecticut, in 1659, we are not informed; that it did exift, and difturb the People there is very fure, or the following Order would not have been paffed by the General Court of that Colony; namely, that Mr. Samuel Willis "is requefted to goe downe to Sea Brook, to affift ye Maior in examininge the Sufpitions about Witchery, and to act therein as may be requifite."[2] We do not find any Mention of the Cafe afterwards, which leads to the Belief that Mr. Willis did not find enough of Witchery to make any Report upon to the Court.

The "Maior," whofe Affiftance Mr. Willis was to receive, was Major John Mafon, long the chief military Man of Connecticut. He was ftationed at Saybrook in 1647.

Mr. Samuel Willis was Son of Mr. George Willis of Hartford, who came from Fenny Compton, in Warwickfhire, England, and fettled there in 1638, and was Governour of Con-

---

[1] Prime, in his *Hiftory of Long Ifland*, 89.

[2] *Connecticut Colonial Records*, I, 338.

necticut in 1642.[1] The Name was afterwards written *Wyllys*, at least in some Branches of the Family, perhaps presuming this to have been the original Spelling; but George the Emigrant signed his Name *Willis* to his Will, and Elsewhere.

There was a Commotion in Andover, Massachusetts, in 1659, which must have been quite considerable, or it would not have caused the venerable Simon Bradstreet to move in the Matter, as there is clear Evidence that he did.

Two original Papers are at Hand, going to show that one John Godfrey of that Town was accused of Witchcraft, that Evidence was taken by Mr. Bradstreet, and that Godfrey was tried at Boston six Years after. The Minutes of Testimony in Mr. Bradstreet's Hand are as follows:

"The Deposions of Job Tylar, aged about 40 Yeares, Mary his Wife, Moses Tylar his Sonn, aged betwixt 17 and 18 Yeares, and Mary Tylar about 15 Yeares old.

"These Deponants witnesse that they saw a Thing like a Bird to come in at the Dore of there House with John Godfrey, in the Night, about the Bignes of a Black Bird or rather bigger, to wit, as big as a Pigion, and did fly about, John Godfrey labouring to catch it, and the Bird vanished, as they conceived through the Chinck of a jointed Board; and being asked by the Man of the House wherefore it came, he answered, it

[1] *Ibidem*, 468-70.

came to fuck your Wife. This was (as they rember) 5 or 6 Years fince.

"Taken upon Oath of the four aboue menconed Parties, this 27. 4. 59, before me
"SIMON BRADSTREETE."

How it happened that no legal Steps were taken for "five or fix Years" after it was difcovered that John Godfrey was accompanied by an evil Spirit, or Imp, we are unable to explain. And equally unaccountable it is to explain why fix other Years were allowed to pafs before any Action was taken on the above Depofition. Whatever the intermediate Steps may have been, if any, they are quite as invifible as thofe of the preceding "five or fix Years." Yet it is certain that the faid John Godfrey and his four Accufers did, about fix Years after the above Depofition was taken, appear before the Court in Bofton; for Edward Rawfon, under his own Hand, endorfes that Depofition thus: "Owned in Court, 7 March, 1665, by Job Tylar and Mofes Tylar." Then again, "Owned in Court, 13 March, 65, by Mary Tyler, on hir former Oath. E. R., S^c."

It feems that for fome Reafon the Wife of Job Tyler did not arrive as foon as the other Members of the Family, and the Court may have been kept waiting for other Witneffes. At all Events there feems to have been a Backwardnefs among fome of the Witneffes, as will appear by the following Letter from one of them, dated, as will be feen, two Days before two of the Witneffes appeared in Court. They had probably been all fummoned at the fame Time, and one of them may have brought Mr. Dane's Letter of Excufe.

"To the honourable Court at Bofton.

"May it pleafe your Wòrſhips, I received a Warrant under Mr. Secretaries Hand for my Appearance at Bofton this Court, to giue in Evidence, about fome Words that Godfery fpake to mee concerning Witches, the which I underftand were ſhewne in the Court vnder my owne Hand; but confidering ye Neceffity thats incumbent by Reafon of prevailing Infirmity, I humbly crave your favourable Interpretation of my Abfence; tis not Difrefpect, nor Neglect of Dutie, my Confcience witneffing, but Frailtie, Nature, and the Rawnes of the Weather; and now hauing prefented ye Caufe, I Craue Leaue to draw a Vayle, defiring Almighty God to be with you, and to conduct you in Pathes of Juftice and Rightoufnes, and Reft.

    "Your Honours obliged unto
       "all due Seruice in the Lord.
"March 5. 65.   FRANCIS DANE."[1]

It would be highly gratifying to know the Contents of what was *ſhewn* in the Court under Mr. Dane's Hand. It muft have been very unfatisfactory in making out a Cafe of Witchcraft, or Mr. Dane would not have been fummoned to

---

[1] Mr. J. W. Dean has given an excellent Account of the DANE Family, in the *N. Eng. Hiſt. and Gen. Reg.*, VIII, 147-56. The Hon. Nathan Dane was defcended from John, Brother of Francis.

appear in Perfon. His Infirmities from Age could not have been great, for he was fcarcely fifty Years old.

It is very reafonable to fuppofe that the Evidence againft Godfrey was of too ridiculous a Character to be ferioufly confidered, and that he was difcharged. After this he probably left Andover, as the Hiftorian of that Town does not give him a Place in his Work. Whether he belonged to the Hampton Family of Godfrey is not known. He may have been the John Godfrey who came to Newbury in 1634.[1]

In the great and diftreffing Calamity of 1692, Mr. Dane did what he could to allay the Witchcraft Excitement, and had his Obfervations been liftened to, and his Judgment heeded, many Lives would have been faved. But like the Phrenfy engendered in the French Revolution, one hundred Years later, this was a Parallel. His Brother John, of Ipfwich, was one of the Jurors of the Trials of 1692, and with others figned an Apology afterwards.[2]

1660.

An Attempt was made at Scituate, in the old Colony of Plymouth, to inaugurate a Crufade againft a fuppofed Witch, but the Plot was too fhallow, and whatever there was of Deviltry in it was thrown upon the one who made the Attempt.

---

[1] See *Founders of New England*, page 70.

[2] See *The Witchcraft Delufion in New England*, III, 121, 135.

Dinah Sylvester accused the Wife of William Holmes of being a Witch. From the imperfect Record preserved it appears that Dinah swore that Mrs. Holmes appeared to her in the Shape of a Bear, "about a Stones Throw from the Path," perhaps in the Night or Dusk of the Evening, but on this Point the Records are silent. On being questioned "as to what Manner of Tayle the Bear had," Dinah said she could not tell, "because the Bear's Head was towards her." A Blank in the original Record is construed to mean, by the able Historian of the Town[1] where the Case happened, that the Testimony was probably too ridiculous to be entered in full. And the Proceedings at the next Court fully sustain the Remark. Dinah was summoned before the Court, sentenced to pay the Costs of Prosecution, be whipt or make public Acknowledgment for falsely accusing Mrs. Holmes. She chose the latter, and her Acknowledgment was entered on the Records of the Court.

Another Case of recorded Witchcraft in the Old Colony took place in 1676, as will be seen in the Order of Time.

In the Year 1660, Suspicions of Witchcraft fell on Mary Wright of Oyster Bay, Long Island. She was a poor and ignorant Woman, and it became a Matter of grave Necessity, according to the Historian of Long Island,[2] "that an Offence of such enormous Depravity should be fully and

---

[1] Samuel Deane, *History Scituate*, 152.

[2] B. F. Thompson, *History Long Island*, 161-2.

satisfactorily investigated; but as there existed at that Time no domestic Tribunal which the People considered competent to hear and determine a Matter of such Magnitude, or none to which they thought proper to submit the Case, it was finally concluded to transport the accused Party to the General Court of Massachusetts, where Charges of this Sort were more common, and the Proof necessary to support them better understood. She was accordingly arraigned there, and the Matter inquired into with all the Formality usual on such Occasions. The Evidence of her Guilt failed, and she was acquitted of the Crime of Witchcraft. She was nevertheless convicted of being a Quaker, a Crime, in the Estimation of the Court, of almost equal Enormity, and was sentenced to be banished out of the Jurisdiction."

Unfortunately for this Story, Nothing of a legal Proceeding is produced from the Long Island Records, or appears in the General Court Records of Massachusetts. Nor do the Quaker Historians, who let no Name of a persecuted Person escape them, allude to any Charge of Witchcraft having been brought against any one of their Sect at the Period in Question. But under the Year 1664, Sewell,[1] after detailing the Treatment of Christison and others in the "bloody Town of Boston," and lamenting that "no Exhortations seemed to take any Hold of the Persecutors," continues: "For once a Girl of thirteen

---

[1] *Hist. of the Rise, Increase and Progress of the Quakers*, I, 370. Edit. 2 Vols., 8vo., Philadelphia, 1832.

or fourteen Years of Age, called Hannah Wright, whose Sister had been banished for Re'igion, was stirred with such Zeal, that coming from Long Island, some Hundreds of Miles from Boston, into that bloody Town, she appeared in the Court there, and warned the Magistrates to spill no more innocent Blood. The Saying so struck them at first, that they all sat silent; till Rawson, the Secretary, said: "What, shall we be baffled by such a one as this? Come, let us drink a dram. And here the Historian abruptly leaves his Readers. But in Besse, under the Year 1661, it is stated that after Sentence of Death was passed on Wenlock Christeson, and he was remanded to Prison to await Execution, which was to be on June 13th (1661), an Order of Court (probably occasioned by some Intelligence from London, of Complaints against them) was issued for the Enlargement of him, and twenty-seven others then in Prison,"[1] for the Crime of being Quakers. All the Names are given, and among them are found those of Mary Wright and Hannah Wright. Neither does George Bishop,[2] who wrote near the Time, add Anything but the Names before referred to.

1662.

A Woman and her Husband, of the Name of Greensmith, were executed at Hartford in 1662,[3]

---

[1] *Sufferings of the People called Quakers*, II, 223-4. Also *Abstract of the Sufferings*, III, 207-8.

[2] *New England Judged*, 340.

[3] From an Entry in Goffe's *Diary*, extracted by Hutchinson, it appears that on Jan. 20, 1662, three Witches were condemned at Hartford, which doubtless refers to this Affair, and the true Date is 1662-3.

or in purſuance of Acts of Witchcraft begun this Year. From what can be learned from Sources now before us, they may have been put to Death by a Mob, as the General Court Records contain no Account of their Trial nor Condemnation. Mrs. Greenſmith is alleged to have been "a lewd and ignorant Woman;" that the latter Part of the Charge was true is very likely, judging from the Anſwers ſhe gave when queſtioned about the Charge of a League with the Devil. She had been caſt into Priſon under that Charge, and while ſhe lay there a Woman named Ann, Daughter of John Cole, who lived near a Dutch Family, was ſeized in a ſtrange Manner with Fits, "wherein her Tongue was improved by a Demon to expreſs Things which ſhe herſelf knew Nothing of." Among her Incoherencies when in theſe Fits, ſhe ſaid certain "Perſons were conſulting how they might carry on miſchievous Deſigns againſt her; that they would afflict her Body, ſpoile her Name, &c." After which the Demon ſaid, "Let us confound her Language, that ſhe may tell no more Tales." Then ſhe made Utterances in Dutch, of which Language ſhe knew Nothing. "The Rev. Mr. Stone being by, declared, that he thought it impoſſible for one not familiar with the Dutch ſhould ſo exactly imitate the Dutch Tone in the Pronunciation of Engliſh." And "ſeveral worthy Perſons wrote the intelligible Sayings expreſſed by Ann Cole, whileſt ſhe was thus amazingly handled." Among theſe "worthy Perfons" were "Mr. John Whiting, Mr. Samuel Hooker, and Mr. Jofeph Hains."

Among the Attendants on the bewitched Woman, fome one of them mentioned the Name of the poor "lewd and ignorant" Woman then lying in Prifon, as already mentioned. She was immediately fent for, and charged with certain Acts done and intended to be done againft Mrs. Cole; the fame having been written down, and now read by Mr. Whiting and Mr. Haines. And we are told that "the Woman being aftonifhed thereat, confeffed thofe Things to be true, and that fhe and other Perfons named in this preternatural Difcourfe, had had Familiarity with the Devil." But on the next Day, having probably reflected that fhe had fallen into a Snare prepared for her, was in a Rage againft Mr. Haines, and denied all Knowledge of Witchcraft; but at Length, probably bewildered by the ftrange Queftions of her Tormentors, "fhe declared that the Devil firft appeared to her in the Form of a Deer or Fawn;" and that finally "the Devil had frequently carnal Knowledge of her;" that "the Witches had Meetings not far from her Houfe; that fome appeared in one Shape, and others in another. One came flying amongft them in the Shape of a Crow." Upon this Confeffion, with other concurrent Evidence, the Woman was executed; fo likewife was her Hufband, though he did not acknowledge himfelf guilty."[1] There were fome other Perfons accufed at the fame Time, but they had the good Fortune to make their Efcape by Flight.

It is conclufively added, that, as foon as the fufpected Witches were either executed or fled, Mrs. Cole was reftored to Health![2] But the crowning Part of this Tale is to come, from which it will appear that Mr. and Mrs. Greenfmith were not hanged, according to the ufual Cuftom, but "there were fome that had a Mind to try whether the Stories of Witches not being able to fink under Water were true," that accordingly a Man and Woman accufed by Ann Cole, had their Hands and Feet tied together and caft into the Water, and that they "both fwam after the Manner of a Buoy." A third was thrown in, and "he immediately funk right down."

The Preferver and Relator of this Affair in the Style of the Dark Ages, adds concerning thofe thus inhumanly executed, "they very fairly took their Flight, not having been feen in that Part of the World fince."[3]

All we find in the Records in which the Name of Greenfmith appears, occurs feveral Years later,

---

[1] I. Mather, *Remarkable Providences*. Mather compofed his Account from a Communication of Mr. John Whiting, before mentioned. The Story as given by the Latter is now publifhed in *Hift. Colls. Ms. H. Soc.*, XXXVIII, 466-9.

[2] Feb. 24 [1662-3]. After one of the Witches was hanged, the Maid was Well. Goffe's *Diary*, in Hutchinfon, *Hiftory of Maffachufetts Bay*, II, p. 18.

[3] *Remarkable Providences*, as before cited.

and is as follows: "This Court impowers Mr. Sam^ll Willys, Captn Tallcott and the Secretary [Mr. John Allyn] to make a Deed of Sale to Andrew Benton, of Nath: Greenſmith's Houſe and Land, which was ſeized for Charge expended on ſaid Greenſmith, and ſold to G. Benton."[1]

The diabolical Method of determining whether Perſons were Witches by caſting them into the Water with their Limbs tied together with Cords, is aſcribed by ſome to that abominable Miſcreant, Matthew Hopkins, though it is ſaid to have been recommended by King James (if he did not invent it), who aſſigned as a Reaſon, "that as ſuch Perſons have renounced their Baptiſm by Water, ſo the Water refuſes to receive them."

Butler, in his peculiar Manner thus refers to Hopkins, who, it is ſaid, ſuffered by the ſame Ordeal by which he had cauſed the Death, in one Year, of no leſs than ſixty Perſons in his own County of Eſſex:[2]

> "────── the Godly may alledge
> For any Thing their Priviledge;
> And to the Dev'l himſelf may go,
> If they have Motives thereunto.
> For as there is a War between
> The Dev'l and them, it is no Sin,
> If they by ſubtle Stratagem,
> Make uſe of him, as he does them.
> Has not this preſent Parliament

---

[1] *Col. Records of Connecticut*, II, 91.

[2] It not being my Purpoſe to give an Account of Hopkins and his Acts, I will only refer the Reader to Dr. Hutchinſon's *Eſſay*. p. 81-92, where Enough will be found to enable him to underſtand Hudibras fully, in the Lines extracted above.

> A Legar to the Devil fent,
> Fully empower'd to treat about
> Finding revolted Witches out:
> And has not he within a Year,
> Hang'd Threefcore of them in one Shire?
> Some only for not being drown'd,
> And fome for fitting above Ground,
> Whole Days and Nights upon their Breeches,
> And feeling Pain, were hang'd for Witches?
> And fome for putting knavifh Tricks
> Upon Green-Geefe and Turkey Chicks,
> Or Pigs, that fuddenly deceaft,
> Of Griefs unnat'ral, as he gueft;
> Who after prov'd himfelf a Witch,
> And made a Rod for his own Breech."[1]

In this Connection it will be worth While to notice, that, a Queftion went about many Years ago in England, refpecting Perfons formerly burnt for Witchcraft; as to where and when the laft Cafe of the Kind took place? The Anfwer which was given, has not, it is believed, been called in Queftion. It amounted to this: It is not quite certain that Amy Duny, and Rofe Cullender or Callender, condemned by Sir Matthew Hale, at Bury St. Edmunds, were burnt, although by fome Accounts it is fo ftated. In the fame Year (1664) Alice Hudfon was burnt at York,

---

[1] Butler's *Hudibras, Canto* III, p. 333-4, *edition* 1684. It will be feen by the Authority before cited, that when People began to reflect upon Hopkins's Doings, they feized him, tied his own Thumbs and Toes together, as he ufed to tie others; in this Condition caft him into the Water, and he was found to fwim as others did. Thus they cleared the Country of him; "and it was a great deal of Pity," fays the Relator, "that they did not think of the Experiment fooner."— Dr. Francis Hutchinfon, *Hiftorical Effay Concerning Witchcraft*, 87.

having been condemned for receiving ten Shillings on a certain Time of the Devil. As late as 1722, the Ninth of George the Firſt, a Caſe occurred at Little Dean, in Scotland, where a Captain David Roſs was Judge. But a Girl was Burnt at Glarus, in Ireland, in 1786!

The Experiment of caſting into the Water occurred as late as 1785. According to a Report in a Northampton Paper (England), a poor Woman named Sarah Bradſhaw, being proceeded againſt for Witchcraft, was thrown into a Pond. She immediately ſank to the Bottom; and thus the Wretches who acted as Executioners were ſatisfied ſhe had been falſely accuſed. This occurred at a Place called Mears Aſhby.

1665.

During the Adminiſtration of the Government of New York by Richard Nicolls, Eſq., one Caſe of Witchcraft, at leaſt, found its Way into the Courts. That they were as common as in other cotemporary Communities of the Day, there is not much Doubt. That they were not Matters of legal Inveſtigation, poſſibly depended on the Abſence of a ſpecial Law for ſuch a Contingency, or that the Laws in general were leſs regarded than they were among their Neighbours in ſome of the other Colonies. Certainly in New Jerſey, the Legends of an exiſting Witchcraft, or a certain Belief that it had exiſted there is current in many Places, and a Witch Tree is, or was, pointed out not many Years ago, in a certain Locality.

The Cafe which came before the Court of Affizes in New York in 1665, was that of Ralph Hall, and his Wife Mary Hall; and although they were eventually acquitted, they were held in Durance about three Years.[1] The Charge in the Indictment againft Hall was that he "upon the 25th Day of December [1663], being Chriftmas laft was twelve Months, and feveral other Days and Times fince that Day, by fome deteftable and wicked Arts, commonly called Witchcraft and Sorcery, did (as fufpected) malicioufly and felonioufly practife and exercife, at the Town of Seatalcott [fince Setauket, now Brookhaven], in the Eaft Riding of Yorkfhire, on Long Ifland, on the Perfon of George Wood, late of the fame Place, by which wicked and deteftable Arts the faid George Wood (as is fufpected) moft dangeroufly and mortally fickened and languifhed, and not long after, by the aforefaid wicked and deteftable Arts, the faid George Wood (as is likewife fufpected) died." Alfo it was alleged, in the fame Indictment, that an Infant Child of Ann Rogers, Widow of the aforefaid George Wood, had, "fome While after the Death" of Wood, fickened and died, and that its Death was caufed by the faid Hall. The fame Indictment was alfo recited againft the Wife of Hall, and then a Bundle of Depofitions was read to the Court (no

---

[1] It is doubtlefs to this Cafe that Watfon, in his *Annals of New York*, refers, p. 166, though in fuch an obfcure Way it is uncertain.

Witnesses appearing in Person), and the Accused called upon by the Clerk to hold up the right Hand, and the substance of the Charges were reiterated. They pleaded not Guilty, and their Case was committed to the Jury. In due Time the Jury rendered a Verdict, to the Effect that they "found some Suspicions of what the Woman was charged with, but Nothing considerable of Value to take away her Life; but in Reference to the Man, we find Nothing considerable to charge him with."[1]

The Sentence of the Court was, that Hall "should be bound Body and Goods for his Wife's Appearance at the next Sessions, and so on from Sessions to Sessions, as long as they stay in this Government. In the mean While to be of good Behaviour." Under these Bonds they continued until the 21st of August, 1668, at which Time "they were living upon the Great Miniford's Island." And we do not find that they were compelled to pay the Costs, as was often the Case with Parties acquitted elsewhere.

In March of this Year a Woman named Elizabeth Seger was tried for Witchcraft at Hartford, and found Guilty by a Jury. But the Court was not convinced of the Truth of the Charge, or of the Sagacity of the Jury, and the Woman was set at Liberty.[2] Whether she was mulct in Costs,

---

[1] Yates, *Appendix to Smith's Hist. N. York*, 509-11. Spafford's *Gazetteer of N. York*, 61-2. Edition 1824. See a more accurate Account in the *Documentary History of New York*, IV, 133.

[2] Judd, *Hist. Hadley*, 233. Mr. Judd has given us one of the very best Local Histories.

as was frequently the Cafe in fimilar Acquittals, is not known.

1669.

The Profecution of Sufannah Martin, of Salifbury, for Witchcraft, in 1669, very likely was prompted on the Part of certain Perfons by Malice. She was fubfequently, and no Doubt previoufly, engaged in Litigations. Thefe before 1669, it is affumed, were the Caufe of this Profecution. Several Perfons who gave Evidence adverfe to her Claims in fome civil Actions, appeared as fwift Witneffes at her final and fatal Trial afterwards, as will be feen by confulting the *Wonders of the Invifible World.*

In 1672 fhe had the Liberty of the General Court to review her former Action, "and fue at Salifbury Court, fub forma Pauperis." The next Year the following Record is made under the fame Authority: "In Anfwer to the Petition of Sufanna Martyn, humbly defiring the Favour of this Court to grant her further Liberty, and that her Sifter Jones may be joined with her, further to profecute and trye hir Accion in the next County Court in Norfolk, the Court grants hir Petition, and that hir Sifter Jones be joyned with hir in the Profecution and Trjall of Action, as hath binn formerly granted by this Court."

The following Year (1674) the General Court Records recite: "In Anfwer to the Petition of George and Sufanna Martyn and Mary Jones, the Court judgeth it meet to grant the Petitioners a

Hearing of the whole Cafe the next Seffion of this Court, the fajd Peticoners giving Notice to all Partjes concerned." At the next Court Judgment was given againft the Plaintiffs, with Cofts, and "five Pounds for hearing the Cafe, which laft was remitted on the importunat Peticons of faid Sufanna Martyn." Nathaniel Winflow was the Defendant.

The Fate of Sufanna Martin in the memorable Year 1692, is fpecially dwelt upon in the Work before mentioned, and will be found noticed when we come to that Year.

1670.

Some Time previous to the May Term of the General Court of Connecticut, Katharine Harrifon, of Wethersfield, was arrefted, charged with the Crime of Witchcraft, and imprifoned.[1] How long fhe fuffered Imprifonment we have not the Means of ftating. She had been convicted by a Jury, at the May Term of the Court of Affiftants. A fpecial Court was affigned for her Trial, with other Prifoners, charged with other Offences. What we find on Record refpecting her runs thus: The Special Court "hauing confidered the Verdict of the Jury refpecting Kathern Harrifon, cannot concur with them fo as to fentence her to Death, or to a longer Continuance in Reftraynt." The Court thereupon ordered her to

---

[1] According to Judd, fhe was tried by a Jury at Hartford the previous October (1669).—*Hiftory of Hadley*, 233.

be ſet at Liberty; but with the monſtrous Proviſo that ſhe ſhould pay the Coſts of her Impriſonment! Alſo "willing her to minde the Fullfilment of remoueing from Weathersfield, which is that will tend moſt to her owne Safety and the Contentment of the People who are her Neighbours."[1]

From theſe ſcanty Facts it may be conjectured without great Hazard, that Mrs. Harriſon may have been a troubleſome Neighbour, but how the Court juſtified itſelf for ſuch Deciſion a modern Juriſt might find it difficult to determine. As Mrs. Harriſon was obliged to leave Weathersfield, ſhe proceeded to Weſtcheſter in New York, and there probably hoped to remain Quiet, but her evil Genius followed her, and ſhe was proſecuted there the ſame Year, and bound over to good Behaviour. But at the Court in October following (1670), it was ordered, "that in Regard there is no Thing appears againſt Katharine Harryſon, Widow, deſerving the Continuance of that Obligation, ſhe is to be releaſed from it, and hath Liberty to remain in the Towne of Weſtcheſter, where ſhe now reſides, or Anywhere elſe in the Government, during her Pleaſure."[2]

The perſecuted Woman had a Family of Children, but how many is not mentioned. There were ſeveral Petitions ſent to the Governour requeſting that ſhe ſhould be ſent out of Weſtcheſter, and the Complaints againſt her ſeem to

---

[1] *Colonial Records of Connecticut*, II, 132.

[2] Yates, *Appendix to Smith's Hiſt. New York*, 511.

have been very general. She was given an
Afylum in the Houfe of one Captain Richard
Panton,[1] a Name of rare Occurrence in our Annals; but once occurring, and then in Connection
of a moft tragic Event.[2]

1671.

We come now to the Cafe of Elizabeth Knap,[3]
a Maid, of Groton, "who, in the Month of October, 1671, was after a very ftrange Manner,
fometimes weeping, fometimes laughing, fometimes roaring hideoufly, with violent Motions
and Agitations of her Body, crying out, Money!
Money! &c. In November following, her
Tongue for many Hours together was drawn like
a Semicircle up to the Roof of her Mouth, not
to be removed, though Some tried with their
Fingers to do it. Six Men were fcarce able to
hold her in Some of her Fits, but fhe would fkip
about the Houfe, yelling, and looking with a
moft frightful Afpect. On December 17th her
Tongue was drawn out of her Mouth to an ex-

---

[1] *Documentary Hiftory of New York*, IV, 136-8.

[2] See *Hiftory and Antiquities of Bofton*, 765-6.

[3] The Account of this Perfon's "Strange Cafe" is taken from one of extenfive Detail by the Rev. Samuel Willard, who in the Time of it lived at Groton. It occupies fifteen clofely printed octavo Pages, and is in the Form of a Diary. Towards the Clofe he fays: "Shee freely acknowledged that the Devill was wont to appear to her in the Houfe of God and divert her Mind and charge her fhee fhould not give Ear to what that black coated Rogue fpake. Whether fhee have cove-nanted with the Devill or not, I thinke this is a Cafe unanfwerable:" *i. e.*, in this Cafe he believed fhe had. *Colls. Ms. H. Soc.*, XXXVIII, 570.

traordinary Length. And now a Dæmon began
manifeftly to fpeak in her, in a Voice not her
own, and without any Motion of her Lips, and
without the Ufe of any of the Organs of Speech.
The Things then uttered by the Devil were
chiefly Railings againft the Rev. Mr. Samuel
Willard, then the Minifter of Groton. Alfo the
Dæmon belched forth moft horid Blafphemies,
exalting himfelf above the Moft High. After
this fhe was taken Speechlefs for fome Time. In
fome of her Fits fhe accufed one of her Neighbours of being the Caufe of her Afflictions."
But it fo happened that the Perfon thus cried out
upon "was a very fincere holy Woman," who on
hearing that fhe was accufed, went to fee the
"poor Wretch." She found her in one of her
Fits, and though with her Eyes faft clofed, "declared who was there, and could tell the Touch
of that Woman from any One elfe. But the
Party thus accufed and abufed by a malicious
Devil, prayed earneftly with and for the poffeffed
Perfon; after which fhe confeffed that Satan had
deluded her, making her believe Evil of her good
Neighbour, without any Caufe. Nor did fhe
after that complain of any Apparition, yea, fhe
faid, that the Devil had himfelf in the Likenefs
and Shape of Divers, tormented her very Diverfly
and cruelly, and then told her it was not He but
They that were her Tormentors."[1]

This Story has been given to fhow how, in

---

[1] I. Mather, D. D., *Remarkable Providences*, and *Magnalia*, B. VI, 67.

thofe Times, a tolerably fevere Cafe of Hyfterics[1] could be magnified by thofe who had an exceedingly large Maggot of Credulity in their Brains. Groton is only thirty-three Miles from Bofton, but the Story, in travelling even that fhort Diftance, had no Doubt fwollen into fuch Proportions, as to have but a faint Likenefs to the Original.

The Condition of Elizabeth Knap was probably very fimilar to that of Elizabeth Barton (the Holy Maid of Kent), who, for her Pretenfions to Infpiration, "Convulfions and ftrange Motions of Body," was put to Death in the Time of Henry the Eighth, 1584.

1672.

A Cafe of Witchcraft is reported to have occurred in Weftchefter County, New York, in 1672. A Complaint was preferred "to the Governour and Council againft a Witch which had come among them." This has Reference, without Queftion, to Katharine Harrifon, whofe Profecution has been detailed under the Year 1670.

1673.

The Cafe of Katharine Harrifon is fuppofed to have been revived again this Year; and the Complaint againft her happened to be prefented juft after the Dutch had repoffeffed themfelves of

---

[1] Hutchinfon calls her "another *Ventriloqua*."—*Hift. of Mafs.*, II, 17.

New Amsterdam. At the Time of the Complaint Captain Anthony Colve, who was in Command of one of the Dutch Men of War at the Capture of the Fort, seems to have had the Government in his Hands, as the Complaint was presented to him for Action. He treated it with Contempt, and thus the Affair ended.

1674.

Mrs. Mary Bartlett, Wife of Mr. Samuel Bartlett, of Northampton, having died in July of this Year, and as her Complaint was not understood by such "Chirurgeons" as the Neighbourhood afforded, a ready Solution of the Case was found by attributing it to Witchcraft. The next Step was to fix upon the Witch; and strange to say, in this Instance, one of the most, if not the most accomplished, and of the highest Standing in the Place, was fixed upon. This was Mrs. Mary Parsons, whose Husband, Mr. Joseph Parsons, was one of the wealthiest Men in Northampton.[1]

It is conjectured that the Standing of Mrs. Parsons had much to do with the Accusation. She may have been somewhat Exclusive in the Choice of her Associates, and even of haughty Manners towards the Parties by whom she was singled out for Persecution; but as to this Nothing is positively known.

On the 29th of September, about two Months

---

[1] As these were the maternal Ancestors of the Writer, he has been as Particular in detailing the Facts as the Documents warrant.

after the Death of Mrs. Bartlett, a Court met at Springfield. Mr. Bartlett in the Meantime had beſtirred himſelf to procure Evidence to ſuſtain his Charge of Witchcraft againſt Mrs. Parſons, in the Shape of Depoſitions. This Lady knowing what was going on, did not wait to be ſummoned, but appeared before the Court in Perſon. The Subſtance of her Speech was, that "ſhe did aſſert her own Innocency, often mentioning how clear ſhe was of ſuch a Crime, and that the righteous God knew her Innocency, and ſhe left her Cauſe in his Hand." But her Proteſtations and Diſclamations of all Knowledge of Witchcraft had little or no Effect upon the Court of Springfield, and that Court at once proceeded to do all which lay in its Juriſdiction. It "appointed a Jury of ſoberdized, chaſte Women to make diligent Search upon the Body of Mary Parſons, whether any Marks of Witchcraft appear, who gave in their Account to the Court on Oath, of what they found." Whether they found Anything extraordinary in their Search is not known, although it is ſaid, that the Report which they made, together with the Evidence, was forwarded to the Governour and Magiſtrates at Boſton. The Accuſed was alſo ordered to appear before them, and was bound over for her further Appearance, in the Sum of fifty Pounds, her Huſband becoming bound in that Sum.

On the 2d of March, 1675, ſhe was indicted by the Grand Jury, and ſent to Priſon to await Trial. On the 13th of May following ſhe was tried, on the Charge of Witchcraft, "in that she had, not having the Fear of God before her Eyes, entered into Familiarity with the Devil, and committed sundry Acts of Witchcraft on the Person or Persons of one or more." She of Course pleaded "not Guilty," and she was cleared by the Jury.[1]

It may be worthy of Notice that at this Time the Hon. John Leverett was Governour, and Generals Gookin and Denison were Assistants. These were three of the most enlightened Men of the Time, and they doubtless exerted a benign Influence on the Jury. Hence Witch Finders were discouraged, and the Country was relieved for a Time. An Attempt was however made against John Parsons, Son of Joseph and Mary Parsons, and a Quantity of Evidence was made up to prove his "Familiarity with the Devil," but the County Court did not think the Evidence strong enough, or they had not Faith enough in the Weakness of the Governour and his Assistants to send the Accused down to Boston, and thus the Case was abandoned.

1675.

The Practice of Witchcraft among the Indians gave the English a good deal of Trouble. Perhaps it did not occur to them that it was a Child of Barbarism, and that in Proportion to the Prevalence of Knowledge it would disappear. But

[1] Chiefly from Facts found in Judd's *History of Hadley*.

when Mankind at any given Period take a retrospective View, they have assumed that all Men previous to their own Age and Country were wallowing in an Ignorance far greater than that by which they were beset. Hence, in the Year 1675, among other Laws for the Government of the Pequot Indians, this was enacted by the General Court of Connecticut: "Whosoever shall Powau or vse Witchcraft, or any Worship of the Devill, or any fals Gods, shall be convented and punished."

1676.

Notwithstanding her stringent Laws against Witchcraft, the Old Colony of Plymouth never found itself obliged to execute any one for that Crime, as is believed. And for about sixteen Years no Case of the Kind, so far as known, was ever carried into Court. But, in the Midst of the terrible War with King Philip, namely, in March, 1676, one Mary Ingham, Wife of Thomas Ingham, of Scituate, was indicted and arraigned before the Court. The Indictment runs thus: "Mary Ingham: thou art indited by the Name of Mary Ingham, of the Towne of Scittuate, in the Jurisdiction of New Plymouth, for that thou, haueing not the Feare of God before thyne Eyes, hast, by the Healp of the Deuill, in the Way of Witchcraft or Sorcery, malliciously procured much Hurt, Mischeiffe, and Paine vnto the Body of Mehittable Woodworth, the Daughter of Walter

Woodworth, of Scittuate aforesaid and some Others, and particularly causing her, the said Mehittable, to fall into violent Fitts and causing great Paine vnto seuerall Parts of her Body att seuerall Times, soe as shee, the said Mehittable Woodworth, hath bin almost bereaued of her Sences, and hath greatly languished, to her much Suffering therby, and the Procuring of great Greiffe, Sorrow, and Charge to her Parents; all which thou hast procured and don against the Law of God, and to his great Dishonor, and Contrary to our Soueraign Lord the King, his Crowne and Dignitie."

After all this high sounding Manifesto, some Show of a Trial might reasonably be expected, and at least the Names of Witnesses given; but there appears Nothing of the Kind on Record. The Records, however, do say: "The said Mary Ingham did putt herselfe on the Tryall of God and the Countrey," and was cleared of this "Inditement in Processe of Law by a Jury of twelue Men."

It would be exceedingly Interesting to know what the Evidence was against the Accused; for without it we cannot give the Court credit either for Sagacity or Lenity. But in the State of Society of that Time, we may reasonably conclude that the Evidence must have been lame indeed, or the Party would not have escaped Conviction. Josiah Winslow was Governour of the Colony, and the Jury that tried Mary Ingham consisted of Mr. Thomas Haskins, John Wadsworth, John

Howland, Abraham Jackson, Benajah Pratt, John Blacke, Marke Snow, Joseph Bartlett, John Richmond, Jerud Talbutt, John Foster, and Seth Pope.

This Trial took place during the darkest Days of a War, which, of itself was enough, as since viewed, to have diverted the Mind of every Inhabitant from all Subjects excepting what might tend to the Preservation of the Country. But Superstition and Fanaticism cling to the uncultivated Mind, even to the Jaws of Death.

To urge at this Day, the Claim for the People of Plymouth, that it was owing to their "good Sense," or superior Wisdom, that None were put to Death for Witchcraft, is very Preposterous. The simple Reason that no Executions took place in some of the New England Colonies is, the Evidence brought forward was not so strong as was produced in those Colonies where Executions followed Convictions; not that the Authorities were less disposed to such Prosecutions.

1678.

Thomas Mayhew, of Martha's Vineyard, wrote to the Commissioners of the United Colonies, apparently in Answer to Questions relating to the Condition of the Indians of that Island, that there were about one hundred and forty Men there which were "not tainted with

[1] His Letter may be seen in the *New England Historical and Genealogical Register*, Vol. IV, 17.

Drunkenneſſe," and that as to Witchcraft, that was out of Uſe among them. Hence, if this Statement was correct, the Indians of that Locality were much in Advance of their white Neighbours.

1679.

In Northampton the Powers of Darkneſs were again "viſible" in 1679. On the 7th of March of this Year died one John Stebbins in an unuſual Manner, as was alleged by a Jury of Inqueſt, confiſting of twelve Men, among whom was Dr. Thomas Haſtings of Hatfield. The Jury found "ſeveral hundred ſmall Spots on the Body, as if made with ſmall Shot. Thoſe Spots were ſcraped, and Holes found under them into the Body." Whereupon it was ſuſpected that it was done by Witchcraft. The Wife of the Deceaſed was a Siſter to Samuel Bartlett. This Individual, although he had failed to convict Mrs. Parſons, as before detailed, probably hoped now to have better Succeſs. The County Court, as appears by its Acts, had more Faith in this Accuſation than in that of the Caſe of John Parſons, for they received the Evidence and tranſmitted it to Governor Bradſtreet, but the Governor did not take Notice enough of the Accuſation to ſend for the Party, and thus the Matter went by.

Tradition in Hadley ſays, that John Stebbins was at Work in a Saw-mill a little Time before his Death; that the Logs and Boards became bewitched and cut up ſtrange and divers Capers, and that in some of their diabolical Manœuvres they interfered with John, but in what Manner is not stated, though they were supposed to have caused his Death.

Simple, unsuspecting, and honest People have often been the Victims to those who practise malicious Mischief, as well as to those who practise different Kinds of Rascality. There were living at this Time in Newbury several Families of the Name of Morse; the oldest or principal Family was that of William Morse. He had lived in that Town since 1635, having emigrated from Marlborough, in Wiltshire, in the early Part of that Year, and was by Occupation a Shoemaker. He had a Wife Elizabeth whom he probably married after he came to New England.[1] In this Family lived a Boy named John Stiles, a Grandson of William Morse. What was the Age of this Boy, or what instigated him to undertake the tormenting of his Grand-parents, there is no Mention as yet discovered. Perhaps he intended no more at First than to frighten them by some deceptive boyish Pranks, and succeeding fully in that, proceeded till his Pranks became Outrages, by which he deceived nearly Everybody.

It was a Period when, if Anything occurred, the Origin or Reason for which was not understood or comprehended, and appeared stranger than usual, the Mind, instead of investigating,

---

[1] *Founders of New England*, Page 56.

fell back upon the ever ready and easy Solution, that such was caused by Witchcraft.

How long the young Scamp carried on his Annoyances before any Complaint was made to the Authorities, does not appear, but it was for some Time previous to December of this Year (1679), as one Caleb Powell had become acquainted with what was going on, and offered his Services to put a Stop to the mysterious Fall of Brick-bats down the Chimney, Pots and Kettles dancing on the Crane, and Irons jumping in and out of the Kettles, and such like extraordinary Manœuvres. Powell, it seems, was a seafaring Man, and it is supposed, that in Order to give himself large Importance in the Eyes of the People of Newbury, he pretended to a Knowledge in the occult Sciences, and that by Means of this Knowledge he could detect the Witchcraft then going on at Mr. Morse's. However this may have been, Powell said that if he had the Boy in his Custody he could put a Stop to the Trouble; and to test the Truth of what he said, Consent was given, though reluctantly, and he took away the Boy, and the Witch Operations did actually cease. Whether he had Connivance with the Boy Stiles, or failed to accomplish some private End he may have had in View, is not known, but the Tragedy of the dancing of Pots and Kettles, bowing of Chairs, &c., was resumed with more Vigour than ever. Whereupon it was assumed that the said Powell was himself the Witch, was prosecuted and in much Danger of suffering for the Part he had volunteered to take. Morſe was his Proſecutor. By what Means he became ſo is not known, and was bound to appear at the Court in Ipſwich to make good his Charges againſt Powell. There are ſome ſcraps of Teſtimony in Coffin's *Hiſtory of Newbury*,[1] and the Deciſion of the Court, which, being very extraordinary, is here reproduced: "Upon hearing the Complaint againſt Caleb Powell for Suſpicion of working by the Devill, to the moleſting of the Family of William Morſe of Newbury, though this Court cannot find any evident Ground of proceeding farther againſt the ſaid Powell, yett we determine that he hath given ſuch Ground of Suſpicion of his ſo dealing, that we cannot ſo acquit him, but that he juſtly deſerves to beare his owne Shame and the Coſts of Proſecution of the Complaint."

This only adds another to the ridiculous Deciſions of the early Courts to thoſe already noticed. The Judges had put the County to the Expenſe of a Trial, of which they muſt pay their Proportion, unleſs it could be ſaddled on Somebody, and there was Nobody but the Perſecuted Party on whom it could be laid with Impunity.

The Teſtimony given in by Mr. Morſe, before Suſpicion lighted on Powell, is as aſtoniſhing as any of the Details of Witch Tranſactions given by Cotton Mather. So extraordinary is his Teſ-

---

[1] The Reader ſhould bear in Mind that the Teſtimony in that Work is ſeparated and miſplaced, but all between Pages 122 and 135.

timony, that one, on reading it, cannot efcape the Conclufion that fome ftrange Compofition muft have occupied the Place in his Head defigned for Brains.

It appears that about the Time Powell was fixed upon as the one "working by the Devill," it began to be whifpered about that Mrs. Morfe was the Witch; and no fooner was Powell acquitted than the Clamour againft her began openly to be made, and on the 7th of January following Commiffioner Woodbridge commenced taking Evidence in the Cafe, all of which will be found in the Appendix. It has, as will be feen by a Perufal, the ufual Character of fuch Teftimony, altogether too childifh to be worthy of Prefervation, did it not fhow the Character of the People of the Age, and how much Improvement has been fince made in all that is effential to the Happinefs of a People.

A great many Witneffes were fummoned to appear at the May Seffion of the Court in Bofton; many did appear in Perfon, fome walking on Foot the whole Diftance. The poor Accufed (then about 65 Years of Age) was taken from Ipfwich Jail, where fhe had been for fome Time kept, and on the 20th of May conveyed to Bofton, by the Conftable, Thomas Knowlton, who queftioned her on the Way about her Cafe. She faid, among other Things, "fhe was accufed about Witchcraft, but that fhe was as clear of it as God in Heaven."

Fortunately perhaps for the Accufed, Simon

Bradstreet was rechosen Governor; among the other Officers composing the General Court were Thomas Danforth, Deputy Governor, Richard Saltonstall, Daniel Gookin, Daniel Denison, John Pynchon, Edward Tyng, William Stoughton, Joseph Dudley, Peter Bulkley, Nath[l] Saltonstall, Humphrey Davy, James Russell, Samuel Nowell, Peter Tilton, John Richards, John Hull, Bartholomew Gedney, Tho. Savage, Wm. Browne.

The Trial was before the Assistants, but no Record of it appears in the Journals, but fortunately there is found a List of the Jury.[1] A Copy of the Indictment is printed in Coffin's *Newbury*, and is in the usual Form — "instigated by and Familiarity with the Devil." Argument on the Part of the Prisoner there was none, and the Jury brought her in "guilty, according to the Indictment." Whereupon the Governour could do no less than pronounce Judgment, which was performed on the 27th of May, after the Lecture. She was to be "hanged by the Neck till she was dead."

Whether a Question of Law came up from some Quarter, or whether the Governour or some of the Assistants had Doubts in the Matter, does not appear; but in the Course of the Trial the

---

[1] Derived from the Documents in the Appendix. They were Mr. Nathan Heyman, and Mr. John Knight, of Charlestown; Mr. Richard Middlecott, Mr. Jeremiah Cushin, Mr. John Wait, Lt. Richard Waye, and Mr. Thomas Harwood, of Boston; John Stone, and Richard Child, of Watertown; Bro. John Green, and Richard Robins, of Cambridge; Jacob Huen, and John Capen, of Dorchester. The Spelling of these Names is given as in the Originals.

following Queſtion was before the Court: "Whether ſeuerall diſtinct ſingle teſtimonyes of preternaturall and Diabolicall Actions by the priſoner at the barr, though not any two concurring to proue the ſame indiuiduall Act is to be accounted Legall evidence to Convict of Witchcraft. This was Reſolued on the affirmative by ye Court. 22 of May, 1680, as Atteſts EDWARD RAWSON, Secret."[1]

There ſeems to have been no Diſſent on the Part of any one, and why the Time for the Execution was not fixed, muſt for the Preſent, at leaſt, remain unexplained. It has been aſſumed by Coffin and later Writers, that the Life of Mrs. Morſe was ſpared through the Backwardneſs of Governour Bradſtreet to proceed in carrying out his own Sentence. It may have been ſo, but Evidence is wanting to fully warrant the Surmiſe. If he had any Scruples why did he ſo promptly pronounce the Sentence of Death? However this might have been, before the Adjournment of the Court, namely, on June 1ſt, but three Days after Sentence was paſſed, "the Governour and Magiſtrates voted the reprieving" of Mrs. Morſe till the October Seſſion of the Court. But Nothing is heard of the Caſe in October. On the 3d of November, however, the Deputies ſent up an Inquiry, deſiring to know "why Execution of the Sentence" had not been carried into Effect? It is evident that no incon-

---

[1] All in the Autograph of the Secretary, as well as Orthography and Capitalization. So in all other Extracts.

fiderable Movement had been Somewhere made (though but its Shadow is vifible) to ftay Proceedings, for the Deputies clamoured againft a "fecond Repreeval," as beyond what the Law will allow. Still the Magiftrates held out and would not give their Confent to have the Prifoner executed. And, bad as Circumftances appeared againft her, fome Humanity was maintained by a Portion of the Officials. It would feem like the laft Stages of Depravity, had not Documents like the following had fome Effect upon them:

"To the Hon[rble] Gov[r] and Council now fitting in Bofton, June 4th, 1680. The Petition of William Mofs. Humbly fheweth, That whereas his deare Wife was by the Jury found Guilty of Witchcraft, and by the hon[ble] Court Condemned to dye: Yet fince God hath beene pleafed to move yo[r] Honors Harts, to grant her a Reprieve until October next, yo[r] Petitio[r] humbly prayes that yo[r] Hono[rs] be pleafed to fhew her fo much Pitty as to grant her Liberty, in the Day Time to walke in the Prifon Yard, and to y[e] Prifon Houfe, and that in the Night Shee may have Priviledge of a Chamber in the Common Goale, and be freed from the Dungeon w[ch] is Extreame Clofe and hott in this Seafon, and alfo Liberty on the Sabboth to goe to Meeting; he and his Children giveing Security for her fafe Imprifonment. So fhall he be ever Obliged to pray as in Duty bound.   WM. MOOSSE."

How far this Petition was liftened to is not known; nor is it known how it happened to be in the Hand Writing of Isaac Addington (excepting the Signature), a Circumstance which may reasonably lead the Reader to infer that that worthy Man rendered what Service he could in Favour of the Prisoner.

We meet with Nothing farther in the Records relative to the Case of Mrs. Morse till the next Year, when by another Petition from her Husband, dated on the 14th of May (1681) it appears she was still in Prison in Boston. The Petition here mentioned is elaborately drawn up, and is an Argument to explain away the Evidence of certain Persons who had testified against his Wife. But Arguments were of small Avail when it was contended that the Devil might have instigated them. The Petition may be seen entire in the *History of Newbury*, and applies to the Testimonies given in our Appendix.[1]

On the 18th of the same Month Mr. Morse again Petitioned the Governour and Magistrates "in Behalf of his Wife," begging them "to hearken to the Cry of your poor Prisoner, who am a condemned Person," having "pleaded not guilty, and by the Mercy of God and the Goodness of the honored Governor, I am reprieued and brought to this honored Court, praying your Justis. I do not understand Law, and know not how to present my Case, but humbly beg that my Request may not be rejected, it being no

---

[1] These were unknown to the excellent Historian of Newbury.

more but your Sentence upon my Trial whether I fhall live or dy."

Six Days later the Deputies had fo far overcome their Defire to have the Prifoner executed, that they voted to grant her a new Trial, but the Magiftrates would not confent to it; and it feems that after her fecond Reprieve, her Family was allowed to take her Home, and although fhe was never relieved from the Sentence of the Court, it does not appear that fhe was further molefted, and finally clofed her Life at Home and in Peace, but at what time is not afcertained. The Hufband furvived the haraffing period of his Wife's Perfecutions, about two Years, dying November 29th, 1683, aged 69, according to Coffin, but according to the more recent Inveftigations of a Genealogift,[1] he was 76; the latter Account feeming more Probable.

A View of the old Houfe in which the Morfe Family lived, is given in the *Hiftory of Newbury*. The Time of Erection has not been found, though the Lot on which it was built was granted to William Morfe in 1645. A Part, if not the whole Houfe, was built foon after the Lot was granted. It ftands at the Corner of Market Street, oppofite St. Paul's Church.[2]

That Mifs Gould had this old Houfe in her Mind, and the Traditions of the Days when Mrs. Morfe was reputed a Witch, when fhe wrote the

---

[1] The Rev. Abner Morfe, in his *Memorial of the Morfes*, Bofton, 1850. 8 vo.
[2] See Coffin, 134.

following Lines, will scarcely be doubted.[1] She thus represents her Visit to a Fortune-teller:

"When I came near the Hut I began to relent,
And how, though I'd run, till my Breath was nigh spent!
For Nightshade and Hemlock grew under the Eaves,
And seemed to have 'Sorcery' writ on their leaves.
When the feathery Group gave their ominous shout,
I thought of the Chicks Mother Carey sent out!
Then there lay old Growler at Length on the Floor,
And looked like the Wicked One keeping the Door;
With Eyes semi-closed, as inclining to Sleep,
But ope'd now and then for an impious Peep;
And even the Puss, as she dozed on the Hearth,
I thought had a Spice of the Witch from her Birth."

1680.

While Witchcraft was flourishing in Newbury, a most exciting Case of it broke forth in Hampton, in 1680. Rachel, the Wife of John Fuller, of that Town, was charged with causing the Death of a Child by the Practice of Sorcery. A Jury of twelve Men was impanneled to investigate the Charge, and the Result as recorded is briefly as follows:

The Jurors say, "being called by Authority to view a dead Child of John Godfres, being about a Year old, which was suspected to be murdered, we find Grounds of Suspicion that the said Child was murdered by Witchcraft: first, in Part by what we saw by the dead Corpse; second, Something we perceived by the Party suspected, which

---

[1] Madam Hooper was nearly Cotemporary with Miss Gould, and her Lines may have Reference to her, as more applicable.

was then prefent, and was examined by Authority; and third, by what was faid by the Witnefs."

The Names of the Jury were: "Henry Roby, *forman;* Tho. Marfton, Willyam Marfton, Abraham Drake, Abraham Perkins, Anthony Taylor, John Smith, Tho. Levet, Aratus Levet, Gerfhom Elkins, Henry Derbond, and John Sanborne.

"This true Lift was given in upon Oath, the 13th of July, 1680, before me,

"SAMUEL DALTON, *of the Council.*"

The next Day John Fuller, the Hufband of the Accufed, entered into Bonds of £100, for her Appearance "to anfwer to what fhall be charged againft her in Point of Witchcraft," when called for. The Cognizance is thus underwritten: "Owned before me 14 July, 1680.

"CHRISTOPHER LUX,[1]

"SAMUEL DALTON, *of the Council.*"

The fame Day Elizabeth Denham and Mary Godfrey depofed, "that we, being in Difcourfe with Rachel Fuller, fhe told us how thofe that were Witches did fo go abroad at Night; they

---

[1] There was a Family of this Name living at Great Ifland (Newcaftle) a little later. "Audrey Lux, of Portfmouth on Great Ifland, Widow," made her Will 9 June, 1688; mentions Grand Children, John and Elizabeth Cranch, Children of Andrew Cranch, of Great Ifland; faid Children not then 21. If they died before 21, then the Property to go to "Abifhag Marfhall, my dau., wf. of Tho. Marfhall, of Great Ifland." To Son-in-law, Adrew Cranch, 5 Shillings. To dau. Abifhag Marfhall, all my Houfes, Lands, Wharues and Orchards. Witneffes, Geo. Pearfon, Ja^s. Booth, Geo. Payne, Proved, 18 March, 1692-3. Lux is not found in the *N. Eng. Gen. Dict.*

did lay their Husbands and Children asleep; and she said Rachel Fuller told us of several Persons that she reckoned for Witches and Wizzards in this Town, to the number of seven or eight. She said eight Women and two Men; some of whom she expressed by name, as Eunice Cole, Benjamin Evans Wife and her Daughters, Goodwife Coulter and her Daughter Prescott, and Goodwife Towle, and one that is now dead."

"Nathaniel Smith, aged about twenty Years, saith, that going to the House of John Fuller, as he was coming Home with his Herd, the said Fuller's Wife asked him what was the News in the Town? The said Smith said he knew none. She told him that the other Night there was a great Route at Goodman Roby's.[1] This was at the first Time when Dr. Reed was at this Town. She said they had pulled Dr. Reed out of the Bed, and with an enchanted Bridle did intend to lead a Jaunt; and he got her by the Coat, but could not hold her. I asked her who it was? and she turned from me, and as I thought did laugh.[2] Sworn the 14th of July, 1680, before me,

"SAMUEL DALTION, *of the Council.*"

Mary, the Wife of John Godfrey, and Sarah her Daughter, aged about 16 Years, gave Testimonies too loathsome for Recital. They speak of a Circumstance which took place "the same

---

[1] This was doubtless Henry Roby, a Justice of the Court of Sessions. He was in the Interest of Cranfield at one Period, and generally in some Kind of Trouble. He was at Exeter as early as 1638. See Belknap, *Hist. N. Hampshire.*

[2] No doubt she laughed to think he was so easily made a fool of.

Day that Mr. Buff went through the Town, about three Weeks or a Month ago." They attempted some Experiments with the Water of the Child; and "by and by Rachel Fuller came in and looked very strangely; bending, daubed her Face with Molasses, as she judged it, so as she almost daubed up one of her Eyes; and she sat down by Goody Godfrey, who had the sick Child in her Lap, and took the Child by the Heand, and Goodwife Godfrey being afraid to see her come in that Manner, put her Hand off from the Child, and wrapped the Child's Hand in her Apron. Then the said Rachel turned her about, and smote the Back of her Hands together sundry Times, and spat in the fire. Then, having Herbs in her Hands, rubbed and strewed them about the Hearth by the Fire. Then she sat down again, and said, Woman, the Child will be well. She then went behind the House. Mehitable Godfrey then told her Mother that Goody Fuller was acting strangely. Then Mary Godfrey and Sarah, looking out, saw Rachel Fuller standing with her Face towards the House, beating herself with her Arms, as Men do to warm their Hands. This she did three Times. Then gathering Something from the Ground, went Home. Sworn the 14th of July, 1680."

The same Day, Mary Godfrey further declared that upon the next Day after Rachel Fuller had been "at her House with her Face daubed with Molasses, the Children told their Mother that Rachel had told them that if they did lay sweet Bays under the Threshold, it would keep a Witch from coming in. One of the Girls faid, Mother I will try it, and fhe laid Bays under the Threfhold of the back Door, all the Way, and half Way of the Breadth of the fore Door; and foon after Rachel Fuller came to the Houfe, and fhe always had formerly come in at the back Door, which is next her Houfe; but now fhe went about to the fore Door, and though the Door ftood open, yet fhe crowded in on that Side where the Bays lay not, and rubbed her Back againft the Poft, fo as that fhe rubbed off her Hat, and then fhe fat her down and made ugly Faces, and neftled about, and would have looked on the Child, but I not fuffering her, fhe went out rubbing againft the Poft of the Door as fhe came in, and beat off her Hat again; and I never faw her in the Houfe fince. Sworn the 14th of July, 1680."

John Godfrey, aged about 48 Years, and his Wife about 36 Years, faid that Rachel Fuller came into their Houfe about eight or nine o'Clock in the Day. Their Child was very ill, at which Mrs. Fuller, feeing the Mother much troubled, faid that "this would be the worft Day with it. To-morrow it will be well." She then "patted the Child's Hand, and took it in hers; at which the Mother fnatched it away and wrapped it in her Apron. Then Mrs. Fuller rofe up, and turning her Back to Mr. Godfrey, did fmite the back Side of her Hand together, and did fpit in the Fire.

"Sworn before SAMUEL DALTION, of the Council, July 14th, 1680, and in the Court at Hampton, Sept. 7th, 1680.

"ELIAS STILEMAN, *Sect.*"

The Depofition of one Hazen Levit clofes the Evidence againſt Rachel Fuller, fo far as Difcovered, and the Proceedings againſt her end with that Depofition. If any further Action was had the Account of it has not been met with. It is probable the Matter was dropped, as the Evidence was too filly and puerile for even thofe benighted Times. Hazen Levit faid he was about thirtyfix Years of Age. "Riding up to his Lot in July laſt, Sun about an Hour high, he faw John Fuller's Wife upon her Hands and Knees, fcrambling too and fro, firſt one Way and then another, and feemed to him to be mighty lazy;[1] but after fhe efpied him fhe left off that Manner of acting, and feemed to take up her Apron with one of her Hands, and with the other to gather up Something." It feems fhe had a "little Child with her," and was perhaps gathering up fome Chips. While fhe was thus employed, fhe may have felt annoyed at Leavit's rude Scrutiny, for, he fays, "fhe gave him a frowning Look at Firſt," and when he went along "fhe laughed on him." After that he faw "a Thing like a little Dog," which came from the Gate leading to her Houfe and went to her "who was ſtill in the fame Actions" of fcrambling Something to put in her Apron.

Mrs. Fuller's maiden Name was Rachel Brafbridge. She was married to John Fuller, March 19th, 1677, and had fix or more Children. He

---

[1] It could be wifhed he had given his Definition of this Word, as it feems to have been the reverfe of that as now underſtood.

died in 1719. His Inventory fhowing confiderable Eftate for the Time, about £460.

Ifabella Towle was committed at the fame Time on the Charge of Witchcraft, but we find Nothing further in Regard to her, or how long fhe and Mrs. Fuller were imprifoned.

At a fomewhat later Day, the People of Hampton gave pretty free Scope to their imaginative Powers; and what one fancied or dreamed, and told to his Neighbour with an ominous Shake of the Head, was by that Neighbour told to another under a full Belief that it was true. Not far back into the laft Century there lived in Hampton, New Hampfhire, a wealthy Gentleman, widely known as Gen. Jonathan Moulton. He was a Man of great Energy and Enterprife, and having by good Luck, Shrewdnefs, or both, fecured a large Eftate in a comparatively brief Period, his ignorant and fuperftitious Neighbours furmifed he had made a League with the Devil, by Virtue of which he received all the Money he wanted. Having met with a Check in his Profperity, by his Houfe taking Fire and being entirely confumed,[1] the Report was at once fpread Far and Wide, that the Fire had been fet by the Devil

---

[1] This was long a memorable Event in the Hiftory of Hampton. It occurred about four o'Clock on Wednefday Morning, March 15th, 1769. A large Manfion Houfe and two Stores were entirely confumed. Of fome 18 Perfons in the Houfe at the Time, all efcaped with their Lives, though with the Lofs of moft of their Clothes. The Owner efcaped with his Cloak only, and a Gentleman was faved only by jumping from a Chamber Window. Colonel Moulton's Lofs was eftimated at £3000 Sterling.— *Newfpapers of the Day.*

becaufe the General had cheated him in a Bargain! No one feemed to know what the Bargain was, but on this or fome other Occafion it was averred that he cheated the Devil, not exactly out of his Boots, but out of Boots full of Money. The *Facts* have been thus ftated: The Devil was to have the General's Soul, after a certain Number of Years; in Confideration of which, at ftated Periods he was to fill the General's Boot with Gold and Silver, the Boot being hung up in the Chimney for that Purpofe. Whether a Bootfull at a Time was not fufficient to meet his Demands for Money, is not ftated; but on a Time when his Majefty came to fill the Boot, he found it took a Quantity fo vaft that he defcended into the Chimney to fee what the Matter was, and to his furprife he found that the General had cut off the Foot of the Boot! and the Room below was fo full of Money that he could not proceed to the Door, and was compelled to go back up Chimney again.

When the General died (which was in the Year 1788) and was put into a Coffin, his Body was miffing immediately afterward. Whereupon all the *knowing* ones hinted that "the Devil had got his own at laft."

There were People within the Remembrance of the Writer who would tell the above, and other equally *credible* Stories refpecting the Operations of the Devil "in the Money Market."

1681.

Plymouth Colony had a Vifitation of "Devilifm" again in the Year 1681. The Tranfactions about to be related have not been claffed hitherto among the Exploits of Witches, yet they clearly belong to them. "One Jonathan Dunen drew away the Wife of a Man to Marfhfield, to follow him, and one Mary Rofs falling into their Company, prefently was poffeffed with as frantick a Dæmon as ever was heard of; fhe burnt her Cloathes; fhe faid fhe was Chrift; fhe gave Names to the Gang with her, as Apoftles, calling one Peter, another Thomas; fhe declared that fhe would be dead for three Days, and then rife again, and accordingly fhe feemed then to die. Dunen then gave out that they fhould fee glorious Things when fhe rofe again; but what fhe then did was thus: Upon her Order Dunen facrificed a Dog. The Men and the two Women then danced naked together; for which, when the Conftable carried them to the Magiftrates, Rofs uttered ftupendous Blafphemies, but Dunen lay for Dead an Hour on the Floor, faying, when he came to himfelf, that Mary Rofs bid him, and he could not refift."

This Dunen, it appears, was a Difciple of Thomas Cafe, who had "bewitched" certain Quakers, detached them from that Sect, and were known as Cafe's Crew. Thefe were eftablifhed at Southold on Long Ifland. From this Company Dunen found his Way into the Old Colony and commenced working Miracles, but his Career was cut fhort in the Manner juft defcribed.[1]

1682.

Had there been a Chronicler in all of the New England Towns in the early Times of New England, and he had diligently recorded all of the Mifchief that was laid to the Charge of the Devil, "the World would hardly have contained the Books," unlefs the People had been aided by the fame Jugglery that caufed them.

There were no lefs than "three Houfes in three feveral Towns," in a ufually quiet Part of New England, befet this Year by Evil Spirits. But the diabolical Manœuvres at only one of the Houfes are preferved, fo far as is known to the Writer, the Preamble to which runs thus: "A brief Narrative of fundry Apparitions of Satan unto, and Affaults at fundry Times and Places upon, the Perfon of Mary, the Wife of Antonio Hortado, dwelling near the Salmon Falls. Taken from her own Mouth, Auguft 13th, 1683."

Satan began his Game in the Month of June, 1682, by a Vifit to the Door of Antonio's Houfe, and hooting out the Queftion to his Wife, "What do you here?" About an Hour later, as Mary was ftanding in the Door, fhe received a Pelt on her Eye "that fettled her Head near to the Door Poft." Two or three Days later, a Stone of

---

[1] From a Work figned "*Anti-Enthufiafticus*," printed in Bofton, in 1742, fmall 8vo., p. 84-86. Said to be by Dr. C. Chauncy.

about an half a Pound's Weight was thrown "along the Houfe within into the Chimney; and going to take it up it was gone. All the Family was in the Houfe, and no Hand appearing which might be inftrumental in throwing the Stone." Soon after, a Frying-pan, then hanging in the Chimney, was heard to ring fo loud that it was heard away acrofs the River, a Diftance of a hundred Rods or more. Upon this Mary and her Hufband embarked in a Canoe and croffed over the faid River; and as they went they faw juft forward of them in the River, a Man's Head fhaven, and two or three Feet behind it, the Tail of a white Cat, but they could fee no Body by which the Head and Tail were connected. After an Hour or fo they returned, and this Time the marvelous bald head and white Tail followed the Canoe, but when it reached the Shore they vanifhed and were feen no more.

Whether before or after the Voyage juft mentioned, is not ftated, nor is it material, "Mary, being in the Yard by her Houfe, in attempting to go into the Houfe, was bitten on both Arms black and blue; the Impreffions of the Teeth being like Men's Teeth were plainly feen by many."

Here was a Cafe fimilar to that of Hudibras, when Ralpho counterfeited the Ghoft:

> "I do believe thee quoth the Knight;
> Thus far I'm fure thou'rt in the Right,
> And know what 'tis that troubles thee,
> Better than thou haft gueffed of me.

> Thou art fome paltry, blackguard Sprite,
> Condemned to Drudgery in the Night;
> Thou haft no Work to do in th' Houfe,
> Nor Half-penny to drop in Shoes;
> Without the receiving of which Sum
> You dare not be fo troublefome;
> To pinch the Slatterns black and blue,
> For leaving you their Work to do."

Mary was not only bitten but fcratched on her Breaft, when the Devil caught her making for the Houfe as juft related. So fhe and her Hufband concluded to abandon their Dwelling. They did fo, and croffed the River, and fojourned for a Time with a Neighbour. They had not been long there before a Woman appeared to Mary, "clothed with a green Safeguard, a fhort blue Cloak and white Cap," brandifhing a Firebrand, as though fhe intended to ftrike her with it, but did not do fo. The next Day the Shape came again. Now fhe had on a gray Gown, white Apron, and a white Head Drefs. She laughed feveral Times, but no one heard any Voice. This we are told was the End of Mary's "fatanical Moleftations." Not fo with Antonio; for on returning to his Houfe the following March, he heard the Noife of a Man walking in the Chamber over his Head, and faw the Boards "buckle" under his Feet; yet no one could be feen there, "for they went on Purpofe to look." So they went again to refide on the other Side of the River, but Antonio carried on his Planting as ufual, notwithftanding the Devil made Spoil upon him in divers Ways. One Time he pulled down "five Rods of good Log-fence," and the Tracks of Cattle were feen between nearly every Row of Corn, yet the Corn was untouched, not even the Leaves cropt. Hence the Conclufion may not be unreafonable, that the Devil was not fond of Corn.

The Narrator faid he was further informed, that Mary., by Advice of fome, "who fhould have been wifer," ftuck her Houfe round with Bayes to keep off the Evil Spirits, and that they had the defired Effect; but as foon as thefe began to wither, they were all carried away by an unfeen Hand, and her Troubles returned as before.

The People of Portfmouth, in New Hampfhire, were again difturbed in 1682. So far as any Record is found to the Contrary, they had had no ferious Annoyance from the Invifible World for about a Quarter of a Century. But "on June 11th, being the Lord's Day, at Night, Showers of Stones were thrown both againft the Sides and Roof of the Houfe of George Walton; fome of the People went abroad, and found the Gate at fome Diftance from the Houfe, wrung off the Hinges, and Stones came thick about them;" and although they feemed to come with great Force, hitting Perfons, yet they hurt no one. The Object which the Witches had in this Management of the Stones feemed to puzzle People. But Matters foon grew more ferious. Stones began to fly about the Rooms within Doors; the Glafs in the Windows was fhattered to Pieces, and the leaden Safhes were bent outward, the Stones being thrown from within. "While the Secretary was walking in the Room, a great Hammer came brushing along against the Chamber Floor that was over his Head, and fell down by him, and a Candlestick was beaten off the Table." Nine of the Stones were gathered up and Marks put upon them, some of which were as hot as if they came out of the Fire; and being laid upon the Table, were soon found to be flying about again. Thus for four Hours the Miscreants kept up the Shower of Stones that Night. The Secretary was not so frightened but that he went to Bed, but a Stone came and smashed through his Chamber Door. Then came a Brick-bat "on the like Errand." And notwithstanding Mr. Walton shut the Stone up in his Room and locked it in, it rushed out "with a great Noise into the next Chamber." The Spit ran or flew up Chimney, and when it came down it came Point first, like a Dart, and stuck in the back Log. Immediately after it was sent out of the Window by an unseen Hand. "This Trade was driven" several Days, but with some Intermissions. It was remarked that the Stones came thickest where the Master of the House was. On one Occasion a black Cat was seen while the Stones were falling, and was shot at; but the unseen Hand that could prevent the Stones from hurting People, could prevent Bullets from Hurting Puss, and she escaped unharmed. On another Time some of the Family "saw the Appearance of a Hand put forth at the Hall Window, throwing

Stones towards the Entry," yet there was Nobody in the Hall at the Time. Difmal Howlings were fometimes heard, and the Trotting and Snorting of Horfes, but nothing could be feen. Mr. Walton went up the Great Bay in his Boat for Timber, but Stones followed him. He carried a Stirrup-iron to his Boat and left it there, but when he left it to return to the Houfe, it "came jingling after him through the Woods." His Anchor leaped overboard without Hands and ftopped the Boat as he was endeavouring to return Home.[1] When he had mown fome Grafs and left it in Cocks, on going into the Field again the Cocks of Hay were found hanging on Trees.

Thefe are only a few of the many Pranks which a Demon played off on Secretary Walton. He was "forely hurt" in fome of them. The Account was written in Auguft of this Year (1682), at which Time it was reported that "during the laft Winter" the Devil was tolerably quiet, but on the Return of Spring he paid Mr. Walton a Vifit, not in Perfon probably, and managed to carry off his Axes, notwithftanding they were under Lock and Key at the Time. What old Clovenfoot wanted of Axes no Conjecture was made.[2]

---

[1] There is a Creek fome Mile and a half from the former "State Houfe," in Portfmouth, known as late as 1769, as Witch Creek. Whether it took its Name from the Incidents of Walton's Voyage, I am unable to fay; but in the Belief of thofe Days, the Devil or his Deputies caufed the Death of two Cows at that Creek eighty-two Years after that Voyage, by Lightning.

[2] Since the Text was written my Attention has been called by a literary Friend to a new Volume of

No Reasons are suggested why Mr. Walton was singled out to be tormented. He was a respectable Gentleman for Anything that is known to the Contrary. His Son Shadrach was a Man of Distinction, and served as a Colonel in the Indian Wars; at one Period with the redoubtable Col. Benjamin Church.[1] He was a Quaker, and it was said that he suspected a certain Woman did by Witchcraft occasion the above preternatural Occurrences.[2]

1683.

Almost a Case of Witchcraft happened in Southampton, on Long Island, "about 1683." One Thomas Travally entered a Complaint against Edward Lacy, in that the said Lacy charged his, the said Travally's Wife with being a Witch; and that he himself had been hag-ridden three Nights by her.[3] The Action appears to have been withdrawn, and the Bill of Costs was ordered to be paid by the Defendant. Hence it would seem that Mrs. Travally was a Witch to the amount of three Shillings and six Pence, that being the Amount of Costs.

Historical Collections, in which there is a Copy of a Letter from Joshua Moody to Increase Mather, noticing this Case of Witchcraft. Amongst the many learned Notes in the Volume, none accompanies this Letter, although the Substance of the Narrative has been long published.

[1] See Church's *Indian Wars*, 184-224. *Edit.* 1827. See also Baylies' *New Plymouth*, IV, 114, V, 96. *Edit.* 1866.

[2] *Magnalia*, VI, 69.

[3] Howell's *History of Southampton*, 98.

In 1683, a Demon, as was alleged by a Contemporary, befet one Nicholas Defborough, of Hartford, in a Way altogether too puerile for ferious Narration, were it not that it affords a Sort of Criterion by which to judge of the Standard of Intelligence of our Anceftors at a given Period in their Hiftory.

It appears from the Narrator[1] of the Story, that Nicholas was caught in the firft Place in a Shower of "Stones, Pieces of Earth, Cobs of Indian Corn, &c.," all "falling upon and about him; which fometimes came in through the Door, fometimes through the Window, fometimes down the Chimney; at other Times they feemed to fall from the Floor of the Chamber, which yet was very clofe; fometimes he met with them in his Shop, the Yard, the Barn, and in the Field when at Work. In the Houfe fuch Things happened frequently, not only in the Night but in the Daytime, if Defborough himfelf was at Home, but never when his Wife was at Home alone." The Devil did not feem to be very furious in the Adminiftration of his Miffiles, for it is faid, that although other Perfons about Nicholas were ftruck, they were not hurt, from which Circumftance we are to infer that an invifible Hand fo reduced their Velocity or Impetus that they loft their Power to injure. But on one Occafion Nicholas received a Blow on his Arm which caufed it to ache a little, and at another

---

[1] Dr. Increafe Mather.

Time he received "a Scratch on one of his Legs," fo as to draw Blood. What the Miffile was that made the Scratch, there is no mention. "Some of the Stones hurled were of confiderable Bignefs; one weighed four Pounds. One Time a Piece of Clay came down Chimney, falling on the Table which ftood at fome Diftance from the Chimney. One of the Family threw it on the Hearth, where it lay a confiderable Time; but while they were at Supper the Piece of Clay was lifted up by an invifible Hand and fell upon the Table," and was quite hot.

After Narrating this childifh Story, as a Marvel, and as the immediate Work of the Devil, the Relator informs us that Nicholas had had an Altercation with a Neighbour; that he had wrongfully withheld fome valuable perfonal Property from that Neighbour, and that after he had made Reftitution the Devil let him alone. The honeft Narrator never imagined, probably, that the Devil was engaged, for this Time at leaft, on the Side of Juftice, and hence was a very good Sort of a Devil. But how Mr. Defbrough viewed the Cafe we are not informed. But from a Record made in 1687,[1] of an Adminiftration on his Eftate, and according to Trumbull, he was one

---

[1] *Colonial Recs. Connecticut*, III, 241. Savage did not meet with him, or overlooked him in his Eagernefs to dilate on Maj. Gen. John Defborough, which afforded him the Pleafure of denouncing the *Ufurper* Cromwell, his **nicknamed** Parliaments, and *fo called Lords*. It may be a Weaknefs of ours, but we believe a Lord made by Cromwell is as much to be regarded as though his Title had come down from the *Ufurper* William the Conqueror.

of the firſt Settlers of Hartford, and died there the ſame Year (1683) in which he had been ſo "moleſted by an inviſible Hand," and in Conſequence of thoſe Moleſtations.

A Caſe of Witchcraft which came up in Hadley this Year, is ſaid to be the moſt notable of any that ever occurred in the County of Hampſhire. The Witch appeared in the Perſon of Mrs. Mary Webſter. Before her Marriage to Mr. William Webſter ſhe was a Reeve. Thirteen Years after they were married, Mary was ſuppoſed to have made a League with the Devil, and could ride through the Air on Broomſticks or without them.

It happened, as is often the Caſe with other Men, that William Webſter became very poor, perhaps lived unhappily with his Wife. Poverty is diſcouraging, and it is intimated that it did not improve the Temper of Mary Webſter; and it is alſo intimated ſhe became ſpiteful, and in ſhort a Termigant, looked upon all thoſe about her as Enemies, and acted accordingly. Neighbours at laſt ſolved the Myſtery of Behaviour by declaring her a Witch. Then numerous hitherto myſterious Circumſtances were explained, and ſimple Occurrences were called to Mind and magnified in the Brains of ſome until their Explanation ended in Sorcery. Cattle refuſed to draw as they approached her Houſe, and Horſes balked, and could not be driven paſt her Door. In ſuch Caſes Drivers would enter the Houſe and beat her, or threaten to do ſo, and then ſhe generally let them pafs. On one occafion fhe overturned a Load of Hay as it was about to pafs, and the Man in Charge of it entered the Houfe to whip her, but in the mean Time his Load of Hay was placed right Side up by an invifible Hand. At another Time, by looking at a Child in a Cradle at a Neighbour's Houfe, fhe caufed it to afcend to the Chamber Floor three fucceffive Times when no vifible Hands touched it. Once a Hen came down (Somebody's) Chimney and was fomewhat fcalded in a Pot which happened to be over the Fire. It was found that Mary Webfter was fuffering from a Scald, about that Time. Thefe are but a fmall Part of the Sorceries attributed to her at the Time.

At Length, the People not being able to endure fuch Horrors any longer, brought Mary before the Court at Northampton, which confifted of Col. John Pynchon, of Springfield (Son of Mr. William Pynchon, who officiated in the Cafe of Hugh Parfons, in 1651), Peter Tilton and Philip Smith,[1] of Hadley, William Clarke and Aaron Cooke, of Northampton. Saml. Partrigg, of Hadley, being Clerk. The Record thus proceeds: "Mary Webfter, of Hadley, being under ftrong Sufpicion of having Familiarity with the Devil, or ufing Witchcraft, and having been in Examination, and many Teftimonies brought in

---

[1] The fame, I fuppofe, who was brought over from Ipfwich to New England, in 1634, by his Father, Samuel Smith, at the Age of one Year. This correfponds with his Age as ftated by Dr. C. Mather, as will be feen prefently. See *Founders of New England*, 53.

againſt her, or that did ſeem to centre upon her, relating to ſuch a Thing; and the worſhipful Mr. Tilton binding her to appear at this Court, and having examined her yet further, and the Teſtimonies aforenamed, look upon her Caſe a Matter belonging to the Court of Aſſiſtants to judge of, and have therefore ordered ſaid Mary to be, by the firſt convenient Opportunity, ſent to Boſton Gaol, and committed there as a Priſoner, to be further examined there, and the Clerk is to gather up all the Evidences and fit them to be ſent down by the Wpf[1] Mr. Tilton to our honored Governour," for his Diſpoſal.

Mary Webſter was accordingly ſent to Boſton in the following April, and on the 22d of May ſhe was taken from the Jail and placed before Governor Bradſtreet, Deputy Gov. Danforth and the nine Aſſiſtants. The Grand Jury then proceed to indict her in the uſual Verboſity of the time, "that, not having the fear of God," &c., " and being inſtigated by the Devil, hath entered into Covenant and had Familiarity with him in the Shape of a *Warraneage*,[1] and had his Imps ſucking her, and Teats or Marks found on her, as in and by ſeveral Teſtimonies may appear, contrary to the Peace," &c. Hence the Grand Jury founded their Indictment mainly perhaps on Teſtimonies of Women who had ſearched her for Witch Teats.

Whether the poor perſecuted Woman lay in

---

[1] An Indian Name for a *black Cat*.—Judd.

Jail from April to September is not certainly declared, but fhe probably did. However, fhe was brought to the Bar for Trial on the 4th of September, in Bofton, and pleaded Not Guilty, making no Exception to any of the Jury. To what Length the Trial extended is not mentioned, but the Jury brought in a Verdict of Acquittal.

By a Note accompanying the Trial of Mrs. Webfter, it is fhown that the Expenfe of it amounted to twenty-three Pounds, fifteen Shillings and two Pence; five Pounds of which were for "bringing her down from Hadley to Prifon," and two Pounds for taking her back to Hadley.

1684.

As ftrong a Cafe of Witchcraft was made out in Pennfylvania, at the Trial of Margaret Matfon, in Delaware County, in 1684, as moft of fuch Trials can fhow. The Parties in the Cafe refided near the Mouth of Crum Creek; and it is faid by the Hiftorian of that County,[1] that the Accufed ftood as well for Refpectability as her Accufers. The Trial took Place in Philadelphia, before William Penn, on the 27th of February, 1684, or 1683, O. S. The Accufations were as ridiculous as any alleged at Witch Trials in New England or Elfewhere. Henry Dryftreet alleged that he was told that the Prifoner was a Witch twenty Years ago, and that

---

[1] George Smith, M. D.

several Cows were bewitched by her; that James Saunderling's Mother told him that she bewitched her Cow.

Charles Ashcom testified that one Night the Daughter of the Prisoner called him up hastily, and when he came she "sayed there was a great Light but just before, and an old Woman with a Knife in her Hand at the Bedds Feet, and therefore she cryed out, and desired Jno. Simcock to take away his Calves, or else she would send them to Hell."

"Annakey Coolin said her Husband tooke the Heart of a Calf that died, as they thought by Witchcraft, and boyled it; whereupon the Prisoner came in and asked them what they were doing? They said boyling of Flesh. She said they had better they had boyled the Bones, with several other unseemly Expressions."

"Annakey Cooling's Attestation about the Gees, saying she was never out of her Conoo; and also that she never said any such Thing about the Calves Heart."

There were other Testimonies neither better nor worse than these, upon which the Jury brought Margaret in "Guilty of haveing the common Fame of a Witch, but not Guilty in Manner and Form as she stands indicted."

The Suggestion that the Verdict was according to the Ruling of Judge Penn, is quite a reasonable one; and "it is to be regretted that the Charge given by the Governour was not preserved, as it doubtless shaped the very righteous, though rather ridiculous Verdict." And, as in some similar Cases, the Accused was bound over in the Sum of one hundred Pounds, for her good Behaviour for six Months. Her Husband, Neels Matson, and her Son-in-law, Anthony Neelson, were her Sureties.[1]

It was probably at this Trial that Governour Penn inquired of the Accused, according to a Tradition, whether it were true that she was a Witch, and whether, as was alleged, she had rid through the Air on a Broomstick? And, on her answering in the Affirmative, the Judge said she was at perfect Liberty to ride on Broomsticks, for he knew of no Law against it, and thereupon ordered her Discharge.

It will be borne in Mind that Pennsylvania was yet a Wilderness, and that Philadelphia had been laid out scarcely three Years,[2] when this Case of Witchcraft occurred.

It has been claimed that this is the only Prosecution for Witchcraft in Pennsylvania, and our Researches are too limited to allow us to question the Assertion. An Annalist of that Locality has rather injudiciously remarked, that by the Verdict in the Case just recorded, "Pennsylvanians have probably escaped the Odium of Salem!" There may be different Degrees of Ignorance and Superstition. Let these afford what Exulta-

---

[1] Smith's *History of Delaware County*, 152-3.
[2] The Year previous (1683) it consisted of three or four little Cottages."— Watson's *Annals of Philadelphia*, 61.

tion they may. The Statute of James I. was acknowledged to be in full Force in the Colony.

A few Years later, namely, in 1695, Robert Reman was complained of at Chester for practising Divination, or, as it was then termed, *Geomanty*. He was "prefented by the Grand Jury, which also prefinted for Prohibition divers Books relating to Witchcraft, Necromancy and so forth; as Hidson's *Temple of Wifdom*, Scott's *Difcovery of Witchcraft*, and *Cornelius Agrippa*.[1]

1685.

How it had fared with Mary Webfter, since her Acquittal in Boston, in 1683, we are not prepared to fay, but in 1685 fhe was again accused of practifing Sorcery, and of the serious Charge of Murder by that Practice. To understand the Feelings entertained by a large Majority of the Community when a Witch was supposed to be discovered, one of the Prefent Day should read some of Dr. Cotton Mather's Descriptions. It is true he may be thought an Extremift of his Time, but it is also true that his Views and Descriptions were nearly univerfally those of Everybody, the World over, at the Time of these Occurrences.

The Name of Mr. Philip Smith has been mentioned before, in Connection with Mary Webfter. He was a Man of confiderable Diftinction in Hadley, was well known as Lieu-

---

[1] Watfon's *Annals*, 228.

tenant Smith, in a Period when Titles of Office were regarded with much Refpect. This Gentleman died after a fhort Illnefs, on the 10th of January, 1685; and as his Malady was not underftood by thofe who attended him, and as he had been among thofe who had brought Mary Webfter to Trial at Bofton, it was at once decided that his Death was occafioned by Witchcraft, and that Mary Webfter was the Witch. And our Narrator,[1] being contemporaneous with the Event, ought to have been well informed with all the Particulars, he fhall therefore fpeak for himfelf:

"Mr. Philip Smith, aged about fifty Years, a Son of eminently vertuous Parents, a Deacon of the Church in Hadley, a Member of the General Court, a Juftice in the Countrey Court, a Select Man for the Affairs of the Town, and which crowns all, a Man for Devotion, Sanctity, Gravity, and all that was honeft, exceeding exemplary. Such a Man was in the Winter of the Year 1684 [1683-4], murdered with an hideous Witchcraft, that filled all thofe Parts of New England with Aftonifhment. He was, by his Office concerned about relieving the Indigencies of a wretched Woman in the Town; who being diffatisfied at fome of his juft Cares about her, expreffed herfelf unto him in fuch a Manner, that he declared himfelf thenceforward apprehenfive of receiving Mifchief at her Hands.

---

[1] Cotton Mather, D. D.

"About the Beginning of January he began to be very valetudinareous, labouring under Pains that feemed ifchiatic. The Standers by could now fee in him, one ripening apace for another World, and filled with Grace and Joy to an high Degree. He fhewed fuch Weanednefs from, and Wearinefs of the World, that he knew not, he faid, whether he might pray for his Continuance here. And fuch an Affurance he had of the Divine Love unto him, that in Raptures he would cry out, 'Lord ftay thine Hand, it is enough, it is more than thy frail Servant can beare.' But in the midft of thefe Things he ftill uttered an hard Sufpicion that the ill Woman had threatened him, had made Impreffions with Inchantments upon him. While he remained yet of a found Mind, he very fedately, but very folemnly charged his Brother, to look well after him. Tho', he faid, he now underftood himfelf, yet he knew not how he might be. 'But be fure' faid he 'to have a Care of me; for you fhall fee ftrange Things. There fhall be a Wonder in Hadley! I fhall not be dead, when 'tis thought I am!' He preffed this Charge over and over, and afterwards became Delirious; upon which he had a Speech inceffant and voluble, and (as was judged) in various Languages. He cried out, not only of Pains, but alfo of Pins tormenting him in feveral Parts of his Body; and the Attendants found one of them.

"In his Diftreffes he exclaimed much upon the Woman aforefaid and others, as being feen by him in the Room; and there was divers Times both in that Room, and over the whole Houſe, a ſtrong Smell of Something like Muſk, which once particularly ſo ſcented an Apple roaſting at the Fire, that it forced them to throw it away. Some of the young Men in the Town being out of their Wits at the ſtrange Calamities thus upon one of the moſt beloved Neighbours, went three or four Times to give Diſturbance unto the Woman thus complained of. And all the While they were diſturbing of her, he was at Eaſe, and ſlept as a weary Man. Yea theſe were the only Times that they perceived him to take any ſleep in all his Illneſs. Gally Pots of Medicines provided for the ſick Man, were unaccountably empty'd. Audible Scratchings were made about the Bed, when his Hands and Feet lay wholly ſtill, and were heard by others. They beheld Fire ſometimes on the Bed, and when the Beholders began to diſcourſe of it, it vaniſhed away. Divers People actually felt Something often ſtir in the Bed, at a conſiderable Diſtance from the Man. It ſeemed as big as a Cat, but they could never graſp it. Several trying to lean on the Bed's Head, tho' the ſick Man lay wholly ſtill, the Bed would ſhake ſo, as to knock their Heads uncomfortably. A very ſtrong Man could not lift the ſick Man to make him lie more eaſily, tho' he applied his utmoſt Strength unto it; and yet he could preſently lift a Bedſted and a Bed, and a Man lying on it, without any Strain to himſelf at all. Mr. Smith dies. The Jury that view'd his Corpfe, found a Swelling on one Breaft, his Privates wounded or burned, his Back full of Bruifes, and feveral Holes that feem'd made with Awls. After the Opinion of all had pronounced him Dead, his Countenance continued as lively as if he had been alive; his Eyes clofed as in Slumber, and his nether Jaw not fallen down.

"Thus he remained from Saturday Morning about Sun-rife, till Sabbath-day in the Afternoon; when thofe who took him out of the Bed, found him ftill warm, tho' the Seafon was as cold as had almoft been known in any Age. And a New England Winter does not want for Cold. On the Night following, his Countenance was yet frefh as before; but on Monday Morning they found the Face extremely *tumifi'd*, and difcolour'd. It was black and blue, and frefh Blood feem'd running down his Cheek upon the Hairs. Divers Noifes were alfo heard in the Room where the Corpfe lay; as the Clattering of Chairs and Stools, whereof no Account could be given."

As in this Recital, fo in all fuch by our Author, the Reader might be led to think him an Eye and Ear Witnefs to all his Narratives; but it fhould be remembered that all, or nearly all his Accounts came to him, at leaft, fecond handed; and often, perhaps, through a third or fourth idle Head, all Lovers of the Marvellous; ready at all Times, efpecially in the Night, to believe the Air full of ill fhapen Monfters, bearing Commiffions from the Devil, to enlift Followers, of whom he might make Witches and fend them forth to vex and torment Mankind.

As a Sort of Sequel to the Tragedy of Mary Webfter, it fhould be related, that the poor and haraffed old Woman lived many Years after fhe was believed to have killed Philip Smith by Sorcery. She died in 1696.[1]

It will be remembered, that, in the Narrative juft extracted, Mention is made of "fome young Men" who "went three or four Times to give Difturbance" to Mrs. Webfter. It is faid by a reliable Hiftorian,[2] that the young Mifcreants went to her Houfe, dragged her out, and hung her up till fhe was almoft dead. They then cut her down, rolled her fome Time in the Snow, and then buried her up in it, leaving her, as they doubtlefs fuppofed, for Dead! But by a Miracle, as it were, fhe furvived this Barbarity. Still more miraculous it was, that the fick Man was greatly relieved during the Time the helplefs old Woman was being fo beaftly abufed by the Ruffians! The Tormentors muft have been Infidels of the worft Type, elfe they would never have dared to moleft one whom they believed to be a Witch, and hence able to afflict them as forely as Mr. Smith was afflicted. And yet they doubtlefs believed that a Witch " could take off her Shoes and

---

[1] As though fhe had been tried for the Murder of Smith (which was not the Cafe), Savage fays, "even though fhe was before a Jury at Bofton, then peculiarly expofed to falfe Impreffions, fhe was acquitted. Years more were needed for the full Triumph of the Devil and Cotton Mather"!

[2] Hutchinfon.

go through a Keyhole" to torment whoever she pleased. Such are the Inconsistencies of Believers in Witchcraft.

A Case very similar to this occurred many Years later, in the County of Hereford, England, namely, in 1751, in the Town of Barkhamsted. "The People of this Place," writes De Foe,[1] "must be believed to be highly addicted to Superstition, if we form our Notions of them from the Barbarity great Numbers of them exercised, in the Month of April, 1751, thro' the Instigation of a Publican, who took himself to be bewitched by one Ruth Osbourne, and her Husband, two poor Creatures, whom, after various Instances of the most diabolical rage, under pretence of the exploded Trial of ducking, they dragged about the Length of two Miles, and threw into a muddy Stream; thro' which ill Usage the Woman died, and for which one Collins suffered Death."

1688.

There are few more remarkable Cases in the Annals of Witchcraft than that related as having happened in Boston, in the Year 1688, in the Family of a reputable Inhabitant of the Name of John Goodwin, living at the North End of the Town. As the Circumstances are minutely detailed by Dr. Cotton Mather, in his *Magnalia*, by Gov. Hutchinson in the *History of Massachu-*

---

[1] Or rather the Editor of his *Tour through Great Britain*, II, 187-8.

setts and in the *History and Antiquities of Boston*, it is not propofed to repeat them here. We therefore will only mention, that one Perfon fuffered Death as the final Refult of the ftrange Infatuation. The Victim appears to have been a poor old Woman, according to Robert Calef, "crazy and ill-conditioned, and an Irifh Roman Catholic." She was arraigned before Judge Jofeph Dudley, condemned and executed. Her Name was Glover, and we have no other Clue to her Hiftory. She was not a *crazy* Perfon, as we now underftand the Word; that is, it was not meant that fhe was infane, but fimply that fhe was weak and infirm. We have, in our Time, heard the Word Crazy applied to aged and feeble Perfons.

It may, however, be interefting to have a few Specimens of what it is alleged that the bewitched Children experienced during the Time of their being tormented by "invifible Hands." And it may be fafely remarked, that if the Half of what is folemnly vouched for, be true, it is no Wonder the Witneffes were amazed and aftounded.

John Goodwin, the Father of the bewitched Children, came to Bofton from Charleftown. His Children were Nathaniel, born 1672, Martha, born 1674, John, 1677, and Mercy, 1681. All thefe were in the Plot of "childifh Mifchief" which fo "fadly perplexed and befooled Cotton Mather," as our Cotemporary expreffes it, as though he were the only one "befooled." The

Commencement of the Trouble did indeed arife from a childifh Circumftance. Some Article of Clothing was miffed by the Family, when Mary Goodwin charged their Wafherwoman's Daughter with purloining it. This Charge the Mother indignantly repelled, and perhaps in rough and irritating Language; whereupon Mary "was immediately taken with odd Fits, that carried in them Something diabolical." Soon after the other Sifter and two Brothers "were horribly taken with the like Fits." What was thought to be extraordinary and preternatural by the moft experienced Phyficians, was the Fact that all the Children "were tormented alike; juft in the fame Part of their Bodies, and at the fame Time," though they were far apart, and neither heard nor faw one another. At the fame Time "their Pains flew like fwift Lightning" from one Part of their Bodies to another. Yet, notwithftanding their Tortures, it was with fupreme Credulity remarked, that they flept well all Night after nine or ten O'clock at Night! Undoubtedly, after performing their Deceptions all Day, they were too tired to keep awake all Night. "But, when the Day came, they were moft miferably handled" again. They would fo affect Blindnefs, Deafnefs and Infenfibility generally, as completely to deceive their credulous and fimple Friends. Their Tongues would be drawn down their Throats and then thruft out upon their Chins, "to a prodigious Length." Their Jaws would be thrown out of Joint, by unavoidable Yawnes, "and anon clap together again like a fpring Lock. They made piteous Outcries, that they were cut with Knives and ftruck with Blows, and the plain Prints of the Wounds were feen upon them."

Their Necks would be broken, fo that the Bone would feem to be diffolved, and then it would become fo ftiff that there was no ftirring of their Heads. At Devotions they were entirely deaf, and could hear Nothing of what was faid; yet the Bofton and Charleftown Minifters held a Faft at Mr. Goodwin's Houfe, which relieved the youngeft Child. It is not ftrange that a Child of eight Years was not able to keep up the juggling Bufinefs any longer, on the other Hand it is ftrange it held out any Length of Time.

But the Magiftrates, "being awakened by the Noife of thefe grievous and horid Occurrences," ordered Mrs. Glover to be taken into Cuftody. At her Trial her pleading "was with owning and bragging rather than Denial of her Guilt," fo that the Court fufpected fhe was under the Influence of another Witch of a higher Grade than herfelf. They caufed her Houfe to be fearched, in which were found feveral Rag-babies. Thefe were decided to be Puppets, being ftuffed with Goats Hair, at which "the vile Woman confeffed that her Way to torment the Objects of her Malice was by wetting of her Finger with her Spittle, and ftroaking of thefe little Immages.

When she was made to take one of these in her Hand, one of the Children fell into sad Fits."

The poor Woman spoke English but poorly, and from her Answers to perplexing Questions it was believed the Devil had deserted her, for Somebody heard her expostulating, the Night following, with a Devil, for thus deserting her, and telling him she had confessed all. Being a strict Catholick, she probably answered with a Sort of Fear that she had somehow gotten into a strange Inquisition. Our Author says, "I did myself give divers Visits unto her, wherein she told me," among other Things, that "her Prince was the Devil." Evidently the poor ignorant Creature thought the Reverend Divine was catechising her upon some Points of her Religion; and from all that can be gathered from their Conversation as reported by the Divine himself, he understood her quite as well as she did him. She was not willing he should pray with her without the Consent of some good Catholick Spirits. This the Reverend Divine construed to mean that she could not allow of it without the Consent of the Devil!

At her Execution she said the Children would not be relieved by her Death, and that it was not she that afflicted them. This was construed into a Threat that "they *should* not be relieved by her Death," and that others as well as she afflicted them. "Accordingly the three Children continued in their Furnace as before, and it grew rather seven Times hotter than it was, and their

Calamities went on, till they barked at one another like Dogs, and then purred like ſo many Cats; would complain that they were in a red-hot Oven, and ſweat and pant as if they had been really ſo. Anon they would ſay cold Water was thrown on them, at which they would ſhiver very much. They would complain of being roaſted on an inviſible Spit, and then that their Heads were nailed to the Floor, and it was beyond an ordinary Strength to pull them from it."

"One of them dreamt that Something was growing within his Skin, acroſs one of his Ribs. An expert Chirurgeon found there a braſs Pin, which could not poſſibly come to lie there as it did, without a preſtigious and myſterious Conveyance. Sometimes they would fly like Geeſe, and be carried with an incredible Swiftneſs through the Air, having but juſt their Toes upon the Ground (not once in twenty Feet), and their Arms waved like the Wings of a Bird."

Thus are ſketched but a ſmall Part of the Wonders performed by the Goodwin Children, yet theſe will probably ſatisfy our Readers, as we have not Room for more.

1691.

At a Court in Springfield, on the 29th of September, 1691, Mary Randall was charged with Witchcraft. The Court entertained the Complaint, but why the Caſe was put off for a Year, unleſs the Evidence was deemed inſufficient immediately to try her, is left to Conjecture. At the end of a Year no Trial was had, but the Father of the Accused, William Randall, became bound for her good Behaviour; and this seems to be the Last heard of the Action, and the last Case of Witchcraft in the County of Hampshire.

1692.

So far as we have been able to learn, thirty Years had elapsed since the experimental Trial of a Witch by Water had taken Place in the Colonies. That related by Dr. Increase Mather, of 1662, was the first and only one up to that Date, so far as known. However hard it may be to believe that such Things ever happened in this Land, that comes to us so direct, and from so veracious a Contemporary of it, that a Disbelief in it cannot be entertained for a Moment. And as we have one other well authenticated Case it is here given. This, according to our Authority,[1] took place in Fairfield, Connecticut. In September of this Year (1692) Mercy Disborough, Wife of Thomas Disborough, of Campo, in Fairfield, and two or three other Women, were tried at Fairfield for Witchcraft, and all were acquitted except Mercy Disborough, who was found Guilty and sentenced to die. She is supposed to have been acquitted; and why she should have been subjected to the Ordeal of being thrown into the Water it is not easy to see; but our

[1] Sylvester Judd, Esq., in his *History of Hadley*, 233-4.

Authority goes on: "Mercy Disborough and Elizabeth Clauffon were bound, Hands and Feet, and put into the Water; and Witneffes teftified that they 'fwam like Cork;' yet Elifabeth was acquitted, and Mary was not condemned, becaufe fhe floated."

Notwithftanding the Record of this Barbarity is unimpeachable, and may have been fuppofed unparalleled in this Country, it will fubfequently appear that a fimilar one tranfpired in Virginia, and at a Date allowing lefs Excufe for its Perpetration.

So much has been written and publifhed upon the great Outbreak of 1692, that only a brief Outline will be attempted in this Treatife. All Things confidered, it is one of the moft furprifing Events in Hiftory. The Smallnefs of the Number of thofe engaged in it, in its Beginning, their Youth and Pofition in Society, their Ability to deceive Everybody for fo long a Time! In any View that has yet been taken of it, its Narrator has found himfelf baffled to a Degree beyond that of any other Event in the whole Range of Hiftory, to account fatisfactorily for the Conduct of the young Females through whofe Inftrumentality it was carried on. It required more *devilifh* Ability to deceive, Adroitnefs to blind the Underftanding, and to keep up a Confcioufnefs of that Ability among themfelves, than ever fell to the Lot of a like Number of Impoftors in any Age of which the Writer has ever read; and he can only say, if there are parallel Cases they have not fallen under his Observation.

It is true, that when once the Imagination is excited, the Reason may become confused, and a Loss of Judgment follows. These Circumstances happening in a Community bound in a Spell of superstitious Awe, may account in some Degree for the total Want of Judgment, common Sense and Humanity, so prominent in all Prosecutions for Witchcraft. Such, however, is believed to be the Master-Key to the Prosecutions and Persecutions to which a Belief in Witchcraft has given rise.

That which gave the Accusers great Advantage over all Opposition from every Quarter, was the religious Belief that nearly Everybody had in its Reality. It was at the Hazard of being denounced by every Christian as an Infidel, to utter a Word against its Existence, and it was believed that any Person might become a Witch. So thoroughly imbued with that preposterous and pernicious Belief, were all Parties, that not only the Court and Juries were demented by it, but the Accused also; for not one is remembered, who, in their last Moments, even questioned the Reality of Witchcraft; but on the other Hand, directly or indirectly acknowledged that there were Witches, and hoped they would be found out and punished, while they themselves disclaimed all Knowledge of it.

The principal Accusers and Witnesses, too, in the whole Term of the Witchcraft Prosecutions were eight Females, nearly all young Girls, from eleven to twenty Years of Age. Thefe were Abigail Williams, eleven; Mary Walcut, feventeen; Ann Putnam, twelve; Mercy Lewis, feventeen; Mary Warren, twenty; Elizabeth Booth, eighteen; Sarah Churchill, twenty; and Sufannah Sheldon.

Mary Walcutt was Daughter of Captain John Walcutt; Ann Putnam was a Daughter of Thomas Putnam; Mercy Lewis was a Servant living in Mr. Putnam's Family; Mary Warren lived in the Family of Mr. John Procter; Elizabeth Booth lived near John Procter; Sarah Churchill lived in the Family of George Jacobs, Sen[r].; Sufannah Sheldon lived in the Village.

Thefe Females inftituted frequent Meetings, or got up, as it would now be ftyled, a Club, which was called a Circle. How frequent they had thefe Meetings is not ftated, but it was foon afcertained that they met "to try Projects," or to do or produce fuperhuman Acts. They doubtlefs had among them fome Book or Books on Magic, and Stories of Witchcraft, which fome one or more of their Circle profeffed to underftand, and pretended to teach the Reft. Yet they were generally very ignorant, for out of the eight but two could write their Names. Such were the Characters which fet in Motion that ftupendous Tragedy, which ended in Blood and Ruin.

Inquiry as to thefe Accufers muft have early occurred. Whether they or any of them were ever punifhed? They were not, becaufe the

Party which had believed in them in the firſt Place, believed in Witchcraft ſtill. The Believers and Infidels died out together. Years aſſuaged the aggrieved Minds of ſuch as were living long after, and Nothing was done, excepting the Beſtowal of a few paltry Pounds on ſome clamorous pretended Sufferers, and a few Shillings on thoſe who needed it more, and were far greater Sufferers. And as to thoſe who cauſed the Proſecutions, adds Hutchinſon, "ſome of them proved Profligates, abandoned to all Vice, others paſſed their Days in Obſcurity or Contempt."

March 1ſt. Sarah Good is apprehended and committed to Jail. On the ſame Day an Indian Woman is brought before Juſtices Hathorne and Corwin, who examined her reſpecting what had taken Place in the Rev. Samuel Parris's Family.

March 7th. Sarah Good, Sarah Oſburn, and Tituba, are all ſent to Boſton to be there impriſoned. Sarah Oſburn died there (in Jail) on the 10th of May following. Tituba lay in Jail thirteen Months, and was then ſold to pay her Priſon Charges. Beſides Sarah Oſburn, Anne Foſter alſo died in Jail. And it is not unlikely, but on the other Hand is extremely probable, that many others ſuffered Death during the long and cold Winter of 1692-3, after inevitable Privations, and in many Caſes loaded with Iron Chains!

From March, 1692, to May, 1693, nearly, if not more than two hundred Perſons had been dragged to Priſon, under color of Law and the

Mockery of a Trial. Some it is certain escaped through the good Offices of Friends outside, and some by Connivance with their Jailors. These, added to the Number which had died in Duress, could hardly have been less than fifty. and we know from good Authority, that the Number set at Liberty in May, 1693, by Governour Phips' Proclamation was one hundred and fifty! most of whom, if not all, had lain all Winter in Jail.

It requires no Flexibility of Imagination to presume that many Families had been utterly ruined. The Imprisoned were generally Persons of small Estates, and small as they were, Confiscation fell upon them. Besides that Besom of Destruction, Jailor's Fees and Court Expenses were added to their Burthens.

The Number that perished by violent Deaths is shown to have been twenty, and of each of them follows brief Notices.

1. Bridget Bishop, said to have "long undergone the Repute of a Witch." One Samuel Gray testified to her having performed Witchcraft twenty Years previous. But on his Death Bed he acknowledged his Perfidy, and that his Accusations were wholly groundless. She was executed protesting her Innocence, June 10th, 1692.

2. George Burroughs, a Minister of the Gospel, was executed August 19th, 1692, under Circumstances which must ever cause a Thrill of indignant Horror, and the deepest Commiseration

to all who have, and ever hereafter may read the Story of his laſt and dying Scene.

3. Martha Carrier, of Andover, was executed the ſame Time with the Rev. Mr. Burroughs. She was the Wife of Thomas Carrier, Huſbandman. The Number of Teſtimonies againſt her were many and ſurpriſing, but not ſo ſurpriſing as that any were weak enough to believe them.

4. Giles Cory was by an old Law put to the moſt cruel Death. When arraigned before the Court he refuſed to plead, or anſwer Queſtions; for he knew what his Fate would be in either Caſe. So to avoid giving the Proſecution any Advantage, he would anſwer Nothing. Whereupon he was ſentenced to be preſſed to Death. Hence, refuſing to put himſelf on Trial, no Trial actually took place, and his Death was the Reſult of his Obſtinacy, and a Firmneſs with ſcarcely a Parallel, certainly not in American Annals. At the Time of his Death (September 16th, 1692) he was over eighty Years old. He had been an "Iron Man," as would be ſaid of ſuch in our Times. In the Commencement of the Troubles he acted a ſingular Part, and in his earlier Career had acquired, whether juſtly or not it is difficult to determine, the Ill-will and Envy of many of his Neighbours, ſome of whom were glad of an Opportunity to ſee him troubled and humbled. But in the latter Particular they ſignally failed, for he ſtood firm to the laſt Breath. Whether he was more than once required to plead "Guilty," or "Not Guilty," our Records do not ſtate, but it

is likely the old Englifh Law was obferved, and that he was brought before the Court three Times, and three Times required to plead.[1]

Well, though ironically, has the Ballad perpetuated the Memory of Giles Cory, in the Lines which follow:

> "Giles Corey was a Wizzard ftrong,
>   A ftubborn Wretch was he,
> And fitt was he to hang on high
>   Upon the Locuft Tree.
>
> So when before the Magiftrates
>   For Triall he did come,
> He would no true Confeffion make
>   But was compleatlie dumbe.
>
> 'Giles Corey,' faid the Magiftrate,
>   'What haft thou heare to pleade
> To thefe that now accufe thy Soule
>   Of Crimes and horrid Deed?'
>
> Giles Corey — he faid not a Worde,
>   No fingle Worde fpake he;
> 'Giles Corey,' fayth the Magiftrate,
>   'We'll prefs it out of thee.'
>
> They got them then a heavy Beam,
>   They laid it on his Breaft;
> They loaded it with heavie Stones,
>   And hard upon him preft.
>
> 'More Weight,' now faid this wretched Man,
>   'More Weight,' again he cryed,
> And he did no Confeffion make,
>   But wickedly he dyed."

---

[1] Mather fays he was often before the Court.—*Wonders of the Invifible World,* 210, Edition 1866.

He laid in the Jail at Ipſwich from the 19th of April till the 16th of September, excepting the Time occupied in his Examination and Execution.

5. Martha Cory was the Wife of Giles Cory, a Woman of blameleſs Life, a pious and worthy Woman. She was "cried out upon" for that very Reaſon; for hitherto the miſcreant Accuſers had ſtruck at Perſons in more humble Circumſtances, and now to raiſe their own Importance began to accuſe Perſons whom they did not dare to attempt at firſt. She was executed September 22d, 1692, "proteſting her Innocency, concluding her Life with an eminent Prayer upon the Ladder."

Upon her Caſe our Balladiſt ſays:

> "Dame Corey lived but ſix Dayes more,
> But ſix Dayes more lived ſhe,
> For ſhe was hanged at Gallows Hill
> Upon the Locuſt Tree."

6. Mary Eaſty was Wife of Iſaac Eaſty, about fifty-eight Years of Age, and the Mother of ſeven Children. She was Siſter of Rebecca Nurſe and Sarah Cloyſe. She appears to have been a meek and amiable Lady, and the Judges ſeemed ſomewhat ſtaggered when in this Character ſhe ſtood before her Accuſers. But as yet the Monſters had met with no Check, and their Teſtimony was believed by the imbecile Court. After her Condemnation, ſhe made a moſt touching Petition to the Judges "and the Reverend

Minifters," in which fhe befought them, "not for my own Life," fhe urged, "for I know I muft die, and my appointed Time is fet; but, if it be poffible, that no more Innocent Blood be fhed, which cannot be avoided in the Way and Courfe you go in." All availed Nothing. She was one of the eight hung at the fame Time, namely, September 22d, 1692. It was upon this Occafion that the Rev. Nicholas Noyes, then prefent, and viewing the Victims, remarked to the Byftanders: "What a fad Thing it is to fee eight Firebrands of Hell hanging there!" What could be expected of Followers when fuch were the Leaders? Mr. Noyes was a fingle Man, and in great Repute elfewhere as well as in the Community in which he then was. He is faid to have acknowledged his Error refpecting the Witchcraft Profecutions; but whether he made any Atonement by affifting thofe he had helped to ruin, we have no Evidence. His Election Sermon of 1698 fhows a great Amount "of Heathen Learning," and by fome Paffages in it he evidently had the Horrors of 1692 before the Eye of his Imagination. "With Grief and Shame we read over and meditate upon fome Texts fpoke of Ifrael: 'as they were increafed fo they finned,' &c. So hath it been with us. As for our Degeneracy, it is too palpable to be denied, and too grofs to be excufed." Again, "God is a very great Stranger to the Affairs of New England. Inftead of Plenty we have had Scarcity; inftead of Health, Sickness; inftead of Peace,

War; impoverished and brought low. We have had remarkable Trouble from Heaven and Hell."

7. Sarah Good, of Salem Village, was one of the first of the Victims of the Delusion. Being poor and friendless, and of general bad Repute, her Persecution was not regarded as such, and thus a Beginning of the nefarious Work was easily accomplished. Although despised and treated with all Manner of Indignities, her Spirit was not broken, as appears from her Answer to Mr. Noyes at the Place of Execution. He insultingly told her she was a Witch, and that she knew it. She indignantly replied, "You are a Liar. I am no more a Witch than you are a Wizzard, and if you take away my Life, God will give you Blood to drink." She was hanged July 19th, 1692.

8. Elizabeth, Wife of James How of Ipswich, was arraigned on the 30th of June, 1692. The Testimony against her was very voluminous, but was absurd and childish as on all similar Occasions. She was a pious and amiable Woman, but Nothing could save her, and on the 19th of July she was hanged.

9. George Jacobs, Sen., of Salem, was executed at the same Time with the last mentioned. His Grand-daughter, Margaret Jacobs, testified against him at his Trial, but when it was too late, acknowledged her Perfidy, in a piteous Letter, still extant.

10. Susanna Martin had long been under the Imputation of being a Witch, and has been

noticed in the Events of 1669. She was one of thofe executed on the 19th of July. She belónged to Amefbury, and appears to have been a Woman of great Spirit and bufinefs Capacity, and perhaps fomewhat prone to wordy Contefts, by which fhe had excited the Jealoufy of envious Neighbours. Her Trial took place on the 29th of June, in which fhe was found Guilty, and was hanged on the 19th of July following. At her Examination her Replies to the Judge's Queftions fhow a Mind far fuperior to that of the Court; and for Directnefs, Concifenefs, and common Senfe, has commended itfelf to all Readers from that Day to this, and has thoufands of Times been quoted.

11. Rebecca Nurfe, of Salem Village, a Lady of great Worth, but aged and in poor Health, was drawn into the awful Vortex in what would appear at this Time, but from a Knowledge of the Exiftence of Feuds which arofe from various Caufes, as a very ftrange Occurrence. She was facrificed in a Manner too cruel for Belief. The Jury returned a Verdict of Not Guilty, but the Court, by the moft barefaced Perverfion of her Anfwers, and being determined on her Deftruction, fent the Jury out again and forced a Verdict of Guilty from them! There is Nothing more memorable, or lamentable, in all the Trials and Convictions, than the Cafe of this Poor Woman. She was hanged with the five that fuffered on the 19th of July.

12. Alice Parker, with eight more, received Sentence of Death on the 17th of September,

and was executed five Days after. She belonged to Salem, the Wife of John Parker, Mariner. As Nothing is heard of her Hufband in connection with the Profecutions, he was perhaps away at Sea.

13. Mary Parker was alfo hanged at the fame Time, protefting her Innocence, as did the others, to the Laft. She belonged to Topsfield, and may have been no Connection of Alice. Their Trials do not appear among the Records.

14. John Procter, with fix others, was tried on Auguft 5th, condemned, and executed Auguft 19th following. He was committed to the Prifon in Bofton on the 11th of April preceding. His Refidence was at Salem Farms, but had lived in Ipfwich. He was not fent to the Jail there, doubtlefs becaufe he had many Friends; of thefe, thirty-two figned a Petition for his Reprieve, who gave him a good Character.

15. Ann Pudeater was of Salem. Mr. Upham thinks her Name was originally or really Poindexter, the Widow of Jacob Pudeater, fuppofed to have been about feventy Years old at the Time of her Profecution, and was poffeffed of confiderable real Eftate in Salem, where fhe refided She was brought up for Examination on the 12th of May, and again on the 2d of July, and then fent to Jail, where fhe doubtlefs lay till the 22d of September, when fhe made one of the eight "Firebrands of Hell" upon the Gallows, as the unfeeling and inhuman Noyes expreffed himfelf.

16. Willmet Redd (fo written in the Records)

or Wilmot Reed or Read, belonged to Marblehead. Nothing has reached us concerning this Perſon, but as being one of the *Firebrands* that periſhed proteſting Innocence to the laſt. There was a Read Family at this Period in Marblehead, but no Chriſtian Name appears among them of Willmet or Wilmot.

17. Margaret Scott was of Rowley, Widow, and one of the *eight Firebrands* who ſuffered proteſting Innocence. Of her Family and Connections we have met with Nothing, beyond what is found in Gage's *Hiſtory of Rowley*, from which it ſeems ſhe was poor and old, two important Conditions in the early Proſecutions.

18. Samuel Wardwell was of Andover, was hanged on the 22d of September alſo. He confeſſed himſelf Guilty, and on this and ſpecter Teſtimony he was condemned. Before he was ſwung off he ſpoke to the Multitude of Spectators, declaring his Innocence.

19. Sarah, wife of John Wildes, of Topsfield was executed on the 19th of July, having, with four others, been condemned on the 30th of June preceding. She was arreſted about the 22d of April, and impriſoned till her Execution. The gruff Denunciations and Demand to confeſs of the Court, did not move her, and ſhe died firmly denying all Knowledge of the Crime for which ſhe ſuffered.

20. John Willard, of Salem Village, had been a Deputy in making Arreſts for Witchcraft, until he became ſatisfied that the Perſons accuſed were

above any such Suspicion. As soon as his Decision was known to the miscreant Prosecutors they "cried out on him." And though he attempted to save himself by Flight, he was pursued, brought back, tried, and executed on the 19th of August.

Thus have been briefly noticed those that were executed. But those who suffered Everything but Death, and some even Death itself, in dismal Jails throughout a New England Winter, cannot be noticed here, but the Reader will find all he can desire, probably, in the three Volumes of *The Witchcraft Delusion*, &c., published by Mr. W. E. Woodward, in 1866, and in the Rev. Mr. Upham's *Salem Witchcraft*, published in 1867, both already mentioned.

Of many of the Sufferers very little is known. Some, and perhaps a very considerable Number, fled to other Parts. At Ipswich, Rachel Clinton or Clenton, Wife of Lawrence Clinton, was before the Court there, and there is a Charge for Fetters (Irons) having been made for her. Also Mehitable, wife of John Downing, was arrested on the 23d of September, but was released on her Husband giving Security. Prosecutions had begun to relax, and on the Day following, Mary, Wife of Hugh Row, Phebe, Wife of Timothy Day, and Widow Rachel Dinson, all of Gloucester, were let out of Ipswich Jail on Bail. The following named Persons, all of Gloucester, also, were brought to Ipswich Court for Examination, on the 30th of October; namely, Esther, Wife of Samuel Elwell, Rebeckah, Wife of Richard Dike, and Abigail, daughter of Hugh Row. They were held till the 7th of November, and then fet at Liberty.

Some Others of Gloucefter met with Trouble befides thofe mentioned in the laft Paragraph. One Abigail Soames of that Town was taken on a Charge of Witchcraft, fent to the Jail in Bofton, and there incarcerated from the 23d of May, 1692, to January 3d, 1693. Nothing is found refpecting whom fhe was accufed of bewitching, or her Examination. She was, no doubt, among the one hundred and fifty difcharged, before mentioned.

As Dr. Cotton Mather has been more feverely denounced than any other Perfon connected with the Delufion of that Period, the Reader may wifh, in this Connection, to fee how he fhuffled out of it after the Tempeft had fubfided. To fay the leaft of it, the Author has fhown a Dexterity not furpaffed in any other Cafe with which we are acquainted, "of cafting a Mift" before his Readers' Eyes, by which he hoped to efcape their Animadverfions, and thus to pafs on to Futurity, maintaining a Pofition in the firft Rank of great Men, as he hitherto feems to have done, efpecially in his own Eftimation.

He wrote in 1698: "As to our Cafe at Salem, I conceive it proceeded from fome miftaken Principles; as that Satan cannot affume the Shape of an innocent Perfon, and in that Shape do mifchief to the Bodies and Eftates of Mankind;

and that the Devil when he doth Harm to Persons in their Body or Estate, it is (at least, most commonly, generally and frequently) by the help of our Neighbour, some Witch in Covenant with the Devil; and that when the Party suspected looks on the Parties supposed to be bewitched, and they are thereupon struck down into a Fit, as if struck with a Cudgel, it is a Proof of such a Covenant. *Cum multis aliis.*"

And again: "When this Prosecution ceased, the Lord so chained up Satan, that the Afflicted grew presently well. The Accused are generally quiet; and for five Years since, we have no such Molestation by them." He had previously remarked, that "this Matter was carried on chiefly by the Complaints and Accusations of the Afflicted (bewitched ones, as it was supposed) and then by the Confessions of the Accused condemning themselves and others. Yet Experience shewed, that the more there were apprehended, the more were still afflicted by Satan; and the Number of Confessors increasing, did but increase the Number of the Accused; and the executing of some made way for the apprehending of others; for still the Afflicted complained of being tormented by new Objects, as the Former were removed. So those that were concerned grew amazed at the Number and Quality of the Persons accused, and feared that Satan by his Wiles had enwrapped innocent Persons under the Imputation of that Crime. And at last it was evidently seen that there must be a Stop put, or the

Generation of the Children of God would fall under that Condemnation. Henceforth, therefore, the Juries generally acquitted such as were tried, fearing they had gone too far before."[1]

A disinterested Spectator could hardly have written thus, at that Day, unless he had really been but a Spectator, and had never encouraged the abominable Proceedings. Now, when it is known that the Author was a considerable Promoter of them, his "Mist" becomes too transparent for Concealment, and the third Person can by no Ambidexterity be palmed off for another.

The Account of the Delusion of 1692 will be closed with the following Indictments and Proceedings against Mr. Philip English, of Salem:

"Essex in the Prouince of the Massachusetts Bay in New England. Ss.

"Anno R R^s and Regino Gulielmi and Maria Anglia, &c. Quarto: Annoq. Domini, 1692.

"The Jurors for o^r Sou^r Lord and Lady the King and Queen, doe present, that Phillip English of Salem, in the County of Essex M^rchant vpon the 31st Day of May, in the year aforesaid, and diuers other dayes and times as well before as after, certaine Detestable arts called Witchcraft and sorceries, wickedly, Mallistiously and felloniously hath vsed, practiced and Exercised, at and in

---

[1] Michael Wigglesworth "feared that innocent Blood had been shed," and thus wrote to Increase Mather, in 1705, the same Year in which he died, and makes a very fair Apology for the Judges. Cotton Mather's Letter to John Richards, dated May 31, 1692, should be read in this Connection, in which he makes out a better Case than in our Extract. It is in *Colls. Ms. Hist. Soc.*, XXXVIII, 391-7.

the Towne of Salem in the County of Effex aforefaid, in, upon, and againft one Mary Wallcott of Salem aforefaid, fingle Woman, by faid wicked Acts the faid Mary Wallcott, ye Day and Yeare aforefaid, and diuers other dayes and Times, boath before and after, was and is Tortured, afflicted, Confumed, Pined, wafted and Tormented; againft the Peace of o^r Sou^r Lord and Lady, the King and Queen, their Crowne and dignity, and the Lawes in that Cafe made and Prouided."

Of the fame Tenor and Date there is another Draft of an Indictment againft Mr. Englifh for bewitching "one Elizabeth Booth of Salem." Both of thefe are endorfed, "Ignoramus," and figned, "ROBERT PAYNE, *Foreman.*" Hence thefe Bills were thrown out, or paffed as not true Bills, although Mr. Englifh was arrefted on the fame 31ft of May, and fent to Bofton and caft into Jail, where he, with his Wife, lay fome fix Weeks or more. In the Meantime, while other Evidence was being collected, and other Preparations for his Trial were being made, he was able, through the Advice and Aid of Friends, to efcape from Prifon. He fled to New York, and there found an Afylum till the Folly and Madnefs of Profecutions were at an End.

Thofe Profecutions did not ceafe until near the End of April, 1693. Among our original Papers we find the following, in a remarkably neat Hand, but the Writer of it is not detected.

Robert Payne, the *Foreman* wrote a strange Hand, judging from his Signature.

"The Deposition of mercy Lewis, aged 8tene, this Deponent Testifieth and saith that Last night Philip English and his Wife came to mee, also Goodwife Dasten, Eliz Johnson and old pharo[1] of Linn: said Mrs. English vrged mee to set my Hand to a Booke, and told mee she would Aflict mee Dreadfully, and kill mee if I did not; so also if I would but touch the Booke I should bee well, or else I should never, s^d mrs. English s^d she might bring the Book now she thought ever one of them would bee cleared, and now at this present time before the Grandiury s^d Philip English, his Wife, and old Pharoh, came into the Roome, or their shape, and stroke mee on the Brest; and almost Choaked mee, and s^d they would strangle mee if they could.

"owned before the Grandiury vpon the oath she had taken Jan^{re} 12th 169$\frac{2}{3}$

Attests   ROBERT PAYNE
foreman."

The same Day William Beale gave his Deposition against Mr. English. He had on the preceding August made another, both of which will be found in *The Witchcraft Delusion*, &c., Vol. III, 181-5, preceded by an Account of that Gentleman, to which the Reader is referred.

---

[1] This " Old Pharo " was a Negro, Slave of Zaccheus Collins, of Lynn. Besides Pharoah, Collins owned three other Slaves, whose Names were Essex, Prince and Cato.— Lewis, *Hist. Lynn*, Ed. 1865, Page 344.

Respecting those who saved their Lives by confessing themselves Witches, it may be proper to remark that such Confessions were wrung from them under Circumstances calculated to excite the greatest Pity and Commiseration for those who made such Confessions; for it must be borne in Mind that all Parties believed in Witchcraft, and that some Persons must be Witches, and that the Troubles complained of were caused by them. Imagine feeble Women forced from their Families and cast into cold and damp Prisons with heavy Irons upon them! Six Females of Andover were thus cruelly incarcerated. It came about in this Wise. The Wife of one Joseph Ballard was taken sick, and it was at once surmised that she was bewitched. To find out who were the Witches, two of the "Afflicted" at Salem were brought to Andover to make the Discovery, and thus commenced the "direful Calamity" which befel that Town. At what Time the six Females were first suspected does not appear; but those in Authority ordered them to come together at the Meeting house, where, after a Prayer was had by the Minister, the Accused were blindfolded and led up to the "Aflicted" already in their Fits. The suspected Females being thus led up to them and their Hands placed upon them by their Conductors, the Afflicted were at once free from their Fits, "and said they were well." Whereupon, say the blindfolded, "we were all seized upon as Prisoners, by a Warrant from the Justice of the

Peace," hurried off to Salem, utterly amazed and
aſtoniſhed, and "affrighted even out of their
Reaſon." Such was their Introduction to Irons
upon their Limbs, and a near Proſpect of an
ignominious Death upon the Gallows. This was
their Condition when Friends beſet them on
every Side to confeſs themſelves Witches, as the
only Means of ſaving their Lives. Hour after
Hour, and Day after Day, they were beſought by
dear and near Kindred and Friends to confeſs,
until they were worn out for want of Reſt
and Sleep. It is not ſtrange that their Minds
wandered until they imagined they experienced
what they confeſſed; as that they rode through
the Air on Poles to certain Rivers or Ponds,
where they were baptized by the Devil; that
they had ſigned his Book, and given themſelves
to him Soul and Body, and thus bound themſelves to worſhip him; that in return they could
command him to afflict whomſoever they ſhould
deſignate. Theſe Things being embodied in the
Indictments were a Guide to Confeſſions, and
were forced from them by leading Queſtions. A
Cotemporary[1] ſays he is ſure that moſt of the
Charges in thoſe Indictments "would be better
laid againſt the Judges in the Oyer and Termi-
ner," for that thoſe Judges "ſerved, if they did
not worſhip the Devil, and took him to be their
God, whether they ſigned his Book or not. Had
that Book been brought into Court, as it ought

---

[1] Savage.

to have been, or the Government called on to show, at least, what Means they had used to get the precious Record to the open View of the Jury, the Name of William Stoughton, and more than one of his associate Judges, I doubt not, as clearly as that of any of the Accused, would have flared in the sapphire Blaze." Such an Idea would naturally occur to any ordinary Lawyer of our Times, but the Accused of those Days had no Counsel to demand in their Behalf that the Book be produced in Court. Had such a Demand been made it would doubtless have been scouted by the Judges. Besides, we are told by an able Lawyer[1] of that Time that "the Devil could not be lawfully summoned" to bring his Book into Court.

1700.

An Execution for Witchcraft took place in Albany, in the Year 1700, related in a Communication of the Earl of Bellomont to the Lords of Trade and Plantations. As it is sufficiently Concise for our Purpose, and graphically sketched, it follows in his own Words:

"Aquendero, the chief Sachem of the Onondage Nation, who was Prolocutor for all the Five Nations at the Conference I had two Years ago at Albany, has been forced to fly from thence, and come and live on Coll. Schuyler's Land near Albany. Aquendero's Son is poysoned, and

---

[1] Sir Robert Filmer.

languishes, and there is a Sore broke out on one of his Sides, out of which there comes Handfulls of Hair, so that they recon he has been bewitched, as well as poisoned.

"I met with an old Story from the Gentlemen of Albany, which I think worth relating. Decannissore, one of the Sachems of the Onondages, married one of the Praying Indians in Canada (by Praying Indians is meant such as are instructed by the Jesuits). This Woman was taught to poison, as well as to pray. The Jesuits had furnished her with so subtill a Poison, and taught her a Legerdemain in using it, so that whoever she had a Mind to poison, she would drink to 'em a Cup of Water, and let drop the Poison from under her Nail (which are always very long, for the Indians never pare 'em) into the Cup. This Woman was so true a Disciple to the Jesuits, that she has poisoned a Multitude of our Five Nations that were best affected to us. She lately coming from Canada in Company of some of our Indians, who went to visit their Relations in that Country who have taken Sides with the French; and, there being among others a Protestant Mohack (a proper goodly young Man), him this Woman poisoned so that he died two Days Journey short of Albany, and the Magistrates of that Town sent for his Body and gave it a Christian Burial. The Woman comes to Albany, where some of the Mohacks happening to be, and among 'em a young Man nearly related to the Man that had been poisoned, who espying the Woman, cries out with great Horror, that there was that beaſtly Woman that had poiſoned ſo many of their Friends, and it was not fit ſhe ſhould live any longer in this World to do more Miſchief; and ſo made up to her, and with a Clubb beat out her Brains."[1]

Although Lord Bellomont does not expreſſly ſay he was himſelf a Believer in the Exiſtence of Witches, it is not probable that he would have taken ſo much Pains to detail this Story had he not imagined that thoſe to whom he was communicating it were Believers.

1706.

Few more diſgraceful Scenes were ever enacted in the Proſecutions for Witchcraft, either in Connecticut or Maſſachuſetts, than this which took place in Virginia, next to be related.[2]

There lived in Princeſs Anne County, in that Province, a Female named Grace Sherwood. The Court of that County ſat on the third of January, 1706; preſent as Juſtices, Beno. Burroughs, Col. Moſely, John Cornick, Capt. Hancock and Capt. Chapman. On Complaint of Luke Hill and his Wife, a Warrant was iſſued ſummoning the Woman to appear at the next Court. As ſhe did not appear an Attachment was iſſued to the Sheriff to arreſt and bring her there. According to the Writ the Accuſed was arraigned

---

[1] *New York Colonial Documents,* IV, 689.

[2] See Barber. — *Virginia Hiſtorical Colls.,* and Foreſt's *Norfolk.*

on the 7th of February following, "and ye Matter being after a long Time debated, and ordered y^t ye faid Hill pay all Fees of this Complaint, and y^t ye faid Grace be here next Court to be fearched according to ye Complaint, by a Jury of Women to decide ye faid difference, and ye Sheriff is likewife ordered to fummon an able Jury accordingly."

Nothing further feems to have been done in this fingular Specimen of a back-woods Court till the 7th of March following. The Juftices then prefent were Col. Edward Mofely, Lieut. Adam Thorrowgood, Maj. Henry Sprat, Capt. Horatio Woodhoufe, Mr. John Cornick, Capt. Henry Chapman, Mr. Wm. Smith, Mr. John Richefon, and Capt. Geo. Hancock. The Jury of Women reported that they had fearched Grace Sherwood and found two Things like "Titts," with feveral other Spots. The names of the Women are given in the Records. Here the Court found itfelf in deep Water, and adjourned over without coming to any Decifion; but on the 2d of May, the Record ftates, that "whereas a former Complaint was brought againft Grace Sherwood for Sufpicion of Witchcraft, which by ye Attorney Generall Tomfon's Report to his Excellency in Council was too generall and not charging her with any peticular Act; therefore reprefented to them, y^t Princefs Ann Court, might, if they thought fitt, have her examined de novo; and ye Court being of Opinion y^t there is great Caufe of Sufpicion, doe therefore order y^t ye Sheriff take yᵉ said Grace into his safe Custody, until she shall give Bond and Security for her Appearance to yᵉ next Court to be examined de novo, and yᵗ yᵉ Constable of yᵗ Precinct goe with yᵉ Sheriff and search yᵉ said Grace's House and all suspicious Places carefully for all Images and such like Things."

The Examination and Search by the Jury of Women seems not to have been satisfactory, and the same Jury were ordered to make a new examination and to report at the next Court. But they declined the Service, and a new Jury of Women was empannelled.

On the 5th of July (1706) we find this Record of Proceedings: "Whereas for this [these] severall Courts yᵉ Business between Luke Hill and Grace Sherwood on Suspicion of Witchcraft, have been for severall Things omitted, particularly for want of a Jury to search her, and yᵉ Court being doubtfull that they should not get one yˢ Court, and being willing to have all means possible tryed, either to acquit her or to give more Strenth to yᵉ Suspicion, yᵗ she might be dealt with as deserved."

It was finally decided that the old English Test should be put in Practice, namely, of casting the Accused into the Water. "The Sheriff to take all such convenient Assistance of Boats and Men, as shall be by him thought fitt, to meet at Jno. Harper's Plantacon, in order to take yᵉ said Grace forthwith, and put her into the Water above Mans Depth, and try her how she swims therein."

The *Executioners* were ordered, that if it was found that fhe would fwim to be careful not to drown her, and as foon as fhe came out, "to requeft as many antient and knowing Women as poffible to examine her carefully for Teats, Spots and Marks about her Body not ufuall on others." The Court ordered further, "that fome Women be requefted to fhift and fearch her before fhe goe into ye Water, y^t fhe carry Nothing about her to caufe any further Serfpicion. She was accordingly bound and caft in, and being found to fwim was taken out again.

There feems to have been much halting in the Cafe of the poor doomed Woman, this laft Record being under the 10th of July. Mention is made of many Witneffes that teftified againft her, but what they teftified to, excepting that fhe was a Witch, Nothing appears. If the Teftimony was written down it was not probably preferved; and we find no mention of the Cafe until the 15th of September (1706) when "having had fundry Evidences fworne, proving many Cercumftances againft her which fhe could not make any Excufe, or little or nothing to fay in her own Behalf, only feemed to rely on what ye Court fhould doe; and thereupon confented to be tryed in ye Water, and likewife to be fearched againe, with Experiments: being tryed, and fhe fwiming when therein," as before mentioned, was fearched again "by five antient Weamen, who all declared on Oath, y^t fhe is not like them, nor no other Woman y^t they knew of; having two Things like Titts on her private Parts, of a black coller, being blacker than ye Reſt of her Body. All which Cercumſtances the Court weighing in their Conſideracon, doe therefore order that ye Sheriff take y^e ſaid Grace into his Cuſtody, and to commit her Body to ye common Joal of this County, their to ſecure her by Irons or otherwiſe, there to remain till ſuch Time as he ſhall be otherwiſe directed, in order for her coming to ye common Goal of ye Countey to be brought to a future Tryall there."

What became of Grace Sherwood does not appear to be known to the People of the Region where ſhe was *experimented* upon. A Hiſtorian of an adjacent Part of the Old Domain has a very brief Notice of the Trial, which he ſays was a very *Grace*-leſs Affair! And we muſt be allowed to ſay that it is our deliberate Opinion that he has not detailed the Subject with any *Grace* at all.

Owing to the ſhockingly bungling and illiterate Manner in which the Records of this Affair appear, it is not eaſy to conſtruct an intelligent Narrative out of them. But one Thing is very evident, namely, that the Accuſed was as ſavagely and perſiſtently purſued as any one could have been ſimilarly circumſtanced. Amidſt it all there muſt have been Scenes both comical and highly ludicrous; imagine a Perſon to be thrown into a Lake, to meet a watery Grave, provided the Party did not float upon its Surface, and at the ſame Time the Court "ordering the Sheriff not to expofe her to the Rain, as fhe might take Cold, ye Weather being very rainy and bad"!

The Trial of *finking or fwimming* was ordered on the 5th of July, but it did not then take place, probably by Reafon of the Inability of the Sheriff to get a Jury of Women to attend to the *delicate* Duties affigned them.

The Place where Trial by Water was made is an Inlet of Lynnhaven Bay, in Princefs Anne County, and known to this Day as *Witch Duck*.

1712.

In South Carolina, as late as 1712, the Law "againft Conjuration, Witchcraft, and dealing with evil and wicked Spirits," was declared to be in force. It is quite probable that fome Cafes of Witchcraft had occurred among fome of the South Carolinians, which caufed the Revival of the Act of James the Firft; but what they were, and how extenfive, we have no Means at Hand to determine, as their Chroniclers are filent upon the Subject. But one Thing is very certain, and that is, if they did not raife Witches down there, they raifed the Devil very early.

About this Period fome fufpected of Witchcraft were feized upon by a fort of ruffianly Vigilance Committee, and condemned to be burnt; and were actually roafted by Fire, although we do not learn that the Injuries thus inflicted proved fatal. The Parties fo tortured, or their Friends, brought an Action in the regular Courts for the Recovery of Damages, but the Jury gave them Nothing!

1720.

There was a Cafe of Witchcraft (as fuppofed) in the then fparfely fettled and out of the way Town of Littleton, in Middlefex County, Maffachufetts, in 1720, which was quite as formidable in its firft Stages as that was in Salem Village, but it was too late in the Century for it to make much Headway, and the Inhabitants were too few to allow it to fpread over any confiderable Territory. The Names of thofe who were Actors in it are fuppreffed in the Materials ufed, and not much Pains have been taken to recover them. The principal Impoftor having removed to Medford in the fame County, a few Years after the Affair had blown over, offered herfelf as a Candidate to the Rev. Mr. Ebenezer Turell's Church there. Her "Experience" was confidered fatisfactory, and fhe was about to take her Place among the Members, when, in the Meantime, the reverend Minifter preached a Sermon, the Burthen of which was, that Liars would go ftraight to Hell, be caft into a Lake of Fire and Brimftone, and there to feethe for ever and ever, and fo forth. Happening to hear this Difcourfe fhe was overcome with Remorfe, fuppofing the Preacher had her Cafe in his Mind. So, in great Tribulation fhe went to him, deeply bewailing her Deception, made a new Confeffion, and in due Time was admitted into the Church, and for aught that has appeared to the Contrary, lived a confiftent Chriftian Life ever after.

As in the Cafes of the Goodwin Children of Bofton, and thofe of the Paris Family at Salem, thofe of Littleton were the three Daughters of "one J. B.," whofe Ages ranged five, nine and eleven Years. One of thefe (probably the oldeft) went to refide at Medford, as juft mentioned. She told all the Circumftances to Mr. Turell, who wrote them down. The Paper thus drawn up was in the Hands of Governor Hutchinfon when he was preparing his *Hiftory of Maffachufetts*, who has given a Synopfis of it in that Work.[1]

1728.

There were doubtlefs fome unaccountable Tranfactions in the Colony of Rhode Ifland which caufed the Authorities there to enact or reenact the Law "againft Conjuration, Witchcraft, and dealing with evil and wicked Spirits; that Witchcraft is and fhall be Felony; and whofoever fhall be lawfully convicted thereof fhall fuffer the Pains of Death."

It is here propofed to fufpend thefe Refearches. They might eafily be carried to a much later Period, and pretty ferious Cafes too might be de-

---

[1] See Vol. II, Pages 20 and 21, Edition, Bofton, 1767.

tailed, but what has been done will probably be as much as will ever be read. The Intereſt of the Publick will decide that Queſtion. If more is wanted, it may be forthcoming in future Editions.

APPENDIX.

No. I.

XAMINATION *of Hugh Parfons, of Springfield, on a Charge of Witchcraft, and the Teftimonies given againft him, before Mr. William Pynchon, at Springfield,* 1651.

[NOTE.—The Figures in Brackets denote the Paging of the original Manufcript, which having been put together wrong, was paged before the mifplacing was detected.]

[21] Hugh Parfons Examinations. All thefe Teftimonies now taken vpon Oath
    Before me, WILLIAM PYNCHON.

[23] The Examination of Hugh Parfons. 1. d. of [March?] and his 2d Exam. y^e [obliterated].

HUGH PARSONS you are attached upon Sufpition of Witchcraft.

George Lankton[1] and Hannah his Wife do ioyntly teftifie vpon Oath: that on ffriday laft, being the 21 ffebruary, they had a Pudding in ye fame Bagg, and that as foone as it was flipped out of the Bag, it was cut lengthwife like the former Pudding,[2] and like

---

[1] *Langton*, or perhaps *Langdon* was the original family Name, but they have long been diftinct. This George was an Emigrant. His Wife was a Widow of Edmund Haynes.

[2] The whole Story about the cutting of Puddings is fet in the laft Leaf.— *Note by Mr. Pynchon.*

another on ye 23 ffeb. as fmooth as any Knife could cut it, namely, one Slice al alonge, wantinge but very litle, from End to End.

Alfo Hannah the Wife of George Lanɗon faith vppon Oath, that a Neighbor came in, and fhe fhowed it to him, and that Neighbor took a Peece of it and threw into the Fier: and fhe faith that about an Hower after, phapps a little more, fhe herd one mutter and mumble at the Dore; then fhe afked Goody Sewell who was then at her Houfe (and neere ye Dore) who it was, fhe faid it was Hugh Parfons, and that he afked whether Goodman Lankton were at Home or no. I faid no, and fo he went away, but left not his Arrand, neather did he euer fince come to fignifie his Arrand.

Depofed in Corte by Hanna [Lankton].

Hugh Parfons being afked what his Anfwer was: he fpake to other Thinges and not to the Queftion,[1] being afked the 2^d Tyme what his Arrand was, he fpake againe of other by Matters, and not to the Queftion: being afked the 3^d Tyme what his Arrand was, and charged to make a direɗ Anfwer, then he faid it was to gett fome Hay of him. Being afked againe whether he had ppounded his Arrand fince to Goodman Lankton; he faid he never faw him fince. Then one or two that were prefent teftified that they fee him meete Goodman Lanɗon next Day below.[2] Symon Bemon[3] and Rice Bodorthe[4] fay vppon Oath,

---

[1] Pity we are deprived of knowing thofe "other Things."

[2] At fome Point down the River.

[3] A Name fince written *Beaman*. Savage has "ftrangely" mixed the Families of "Beamond, Beamon, and Beaman."

[4] Savage did not find the Name thus fpelled, but over *Rice* he raifes confiderable Mift. Judd (no Doubt) told him that Rice was the Father of John, who "was drowned, 18 Mar. 1683, with his f. and Lydia, w. of his br. Jofeph, and Mercy, d. of his br. Samuel."

Appendix. 221

that the next Day but one they faw Hugh Parfons meete Goodman Lankin accompanied wth Thomas Sewell[1] in the Streete, and that they faw him fpeak to Goodman Lanketon.

George Lančton faith on Oath that he neuer to this Day afked him for any Hay.

When Hugh Parfons faw himfelf taken tardy [24] in this put of, then he faid that he did not afk him becaufe John Lumbard had tould him that Goodman Lankton had fould more Hay to Goodman Herman than he could fpare. But after inquiry

John Lumbard[2] faith vppon oath, March 17, 1650, That the Wednefday before that Hugh Parfons came to Goodman Lanktons Houfe for Hay, that he had fpeoken to buy fome Hay of Goodman Lankton, namly as he paff'd by where he and Hugh Parfons were at Worke together, and had a Deniall; and then he tould Hugh Parfons that Goodman Lankton could not fpare him any Hay, for he had already fould more to Goodm Herman[3] than he could fpare, and faid he fhould now want himfelf.

John Lumbard alfo faith on Oath, that ye ffriday after, when the faid Pudding was fo ftrangely cut, he tould Hugh Parfons that Lančton had no Hay to fell. Hugh Parfons not being able to replie any further, it is evident that his coming to ye Dore of Goodman Lankton p'fently after the burning of the Pudding, wch was the next Day after Jo. Lumbard had tould

---

[1] To what Family of *Sewell* or Sewall he belonged has not been found. Savage gueffes he left Springfield foon after the Birth of a Dau. (Abigail) 14 March, 1650, but where he went, or "whence he came is wholly uncertain."

[2] Since fpelt Lombard. John is found at Springfield, 1646; the next Year, Sept. 1, he was at New Haven, where he married Joanna Pritchard.— *Savage*.

[3] A Family named *Harman* came to N. England in 1635, in the Ship Love. This was probably *John Herman*.

him that he had no Hay to ſpare, that his Arrand to gett Hay was no true Cauſe of his coming Thither but rather that yᵉ Spirit that bewitched the Pudding brought him thither.¹

Mary Parſons being pſent at yᵉ 2ᵈ Examination, ſaith, one Reaſon why I have ſuſpected my Huſband to be a Witch is becauſe all that he ſells to Anybody doth not proſper. I an ſorry ſaid ſhe for that pore Man, Tho. Millar,² for two Dayes after my Huſband and he had bargained for a Peec of Ground Thomas Millar had that Miſchance of that Cutt in his Legg.

[25] Thomas Millar being pſent, ſaith vppon Oath, that he being in Company with ſeuerall other Workemen about Tymber Trees in the Woods, as we were at Dinner, and merry together, Hugh Parſons ſatt on a Bow ſomewhat higher then the Reſt. Then one of the Company ſtarted this Queſtion: I wonder why he ſitts there: Thomas Millar ſaith he anſwered, To ſee what we have: and then I began to ſpeak of the cuttinge of the Puddinge in Towne.

Thomas Cooper³ being pſent wᵗʰ the ſaid Workmen, ſaith, that he was much troubled in his Minde becauſe Thomas Millar ſpake ſo plainely to Hugh Parſons leaſt ſome ill Euent ſhould follow.

And both Tho. Cooper and Thomas Millar ſay vppon Oath, that Hugh Parſons was as merry and as pleaſant before this Speeche about the Pudding as any

---

¹ As though the Devil could not bewitch a Pudding without being on the Spot!

² He was probably an Emigrant, although at what Time he came over is not known. His Wife was Sarah, Daughter of Thomas Marſhfield, of Springfield, whom he married in 1649. He was killed by the Indians, October 5th, 1675.—*Springfield Records.*

³ The ſame afterwards (5 Oct., 1675) killed by the Indians, as he was paſſing from one Garriſon to another.—See I. Mather, *Brief His.*, p. 98, Note ; and *Hubbard*, I, 107, 121; II, 44.

in the Company, but after this he was wholly filent, and fpake not a Word in replie about ye Pudding: but fatt dumb: and Tho. Millar faith that about half a Quarter of an Hower after, at his firſt fettinge to Worke, his Legg was cutt.

April 3. 1651. Thomas Burneham[1] faith vppon Oath that he faid to Hugh Parfons a Little before his App^rhenfion: here is ſtrange Doings in Towne about cutting of Puddings, and whetting of Sawes in ye Night Tyme: Hugh Parfons herd thefe Thinges much agitated among diuers then p'fent, and was wholly filent, but at laſt he faid, I never herd of this Thinge before this Night. Thomas Burneham faith he faid to him, that is ſtrange, that you ſhould not here of thes Thinges: and I being but a Stranger in Towne, doe here of it in all Places whereuer I come: Att this Hugh Parfons held down his Head and was wholly filent, but he tooke Occafion to fpeak of other by Matters, as pleafantly as Anybody elfe, but to the Matter of the Pudding he would fay Nothing: and yet faith Thomas Burneham, I fpake to him of it feuerall Tymes, and of ye whetting of Sawes on purpofe to fee what Hugh Parfons would fay to it, but ſtill he continued fylent,[2] and would not fpeak any Thinge about thefe Thinges. Then Goodman Mun beinge p^sent faid I would y^t thofe that whet Sawes in the night Tyme, and on ye Lordes Dayes, were found out: Then faith Thomas Burnham, I faid, you Sawyers you had need to look to it: Hugh Parfons being alfo a Sawyer, never returned any Anfwer, but ſtill con-

---

[1] He happened to be at Springfield at this Time, but probably did not remain long. Where he came from, or where he went to, is alike unknown. He may have been of the Ipfwich Family, but Conjectures may not be very fatisfactory.

[2] That any fenfible Man ſhould have been filent at the Repetition of fuch childiſh and contemptible Nonfenfe is not at all ſtrange.

tinued filent: This Matter about the Puddinge and whetting of Sawes was often toffed vp and downe betweene feuerall P^{s}ons, and many faid they neuer herd ye like: and Hugh Parfons was often fpoken to, in pticular, and afked if he euer herd ye like, but ftill he continued wholly filent.

Joane, the Wife of William Warrener,[1] and Abigall ye Wife of Goodman Munn,[2] being p^{s}nt when the faid fpeeches were vfed, do acknowledg that they rember all Thinges that haue bin related by Thomas Burnham, and that Hugh Parfons was wholly fylent, and do teftifie the fame vppon Oath, the Day and Yere aboue faid.

[27] 2dly Blanche Bodorthe[3] faith on Oath, ffeb. 27, and March 1ft. and March 18, 1649. That about two Yeeres fince, Hugh Parfons being at ower Houfe, we had fome Speeches about a Bargaine wth my Hufband about fome Brickes: and then Blanch Bodorthe faith that fhe fpake Somethinge about the faid Bricks that did much difpleafe Hugh Parfons: Therevppon he faid vnto me, Gammer, you neded not haue faid Anythinge, I fpake not to you, but I fhall remember you when you little think on it.

Alfo Rice Bodorthe faith vppon Oath, that he took Notice of the faid Threatninge, and was much offended at it, and tould Hugh Parfons that it was no good Speech; but I haue often herd him vfe fuch

---

[1] Suppofed to be the Freeman of 1638. His Wife's maiden Name was Searl, or Something like it, as Genealogifts cannot agree about it, and their great Arbiter does not obtrude a Decifion. They call her *Joanna*.

[2] Doubtlefs Benjamin Munn, previoufly of Hartford, who had ferved in the Pequot War; removed to Springfield, where he married Abigail (Ball) Burt. See *Savage*, III, 254. The Name is lefs common than many others.

[3] Her maiden Name was Lewis, married Rice Bodortha, 1646. It will be remembered that Parfons's Wife was a Lewis.

Threatninge, both againſt myſelf and others when he hath bin diſpleaſed.

Blanch Bodorthe tooke Oath in Corte to all ſhe witneſſeth.

[28] Samuell Marſhfeild[1] being alſo pſent at yᵉ ſame Tyme, teſtifies vppon Oath, that he herd Hugh Parſons vſe the ſaid threatninge Speech to Blanche Bodorthe.

At this Hugh Parſons was wholy ſilent and anſwered not.

Then I tould him of ſome euill Euents that did follow not longe after this Threatninge.

Samuell Marſhfeild teſtifieth in Cort.

Blanch Bodorthe doth teſtifie vppon Oath, that ſoone after this threatninge Speech, as ſhe was going to Bedd, and had put of her Waſtcote made of red ſhag Cotten, and as ſhe was going to hang it vp on a pin, ſhe held it vp betweene her Hands, and then ſhe ſaw a Light as it had bin the Light of a Candle, croſſing the back of her Waſtcote, on the Inſide, three Tymes, one after another, at wᶜʰ ſhe was amazed: and therefore ſhe ſaith, that after ſhe had laid it downe, ſhe tooke it vp againe to try if yᵉ Fierlight might not be the Cauſe of it, but ſhe ſaith that the Fierlight being all one as it was before, ſhe could not prciue any ſuch Light by it, and beſides ſhe ſaith it could not be the Fierlight, becauſe there was a double Indian Matt compaſſing the Bedd and the Place where ſhe was, ſo that it could not be the Fierlight, for this double Matt was betwixt her and the Fier: and ſhe ſaith moreouer that becauſe this Light was ſo ſtrange to her, ſhe took her Waſtcote ſeuerall other Nights to

---

[1] He married Eſther, Daughter of Samuel Wright, 18 Feb., 1652; was Son of Thomas Marſhfield, who was ſuppoſed to have been loſt at Sea. The Name is uniformly Maɾſhfeɨld in the Manuſcript.

try if ye Fierlight would not giue fuch a Light as fhe faw at firft, and held it vp ye fame Way that fhe did at firft but fhe faith fhe could not prciue any fuch Light afterwarde.

[29] 2dly. About a Month after this, fhe faith that when fhe was in Child Bed: and as well as moft Women vfe to be, and better then fhe vfed to be: yet at the Weeks end being defirous to fleepe, fhe lay ftill, that fhe might fleepe, and fhe did fleepe: and yet about an Hower or more after, fhe awaked, and felt a Soreneffe about her Hart, and this Soreneffe increafed more and more in three Places, namely vnder her left Breft, and on her left Shoulder, and in her Necke: and in thefe three Places, the Paine was fo tedious, that it was like the pricking of Knifes, fo that I durft not lie downe, but was faint to be fhored vp wth a Bagg of Cotten Wool, and with other Thinges: and this Extremity continued from Friday in the Forenoone till Monday about Noone, and then the Extremity of the Paine began a little to abate, and by Tufday it was pritty well gon: and fuddenly after, my Thoughtes were, that this Euill might come vppon me from the faid threatning Speech of Hugh Parfons.

I do not app^{r}hend that I was fick in any other p^t of my Body, but in the faid three Places only, and by the Extremity of thefe Prickinges only.

The Widdow Marfhfeild[1] teftifies vppon Oath, March 22, 1650, that when fhe *kept* (?) in Rice Bodorthes Wife, fhe was not there in ye Night, but in the Daytyme only: when I went Home at Night I left her well, as could be expected of a Woman in Child Bed, but in the Morning when I came fhe was in lamentable Torment; fhe grew worfe and worfe for two or three Dayes, and fhe cryed out as if fhe had bin

---

[1] Perhaps the Widow of Thomas Marfhfield   See *Note, ante*.

pricked with Knifes in such a lamentable Manner that I did much feare her Life: I neuer saw a Woman in such a Condition in Child Bed, for she could not lie downe in her Bed, neather doe I aperhend that she had any other Kind of Sicknesse, but that pricking Paine only in her Side and Shoulder.

3^{ly}. Blanch Bodorthe saith vppon Oath, that my Child being about two Yeeres ould, as he was standing neere to his Father, did hastily run to him, and striued to gett vp vppon his Knees, and cryed I am afraide of the Dogg, and yet there was no Dogg there: his ffather asked him where the Dogg was, he said it was goun vnder the Bedd: his ffather asked him whose Dogg it was: [30] he said it was Lumbardes Dogg: his ffather said that Lumbard had no Dogg: y^n he said again it was Parsons Dogg: but ye Child's Meaning was at first that it was Parsons Dogg: I know it by this becaufe when Parsons did after vse to come to ower Howse he did often cale him Lumbard: and euer and anon he is much affrited with this Dogg, and doth often speak of it: and yet Parsons hath no Dogg, neather was there any Dogg in the Howse: but the Earnestnesse of ye Child, both then and since, doth make me conceiue it might be some euill Thing from Hugh Parsons.

Hugh Parsons hauing herd all thes Testimonies alledgd, stood still at his 2^d Examination, as at ye first, and made no Answer.

Rice Bodorthee saith vppon Oath, that euer since ye first Tyme the Child was afraid of this Dogg he will often speak of it and point at it wth such Earnestnesse that he hath often made me afraid wth his earnest pointing at it; sometymes he saith it is there vunder the Stoole, and sometymes it is there vnder the Cradle, and so vnder other Places.

[31] 3^{ly}. Your Wife saith that she suspects you may

be ye Caufe of all the Euill that is befallen to Mr. Moxons Childerne, becaufe when fhe hath fpoken to you about the Bargaine of Bricks that you vendertook to make for Mr. Moxons Chimnies, and that fhe thought Mr. Moxon would expect the pformance of the faid Bargaine: therevppon you faid, if Mr. Moxon do force me to make Brickes according to Bargaine, I will be euen with him, or he fhall get Nothinge by it, for fhe faith that thes two Speeches are very vfuall with you when you are difpleafed wth any Body.

Anf^r. Hugh Parfons faith, I faid not that I would be euen wth him, but this I faid, if he would hould me to my Bargaine, I could puffle him in the Bargaine.

John Mathewes[1] being p^{s}ent, faith vppon Oath, that when he went with Hugh Parfons to fetch fome of his *fannell* (?) Brickes, he faid to Hugh Parfons, doe not you make more Brickes for Mr. Moxons Chimnies, he will ftay with vs now, and then I beleue he will haue vp his Chimnies: Hugh Parfons faid, no, that I know of, then faid I, Mr. Moxon will hould you to your Bargane about the faid Brickes; then faid he, if he doe, I will be euen with him: And when Hugh Parfons made my Chimnies he did often vfe the fame Speech: and when he is difpleafed wth any Body it is his vufuall Speech.

At y^s Teftimony of Jo: Mathewes Hugh Parfons was filent and made no Replie.

Mr Moxon being p^{s}ent, faith the fame Week that I fpake to Hugh Parfons about the Brickes, and to his Wife about another Bufineffe, my Daughter Martha was taken ill wth her Fittes. I confefs alfo that when I fpake to him of the faid Bargaine, that Hugh faid I

---

[1] He was previoufly at Rehoboth. His Wife was Penticoft Bond, but who her Father was is unknown. She was maffacred by the Indians at the fame Time Lieut. Cooper and Thomas Miller were killed, Oct. 5th, 1675. *Springfield Records*, and Hubbard's *Narrative*.

could not, in Strictness, hould him to ye Bargaine: But this laft Anfwere doth not take of the ill Purpofe of his former Threatning.

[32] 4th Sarah the Wife of Alexander Edwardes[1] teftifies vppon Oath, ffeb. 27, 1650, that about two Years agoe, more or leffe, Hugh Parfons being then at the Long Meddow, came to her Howfe to buy fome Milke: fhe faid I will giue you a Halfpenny worth, but I cannot let you haue any more at this Tyme: This was at that Tyme when my Cow gave three Quartes at a Meale; but the next Meale after fhe gave not aboue a Quart, and it was as yellow as Saffron, and yet ye Cow ayld Nothing that I could difcerne: the next Meale it altred to another ftrange odd Cullor, and fo it did euery Meale for a Week together it ftill altred to fome od Cullor or other and alfo it grew leffe and leffe: and yet all the While ye Cow was as well as at any Tyme before, as far as I could difcerne: and about a Weeke after fhe began to mend her Milk againe w^thout any Meanes vfed: vppon this I had Thoughts that Hugh Parfons might be the Caufe of it.

Alexander Edwards fwore that George Coulton[2] faw ye Milke in ftrang Colors.

Ans. Hugh Parfons faith that he did not lie one Night at ye Long Meddow that Somer, but only in the Spring of the Yeere, eather in March or in the Beginning of Aprill, when he fet vp Fencinge there, and that he neuer had Milk of her but that one Tyme; and at that Tyme of the Yeere he thinks her Cow could not giue three Quarts at a Meale.

But now, at his 2d Examination, May the 18, 1650,

---

[1] He came from Wales, by way of Briftol. His Wife was Sarah, Widow of John Searl, whom he married April 28, 1642.—*Savage*.

[2] George *Colton* died at Springfield, December 17th, 1699. He was recorded as Quartermafter.—*Springfield Records*.

he seeing Alexander Edwardes about to testifie ye Contrary, he confesseth that he lay a Night there in plantinge Tyme, about the End of May. I remember y^t Alexander Edwards came to me to tell me of this Accident, and said that he was p^swaded the Cow was bewitched by Hugh Parsons: but I did not beleue him at that Tyme, I rather conceiued that the Cow was falling into some dangerous Sicknesse; for such a sudden Abatement I tould him was a Sign of some dangerous Sickness at Hand: but seeing no Sicknesse followed, I told Hugh Parsons that such a sudden Change could not come from a naturall Cause. [33] 5^{ly} Anthony Dorchester[1] saith vppon Oath ffeb. 25, 1650, the 1. Day of the 1. Month and the 18 Day, that about September was twelve Monthes, four Men had equall Shares in a Cow: each had a Quarter, and ye Offall was to be diuided also: and Hugh Parsons desyred to haue the Roote of the Tounge: but he had it not: it fell to my Share: and a certaine Tyme after I had salted it, I tooke the said Roote and another Peece of Meate, and put it into the Kettle as it was boylinge ouer the Fier at Hugh Parsons Howse where I liued at y^t p^rsent: and there was no Body there but he and his Wife, and I and my Wife who was sick of a Consumption, sittinge on her Bedd, and not able to gett of without Help: neather were any of my Children able to take such a Thinge out of a boyling Kettle: this being the Sabbath Day, Hugh Parsons and his Wife went to the Church before me, then I made myselfe ready and went p^rsently after them, and came Home before them: and tooke vp my Meate before they came Home, but the Roote of the Tounge w^h Hugh Parsons formerly desyred was gonn:

---

[1] He died at Springfield, August 28th, 1683. His Wife, Sarah, died Aug. 11th, 1649. A Wife Martha, died 17 Dec., 1662.

Appendix.

his Wife came Home p^rfently after me (but he came not with her.) Then I tould her, and fhe wondred how it could be gonn: and fhe went to ye Tubb where it was falted to fee if it might not be forgotten, and it was not there: Then faid I to her, I am fure I put it into the boyling Kettle, and fhe confeffed that fhe faw me pick it and wafh it, and being p^rfent did much wonder ye ftrange going of it away; and faid that fhe feared her Hufband might convey it away: fhe tould me that her Hufband went along with her till we came neere to Goodman Merickes, and was very pleafing to her, more then vfually he had bin a great while before: but there he laid the Child downe and went no further with her: and fhe faw him no more till ye Meeting was almoft donn: (all this, Mary Parfons being p^rfent doth acknowledge.) p^rfently after this he came home: Then I fpake of it to him, and all that he faid was, that he thought I [34] did not put it in: but I tould him that I was fure I put it into the boyling Kettle: And I haue euer fince belieued that no Hand of Man did take it away: but that it was taken away by Witchcraft.

Ans. Hugh Parfons confeffeth that he defyred the Roote of ye Toung, but withall faith he is ignorant as ye Child vnborne wch way it went.

Some by Standard objected it might be taken away by his Wife as well as by him; But that is not fo likely becaufe Hugh Parfons went not with her to ye Meeting, but laid down her Child and went from her, and fhe faw him no more till Meeting was almoft don.

Ans. Hugh Parfons faith, that he doth not remember that he went any whither, unleffe he might go into Goodman Merikes[1] Howfe to take a Pipe of To-

---

[1] Thomas *Merrick* was among the early Settlers of Springfield. His Wife was Sarah, Daughter of Rowland Stebbins.

bacco, and though his Wife faw him no more till the Meeting was almoſt donn, yet he faith he might be ſtanding wthout the Dore, though ſhe faw him not; And, at his 2d Examination, he aſked how it did appeere that he came not to the Meeting till it was almoſt don.

Abigall Mun being p^{r}fent doth teſtifie vppon Oath, that ſhe knew by the Talk about the ſtrange going away of this Roote of the Tounge, what Sab. was ment, and ſhe faith that ſhe faw him come that Sabbath to ye Meeting, when ye Sermon was well onward.

Jonathan Taylor depofed in open Courte: faith that he heard the faid Parfons fay (notwithſtanding the Roote of the Toung was defired by Anthony Dorcheſter, for his Wife, being ficke) yett he faid I will haue it. EDWD: RAWSON *fecry*.[1]

[35] 6^{ly} Griffin Jones[2] doth fufpect you for Witchcraft about Knife. Griffin Jones faith vppon Oath, ffeb 25, 1650, March 1. and 18 Day that when he liued at his Howfe neere Hugh Parfons Howfe, about 2 y. agoe: on a Lordes Day, I went Home to Dinner, but my Wife ſtaid behind at a Neighbors Howfe to Dinner. I took vp my Dinner, and laid it on a little Table made on ye Cradle Head. I fought for a Knife, but I could not find any. I cleered the Table where I dined to fee if any were there, and I ferched euery where about ye Howfe, and I could find none, yet I knew I had more than two, and when I could find none I went to an ould Baſket where I had Things to mend Shoes wthall, and there was a ruſty Knife, and with that I was faine to eate my Dinner.

---

[1] Only this Teſtimony of Taylor is in the Hand of Rawfon, all the other in that of Pynchon except otherwife noted. Taylor died at Suffield, 1683. Had Wife Mary, who died a few Weeks before him.

[2] In other Records his Name ſtands *Griffith* Jones. He had a large Family of Children, and died in 1677.

Appendix. 233

After I had dined I took away ye Victualls that were left, and laid it vp; and then I laid the rusty Knife on the Corner of the Table to cutt a Pip of Tobacco w^{th}all. But before I cut my Tobacco I first went out of Dore to serue a Pigg that was but a very little of the Dore, and no Man could come in but I must see them, and as soone as I came in to cutt my Tobacco wth the said rusty Knife, there lay three Knifes together on ye Table, wch made me blush:[1] wondering how they came there seeing no Body was in ye Howse but myself: and as I was going to cut ye Tobacco, Hugh Parsons came in, and said, where is the Man. Are you ready to go to ye Meetinge: I said by and by; as soone as I haue taken a Pipe of Tobacco. So he staid and took some wth me.

Ans. Hugh Parsons saith he is ignorant of any such Thing, and in the Sight of God can cleare his Consience.

It was tould him that such a strange Thinge falling out iust at his coming in, did minister iust Occasion of Susp:tion of Witchcraft: he replyed that one Witness was not sufficient.[2]

[36] 7^{ly}. Mary Parsons his Wife saith that one Reason why she doth suspect you to be a Witch, is becaufe you cannot abide that any Thing should be spoken against Witches. She saith that you tould her that you were at a Neighbors Howse a little before Lecture, when they were speaking of Carrington[3] and his Wife, that were now app^rhended for Witches, she

---

[1] The Fellow was doubtless too drunk to know very precisely what he was about.

[2] Here was *common* Sense against *Non*sense. He doubtless viewed these Accusations with too much Contempt to speak of them complacently.

[3] Perhaps John Carrington, of Wethersfield, in Connecticut. I have found no Record of the Case. See *Public Records of Connecticut*.

faith that when you came Home and fpake thes Speeches to her, fhe faid to you, I hope that God will find out all fuch wicked Pſons and purge New England of all Witches ere it be long: to this fhe faith you gaue her a naughty Looke, but neuer a Word; but pſently after, on a leight Occafion, you took vp a Block, and made as if you would throw it at her Head, but yet, in yᵉ End, you did not, but threw it downe on yᵉ Hearth of the Chimney. This Expreffion of yʳ Anger was becaufe fhe wifhed the Ruine of all Witches.

Mary Afhley[1] teftifies this fubftance, vppon Oath.

Ans. Hugh Parfons faith he does not rember that euer he took vp a Block to throw at her, but vppon further Debate he faid at laft that he tooke vp a Block but remembered not the Occafion: at his 2ᵈ Anfwer he faith that he took vp no Block on that Occafion.

Replie: it might well be on that Occafion, for not long fince fhe faith that you faid to her, if euer any Trouble doe come vnto you, it will be by her Meanes, and that fhe would be the Meanes to hang you.

Ans. Hugh Parfons faith that he might fay fo, becaufe, in his Anger he is impatient, and doth fpeak what he fhould not: At his 2ᵈ Examination, he fᵈ he might fay fo, becaufe fhe is the worft Enimy that I haue, confidering the Relation that is betweene vs: [37] and if any Body befpeake Euill of me fhe will fpeake as ill, and as much as any Body elfe.

Mary Parfons replied, I haue often intreated him to confeffe whether he were a Witch or no, I tould him that if he would acknowledge it I would begg the Prayers of Gods People on my Knees for him, and that we are not our owne, we are bought with a

---

[1] Probably the Wife of Robert Afhley, one of the firft Settlers of Springfield. The Afhleys were an early Family there.

Price, and that God would redeeme from the Power of Sathan, &c.

Hugh Parsons was asked if his Wife had spoken Anything to him at any Tyme to confess Witchcraft.

Ans. Not Anything to me about Witchcraft that I rember.

8^{ly}. Mary Parsons saith, did not I speak of it to you vppon the death of my Child: did not I tell you then that I had iealousies that you had bewitched y^r owne Child to Death.

To this he was sylent and made no Answer.

Then she desyred Antony Dorchester that liued then in their Howse whether he could not remember that she had charged her Husband wth the bewitching of his Child.

Anthony Dorchester said that he did not rember that euer she spake directly to him of bewitching his Child, but that she had Ielousies that he had bewitched his Child to Death.

Mary Parsons said, that when her last Child was ill she tould him that she suspected he had bewitched that, as he had done his other Child, and said, I haue spoken of it to him, and to other Folkes, together aboue forty Tymes.

It was alledged that he might well be suspected to haue bewitched his former Child to Death, becaufe he expressed no Kind of Sorrow at the Death of it.

[38] Ans. Hugh Parsons saith that he was loath to expresse any Sorrow before his Wife, becaufe of the weak Condition that she was in at that Tyme.

Mr. Moxon desyred to ask him a Question wch was this: It seemes he had Conference with his Wife about his sick Child, and about her Greefe for it, or else why should he forbeare to expresse the Affection of Sorrow before her, that he might not grieue her.

Hugh Parsons saith that his Wife might wonder at it, but yet that was the true Reason of it.

It was asked him why he did not show more Respect to his Wife and Child, but went into the long Meddow and lay there all Night when his Child lay at the Point of Death, and when he herd of the Death of it he next Morning neuer shewed any Sorrow for it.

George Coalton stood forth to testifie on Oath, that coming to Hugh Parsons House where his Wife was sitting by the Fier wth the Child in her Lapp, and she shewed to me the strange Condition of the Child, and I was amazed at it, for ye Childs Secretts did rott, or were consuminge: and she said, though my Child be so ill, and I haue much to do with it, yet my Husband keepes adoe at me to help him about his Corne: I said to her, y^o Husband had more need to get you some Help then to keepe adoe at you to help him: and she spake very harsh Things against him before his Face; and if he had bin inocent he would haue blamed her for her Speeches, for she spake such Things against him as are not ordinary for Psons to speak one of another, and yet he beinge p^{s}ent said Nothing for himself in way of blaminge any Thing that she had spoken against him.

Sworne in Corte.

It was also objected to Hugh Parsons, that if he had bin inocent about the Death of his Child, he would haue reproued her Speeches.

[39] Ans. Hugh Parsons saith that he had such Speeches from her dayly, and therefore he made the best of it now, and he also saith, I sett her not about Businefs, I required none at her Hands, except it were to throw in some Indian Corn from ye Dore. I haue often blamed her for doinge Worke, and bidd her do lesse.

Anthony Dorchester, who liued in their Howse,

ftood forth to teftifie that he neuer knew him blame her for doinge to much Worke, except (faith he) that fhe helped my Wife at any Tyme, wch Worke did not bring in any pffit to him. But, faith Anthony Dorchefter, he need not fay that he forebore Greefe for his fick Child before his Wife, for feare it fhould trouble her in her weak Condition, for he neuer feared eather to greeue or difpleafe his Wife any Tyme.

Being afked whether he did euer do any Thinge to comfort his Wife in her Sorrow for ye Death of her Child, he anfwered not.

Mary Parfons faid no, he did Nothing to comfort me, but ftill, when he came Home he kept adoe at me to throw in the Corne from the Dore, and when I faw my Hufband in this Frame, it added more Greefe to my Sorrow.

Anthony Dorchefter faith, I faw Nothing he did to comfort his Wife, but he did often blame her that fhe did not throw in the Corne from the Dore.

It was euidenced by George Coulton vppon Oath, that he fhewed no naturall Sorrow for ye Death of his Child when he firft herd of it in ye longe Meddow.

Jonathans Burtes Teftimony vppon Oath was for the Tyme of the Morning when he brought Word to Hugh Parfons of the Death of his Child: Jonathan faith it was as he thought, about eight or nine a Clock in the Morning; and the Place where he was firft tould of ye Death of it was at a great Oake [40] about 16 or 20 Poles from George Coulton's Howfe.

George Coulton teftifies vppon Oath, March. 1. and March 18, 1650, that Hugh Parfons came into ye long Meddow when his Child lay at ye Point of Death; and that hauing Word of ye Death of it the next Morning, by Jonathan Burt, he was not affected wth it, but he came, after a light Manner, rufhing into my Howfe, and faid, I here my Child is dead: but I will cutt a Pipe of Tobacco firſt before I goe Home: and after he was goun my Wife and myſelf did mch wonder at yᵉ lightneſſe of his Carriage, becauſe he ſhewed no Affection of Sorrow for yᵉ Death of his Child.

Sworne in Corte.

Ans. Hugh Parſons faith that he was very full of Sorrow for the Death of it in Private, though not in Publik; he faith that he was much troubled for the Death of it when he firſt herd of it before he came into Goodm Coultons Howſe:

George Coulton being pˢent doth teſtifie, that Hugh Parſons came to his Howſe, he thinks, about 8 a Clock in the Morning, and therefore he is very ſure of it, that he herd of it but a litle While before he came to his Howſe; for Jonathan Burt, that brought the Newes of it, ſpake of it to Hugh Parſons, but about 12 or 20 Poles from George Coultons Howſe, and he came pˢently thither: and therefore if he had had any Sorrow for the Death of his Child he could not but haue ſhewed ſome Signe of it when he came to his Howſe; but he faith that both he and his Wife diſcerned no Signe of Sorrow at all.

Sworne in Corte.

Hugh Parſons defyred that Goodman Cooly would teſtifie whether he was not affected wᵗʰ the Death of his Child when he came to ſpeak to him to go to the Buriall of it, he faith he could not ſpeak to him for weeping.

[41. Beniamin Cooly faith that when he ſpake to him to go to the Buriall of his Child he cannot rember any Sorrow that he ſhewed, for he came to him taking a Pipe of Tobacco.

Anthony Dorcheſter teſtifies vppon Oath, March 1 and 18, 1650, that when Hugh Parſons Child was dead, wᶜʰ was laſt Indian Harueſt was 12 Monthes, he then liuing at the Howfe of Hugh Parfons, did much wonder that when the faid Hugh Parfons came Home from the long Meddow, he expreffed no Kind of Sorrow for his Child after he came Home; but carried himfelf as at other Tymes without any regard of it, that eather I or my Wife could difcouer.

Alfo, Blanch Bodorthe faith, on oath, that fhe was at Hugh Parfons Howfe when he came from ye long Meddow and he fhewed no kind of Sorrow for ye Death of his Child.

Hugh Parfons faith, that when his Child was fick and like to dye, he run barefoote and barelegged, and with Teares to defyre Goody Cooly to come to his Wife, becaufe his Child was fo ill.

Mary Parfons faith, that this was out of a fudden Feare, at the very firft Tyme that ye Child was taken, for it was fuddenly and ftrangely taken with a Trembling, beginning at the Toes, and coming vpwardes, and fo it ftopped the Childes Breath.

Goody Cooly alfo teftifies, that this was at the firft Tyme that the Child was taken. There was fome Speeches vfed, that it might be bewitched, for thefe that are now bewitched haue often Tymes Something rife up into their Throates that doth ftopp their Breath: and it feemes by George Coultons Teftimony, that the Child was ftrangely taken.

Mary Afhly and Sara Leonard ftood vp to giue Teftimony, that they faw the Child in ye Tyme of its Sickneffe, and that they app^{r}hended the Secrets of the Child to confume and waft away.

[42] Mary Parfons being afked what Reafons fhe had to fufpect her Hufband for a Witch, gaue thefe Reafons:—

1. Becaufe when I fay Anything to any Body, neuer fo fecretly, to fuch ffreinde as I am fure would not fpeak of it, yet he would come to know it; by what

Meanes I cannot tell: I haue fpoken fome Thinges to Mrs. Smith, that goes litle Abroad, and I am fure would not fpeak of it, yet he hath knowen it, and would fpeak of it to me as foone as I came Home.

2^{ly}. Becaufe he vfeth to be out a Nights till Midnight (till of Late), and about half an Hower before he comes Home, I fhall here fome Noyfe or other about the Dore, or about the Howfe.

3^{ly}. Becaufe he vfeth to come Home in a diftempered Frame, fo that I could not tell how to pleafe him; fometymes he hath puld of the Bed Clothes and left me naked a Bed, and hath quenched the Fier; fometymes he hath thrown Peafe about ye Howfe and made me pick them vp.

4. Becaufe oftentymes in his Sleepe he makes a gablinge Noyfe, but I cannot vnderftand one Word that he fays, and when I did afke what it was that he talked in his Sleepe, he would fay that he had ftrange Dreames; and one Tyme he faid that the Diuell and he were fighting, and that the Diuill had almoft ouercome him, but at laft he got the Maftery of the Diuill.

Being afked if euer fhe knew her Hufband doe any Thing beyond the Power of Nature: fhe faid on a Tyme her Hufband fent her to Jonathan Taylor to get him to worke on the Morrow, and as I returned Home in ye Twilight, I faw a Thing like a great nafty Dogg by the Path Side. I fufpected it was donn by Witchcraft from my Hufband he fent me out [worn from the Margin] but vfually he doth fuch Thinges himfelf.

[43] ffeb. 27, 1650. Beniamin Coly faith vppon Oath that Mary Parfons tould him aboue a Yeere fince, that fhe feared her Hufband was a Witch, and that fhe fo far fufpected him that fhe hath ferched him when he hath bin afleepe in Bedd, and could not find Anythin about him vnleffe it be in his fecret Ptes.

ffeb. 27, 1650. Anthony Dorchester faith vppon Oath, that about a Yeere and a Quarter fince, I and my Wife liued for a Tyme at Hugh Parfons Howfe, and that I haue feuerall Tymes herd Mary Parfons fay that fhe fufpected, and greately fufpected, her Hufband to be a Witch, and that her Hufband once in 24 Howers would be from Home, if not in the Day Tyme then in the Night Tyme, what euer Weather it was: and that in his Abfence fhe hath herd a rumbling Noyfe in the Howfe, fometymes in one Place and fometymes in another; and that fhe did much fufpect him to be a Witch, becaufe if fhe had any priuate Talk wth any he would come to know it, by what Meanes fhe could not tell, being confident that thofe fhe reuealed herfelf vnto would neuer tell it.

Beniamin Cooly and Anthony Dorchefter fay vppon Oath, that being charged by ye Conftable to Watch Mary Parfons this laft Night, fhe tould them that if her Hufband had fallen out with any Body he would fay that he would be euen wth them, and then fhe found he did bewitch his owne Child that fhe might be at Liberty to help him in his Indian Harueft; for he expected help from her, and becaufe her Tyme was taken vp about her Child, he being egar after the World, feemed to be troubled at it, and fhe fufpected that he was a Meanes to make an End of his Child quickly, that fhe might be at Liberty to help him: another Thing fhe faid made her to fufpect her Hufband to be a Witch was, becaufe moft Things he fould to Others did not profper: another Ground of fufpition was, becaufe he was fo backward to go to the Ordenances, eather to the Lecture or to any other [44] Meetinge, and fhe hath bin faint to threaten him that fhe would complaine to the Magiftrate, or elfe fhe thought he would not let her go once in the Yeere: another Thinge made her fufpect him to be a

Witch was becaufe of the great Noyfe that fhe fhould here in the Howfe when he was abroad; and fhe faid, that laft Tufday at Night, when he was abroad fhe herd a Noyfe in the Howfe as if 40 Horfes had bin there, and after he was come to Bedd he kept a Noyfe and a galling in his Sleepe but fhe could not vnderftand one Word and fo he hath done many Tymes formerly and when fhe afked him what he ayled, he would fay he had ftrange Dreames, and one Tyme he faid that the Diuill and he were a fighting, and once he had almoft ouercome him, but at laft he ouercome the Diuill.

ffrancis Pepper faith vppon Oath: when I came to fee Mary Parfons that Sabbath that fhe kept at Robert Afhlies Howfe, as foone as fhe faw me fhe faid vnto me, ye Heffer was bewitched. I afked her how fhe could tell, fhe faid her Hufband had bewitched it, and now he had bewitched me, and he knows now what I fay, and he now terrifies me in this Place, ftriking her Hand vppon her Thigh.

ffeb. 27, 1650. Mary the Wife of Robert Afhly faith vppon Oath, that Mary Parfons was at her Howfe, laft Lecture Day was Sen'ight, before Meeting, and among other Speeches fhe faid, as for the Death of Mr. Smithes Children,[1] it lay very fad vppon her, very, fhe faid becaufe my Hufband would haue had me to haue nurfed his Children: but, faid fhe, doth Any one think me a fitt Nurfe for them: I afked her why he would haue her to nurfe them: fhe faid for Luker and Gaine; one may well know his Reafon: after this fhe fetched a great Sigh and faid, litle doth Any one think how the Death of thofe Children lies

---

[1] Mary, Dau. of Mr. Henry Smith, buried at Springfield, Nov. 9th, 1641 ; Margaret, Dau. of Mr. Henry Smith, died 24th June, 1648 ; Sarah, died 30 June, 1648. — *Springfield Records.*

vppon me: and she said it was her neere Relation; but, said she, it is better for others to bring him out then for me, but I can speak a great Deale of him if others bring him out.

Mary Parsons was asked what Grounde she had to think that her Husband bewitched Mr. Smithes Children: becaufe, my Husband would often say that he would be euen wth Mr. Smith if he denied to let him haue any Peafe, or to plow his Ground or to do any other Thing for him that he defyred: he would often say I would be euen wth him.

[45] John Lumbard faith vppon Oath, March 17, 1650, that one Day the laft fummer he fett a Trowell and a ftick, wch he vfed to hould to his Clay when he dawbed, on ye Ground iuft without his Dore: after this two Indians came in, and alfo p^{s}ently went away againe; then I alfo went out to look for my Trowell: and there was my faid Stick but my Trowell was gonne: I and my Wife fought for it very narrowly, both in that Place and alfo within the Howfe, and could not find it: But about two Dayes after, as Hugh Parfons was at the Dore of my Howfe I faw the faid two Indians, and I called them to afk them for my Trowell: faid Hugh Parfons what do you want, I faid they haue ftolen my Trowell: faid Hugh Parfons look, here it is, and there it was in the very Place where I laid it. I did not fee him lay it there, but I do really think it came there by Witchcraft.

Hugh Parfons anfwered, that he cannot remember that he laid it there. John Lumbard faith that the Reafon why he did not afk him how it came there was becaufe he had bin at Hugh Parfons but the Day before to borrow a Trowell, to make an end of his Daugbing, for that Trowell he had left was Goodman Lanktons. Hugh Parfons at this ftood dumb and anfwered no more.

John Mathewes saith vppon Oath, ffeb. 27, 1650, that a little before the Tryall wth ye Widdow Marshfeild, wch was about May, 1649, being in Talk with Mary Parsons about Witches, she said to me that her Husband was a Witch: I asked her how she [46] knew it, she said the Diuill came to him in ye Night, at the Bed, and suckt him one Night and made him cry out one Tyme, she could not tell what it should be else but the Diuill. She said also that her Husband was often tormented in his Bowells, and cryed out as though he were pricked with Pins and Daggers, and I know not what else it should be, vnlesse it were the Diuill that should torment him so.

March 3, 1650. Thomas Merick, the Constable saith vppon Oath, that this last Night, towards Morning, Hugh Parsons lyenge by the Fier Side said to him two seuerall Tymes Good[Man?] now come and lance my Belly, for I am in lamentable Paine or Torment. I said to him, if you will goe forth to ease y^slfe Ile take of ye Chaines and let you goe: he said, no, I haue no need that way.

Hugh Parsons answer March 18, that he had a Paine in his Belly, but did not speak of lancinge it.[1]

Sarah, the Wife of Thomas Merick stood forth, and testified that all her Husband had testified was true.

[47] April 3^d, 1651. Thomas Cooper saith vppon Oath that being appointed to watch Mary Parsons, about mid March last, among other Things she tould me that she was now hampered for relatinge so much as she had don against her Husband at Mr. Pynchons. But, said she, if that dumb Dogg could but haue spoken it would haue bin better wth me then it is: but

---

[1] The "lancing it" was unquestionably thrown in by the Constable to give his Testimony more importance.

said she if I might but speak wth him before Mr. Pynchon, Face to Face, I would make that dumb Dogg to speak. I said to her why do you speak so of y^o Husband; me thinkes, if he were a Witch there would some apparant Signe or Mark of it appere vppon his Body, for they say Witches haue Teates vppon some pt or other of their Body, but as far as I heere there is not any such apparant Thinge vppon his Body. She answered, it is not alwayes so: but, said she, why do I say so, I haue no Skill in Witchery: but, said she, why may it not be with him as it was with me; that Night that I was at Goodman Ashlies: the Diuill may come into his Body only like a Wind, and so goe forth againe, for so the Diuill tould me that Night, (for I think I should haue bin a Witch afore now but that I was afraid to see the Diuill, left he should fright me.) But the Diuill tould me that I should not Feare that, (I will not come in any Apparition, but only come into thy Body like a Wind, and trouble thee a litle While, and p^sntly go forth againe:) and so I consented; and that Night I was with my Husband and Goodwife Mericke and Besse Sewell, in Goodman Stebinges his Lott: and we were sometymes like Catts and sometymes in our owne shape, and we were a plodding for some good Cheere; and they made me to go barefoote and mak the Fiers, because I had declared so much at Mr. Pynchons.[1]

[48] April 7, 1651. Jonathan Taylar saith vppon Oath, that in ye Day that Mary Parsons was first examined, Hugh Parsons came to me to Merickes Barne, and desyred to aske me a Question, and to tell him who were his Accusers: I said I cannot tell: said he, why

---

[1] Had not the Brains of Magistrate and People been turning Somersets, nearly as much so as those of the Accused, she would have been treated as one entirely bereft of Reason.

do you fay fo, you can tell, I know you can tell. Was it euer known, faid he, that a Man fhould be accufed and not know his Accufers: Tell me who they are, for what euer you tell me fhall be as in y° owne Breft. I faid I wonder you are fo earneft wth me to tell you; you will know foone enough; I will not tell you any Thinge; but, faid I, I beleeue y° Wife will be y° biggeft Accufar: at this Speech he faw his Wife goe by to be examined, then faid he, it is like I fhall be examined now.

At Night, when I was ready to goe Home, I afked Goody Meerik for fome Beere; fhe faid go down into the Sellar and draw it, fo I did, but could not wringe out ye Tapp wth all ye Strength I had; then I tooke a Peece of an Inch Board and knocked the Tapp on each Side to loofen it, and then I tryed to wringe it out againe wth my Hand, till the Blood ftarted in my Hand wth wringinge at it, and yet I could not get it out: I came vp and tould Goody Merik, and fhe laughed at me, and faid, I am pfuaded I will fetch it out with my litle Finger: I tould her it was impoffible, then fhe faid light a Candle and go fee: fo I lighted a Candle, and fhe and Hugh Parfons went with me, and as foone as euer fhe touched it, the Tapp came out.[1] I faid to her what, are you a Witch (though I did not think fo) but I do verily beleeue it could not haue bin fo ˚xcept it were bewitched. After we were come vp fhe faid let me, fee y° Hand; then, faid fhe, I confeffe y° Hand is very tender, and fhe faid to Hugh Parfons, the Blood ftands in his Hand: but I would not haue you think it was by Witchery, for I think the leaft Child in the Howfe might haue gott it out.

---

[1] There can be no Queftion in this Cafe but that the Witch was Goody Myrick, but poor Hugh Parfons was predoomed.

Appendix. 247

Affore I came Home, and when I was a Bedd, there was a Light in ye Rome, as if it had bin Day-Light: I was amazed to fee fuch a Light: I thought it could not be Day: I fatt vp in the [49] Bed to fee if it were Day or no: and as I looked ouer the Bed I faw three Snakes on the Floore, and I was in a Maze to fee them: I ftranged that Snakes fhould be abroad at this Tyme of the Yeere: two of them were great ones, the other was a litle one, wth blackifh and yellow Streaks: and the little one came to ye Bedd Side and gott vp vppon ye Bedd; wth that I ftrok it downe with my Hand: it came vp againe and I ftruck it downe againe: then I began to feare that if my Wife fhould fee them, being then very neere her Tyme, it would half vndoe her wth Feare: therefore I did not wake her, but lay downe againe: and then I thought thus; lett God doe what he will: and as foone as I was laid downe, ye faid Snake ranne vp a 3^d Tyme, and hitt me on ye Forehead, wch pricked like a Needle; then I herd a Voice that faid, Death, and that Voice was like Hugh Parfons Voice to my beft App^rhenfion; and now I was a little reuiued in Spirit, and I faid Death: that is a Lye, it was neuer knowen that fuch a Snake kild a Man: then it was darke againe: and I was taken with fuch a ftrange Shakinge, as if euery Limb had bin puld in Peeces: then my Wife awaked, and fhe faid Hufband, what ayle you that you fhake fo, are you could: no, faid I, am hot enough, but I am very ill, fhe faid fhall I rife and warm you fome Cloathes, I faid no: but this Extremity continued all Night as if one Limb had bin rent from an other, and in the Morninge fhe arofe, and called in fome neighbors:[1] this was on ffriday Night, and I was held fo till Tuefday Morning, as if I had bin rent in Peeces; one Fitt began at my Forehead, where the Snake bitt me, and ended at my Knees, and then the next Tyme it began at my Knees and ended at my Forehead, and in this Order it continued all ye forefaid Tyme.

Tuefday being a Day of Humiliation, I faid to my Wife, though I be ill, yet I will go thither; I am pfwaded I fhall be better, and fo I was; but yet I haue bin troubled wth griping Paines euer fince, and am not after my former vfuall Manner.

[50] April 7, 1651. Jonathan Tayler faith vppon Oath, that two Nights before Mary Parfons was carried into the Bay, I watched her: fhe faid I haue two Things to fay to you: one is I forgiue you the Wrong you haue done me: the other is about the three Snakes that you faw: they were three Witches f^d fhe: I afked who they were; fhe faid one was my Hufband. I afked her who were the others, fhe faid I haue pointed at them already: but you will not beleeue me; I am counted but as a Dreamer: but when this Dreamer is hanged, then remember what I faid to you: y^o Towne will not be cleere yet: then faid fhe if you had beleeued ye Voice that fpake to you, you had dyed: but feeinge you fpake to it, and refifted it, it had not Power to kill you: for you doe not know how my Hufband hath threatned you.

All fworn in Cort 13, 3.

[51] ffeb. 25, 1650. Georg Lankton faith on Oath, that his Wife made a Pudding in a Bagg, and becaufe my Wife had the Child, I took it and put it out of the Bagg at Dinner this Day Fortnight (wch was the

---

[1] That one attacked with a raging Fever fhould dream of feeing *Snakes* or Anything elfe, is common Experience. That this Fellow embellifhed his Dream afterwards is probably quite as certain as that any fuch Dreams may be and ufually are embellifhed.

11. of ffeb.) and as it flipt out of the Bagg it fell into two Pieces, length wife, and in Apperance it was cutt ftrait along as fmooth as if it had bin cutt with a Knife. It was cutt ftrait along almoft the whole length: it lacked but very little.

Hannah the Wife of George Lanƌton doth vppon Oath concurr with her Hufband in the faid Teftimony. Febb 21, 1650, George Lanƌton and Hannah his Wife doe ioyntly teftifie vppon Oath, that they had another Pudding in the fame Bagg, that was cutt lengthwife like vnto ye former, as fmooth in Appearance as any could cutt it with a Knife, namely one Slice all alonge the Side of the Puddinge wantinge but a very litle, from End to End.

Alfo Hannah the Wife of George Lankton faith on Oath; a neighbor came in and fhe fhewed to him how the Puddinge was cutt: and that Neighbor tooke a Peece of it and threw it into the Fier: and fhe faith, that about an Hower after, phapps a little more, fhe herd one mutter and mumble at the Dore; then fhe afked Goody Sewell, who was then at her Howfe (and neerer the Dore) who it was; fhe faid it was Hugh Parfons, and that he afked whether Goodman Lankton were at Home or no, I faid no, and fo he went away, but left not his Arrand, neather did he euer fince come to fignifie his Arrand.

Hannah Lanƌton fworne in Corte 13. 3 m°.

ffeb. 23, 1650, George Lankton and Hannah his Wife joyntly teftifie vppon Oath that they had another Pudding in the former Bagg, that was cut lengthwife, and as it was flipped out of the Bagg, it fell into three Pts: one Peece being cutt all along on the one Side, and two [53] Peeces all alonge on the other Side: then they fent for fome Neighbors to fee it: Roger Pritchard teftified vppon Oath, that he faw the faid Pudding and it feemed to him to be cutt all the three

Peeces as euident and as plaine to him as that wch George Lankton cut wth his Knife.

Thes Teſtimonies were all taken vppon Oath before me   WILLIAM PYNCHON.

[3] March 12, 18, 22, 1650. Samuell Marſhfeild faith, vppon Oath, that when Hugh Parſons came to pay the 24 Buſhels of Indian to my Mother for the diſcharge of ye Action of Slander againſt Mary Parſons, that he deſyred my Mother to abate 20s, but my Mother ſaid ſhe would not abate, becauſe[1] ſhe herd that he had ſaid the Witneſſes gaue in a falſe Teſtimony. Hugh Parſons replied, well, if you will not it had bin as good you had—it will be but as wild Fier in y^s Howſe, and as a Moth in y^o Garment, and it will doe you no Good, Ile warnt it, and make Account it is but lent you: this Corne was paid in Winter was 12 Months, and the Spring after my Siſter Sara was taken with ſtrange Fitts, at Tymes, but neuer ſo bad as when Mr Moxon's Children were taken.

Sworne in Co^{r}te.

March 22, 1650. The Widdow Marſhfeld teſtifies vppon Oath, that when Hugh came to tender the ſaid Corne, he ſaid, I here that you will abate 20^s of the Money. I told him I would not abate any Thing, becauſe I herd that his Wife had ſaid the Witneſſes had taken a falſe Oath: then ſaid he, if you will not abate, it ſhall be but as lent it ſhall doe you no Good, it ſhall be but as Wildfier in y^o Howſe, and as a Moth in y^o Clothes, and theſe threatning Speeches he uttered with much Anger: and ſhortly after, in the Spring, about May, my Daughter began to be taken with her Fitts of Witchcraft.

John Lumbard ſaith vppon Oath, March 17 and 22. 1650. that I haue herd Hugh Parſons and his Wife

---

[1] This word is abbreuiated *bec^t* throughout the MS. and never ſpelt out.

alſo ſay that the Corne wch they paid to ye Widdow Marſhfeld for the Slander, would do her no Good, and that it had bin better ſhe had never taken it. I haue herd both her and him ſay ſo ſeuerall Tymes, and I haue often herd him ſay, when he hath been diſpleaſed wth any Body, that he would be euen with them for it.

[4] Hugh Parſons being preſent anſwered not, but at laſt he aſked, when did I giue ſuch threatening Wordes. It was told him, when his Corn was paid in.

Hugh Parſons ſaid he did not rember that he gaue ſuch threateing Word: he ſaid that in iuſtice the Corne was due to her: but becauſe we app^rhended my Wife was falſley accuſed. That was the Reaſon of my Speeches.

Mary Parſons alſo ſaid, that when her Huſband came Home, he tould her what Speeches he had vſed to the Widdow Marſhfeild, namely, according to ye Teſtimonies ſhe ſaid it might well be ſo, for ſhe was falſely accuſed.

[5] March 18. 1650. Thomas Miller teſtifies vppon Oath (Hugh Parſons being preſent) that my Wife being in one of her Fitts, March 17, 1650, ſhe ſaid thus: get thee gon Hugh Parſons, get thee gonn, if thow wilt not goe, I will goe to Mr. Pynchon, and he ſhall haue thee away.

Miles Morgan, and Prudence his Wife, and Griffin Jones, being all p^sent, do teſtifie the ſaid Speech vppon their Oathes.

Then all the aforeſaid pſons, and ffrances Pepper do teſtifie vppon Oath, that it is an vſuall Thinge wth Goody Millar, in her Fitts, to vſe the Word Sirra and thow Witch.

Prudence Morgan ſaith vppon Oath, that the 27 of March, 1651, Sara Millar was at her Howſe, and then betweene her Fitts ſhe ſaid, look you, there is a Man, at Goodman Coopers Barne, I faid no there is no Man there that I can fee, fhe faid you might fee him if you would. But now he is gone faid fhe: then fhe fell into a Fitt: and after fhe came to herfelf, fhe faid, look you, there he is. I faid to her who is it, fhe faid it is one in a redd Waftcote and a lynd Capp. It is like Hugh Parfons; then faid fhe he points his Finger at me; he would haue me come to him: but Hugh Parfons was gone into the Bay the Monday before: but he vfed to weare a red Waftcote, and a lynd Capp.

Samuell Marfhfeild faith vppon Oath, that he came into Goody Morgans Howfe the Day aforefaid; and as foone as Sara Millar came to herfelfe out of her Fitt, fhe faid look you, there he is: Goody Morgan afked her who it was, fhe faid, one in a red Waftcote and a lynd Capp: it is like Hugh Parfons: and faid fhe, he pointed his Finger at me, he would haue me come to him. [6] I faid to her there is no Body there that I can fee: fhe faid yes, there he is, two or three times ouer, but there was Nobody there that we could difcouer, though fhe did often affirme it.

Sworne in Courte.

[7] March 18 1650. John Stebbinge[1] teftifies vppon Oath (Hugh Parfons being p^rfent): that as my Wife[2] was entring into one of her Fitts, fhe looked vp the Chimney. I afked her what fhe looked at, and obferuing her Ey fixed on Something, afked her againe (for fhe did not anfwer at firft) what fhe looked on, and fhe faid, with a Gefture of ftrange Wonderment, O deere! there hangs Hugh Parfons vppon ye Pole (for

---

[1] There is an interefting Memoir of the Stebbinge Family, but the Writer had no Knowledge that Members participated in Witch Tranfactions. *Savage* is equally in the Dark. See the *New England Hiftorical and Genealogical Regifter* for the Genealogy of the Stebbins Family, Vol. V, Pages 71 and 351.

[2] I find on the *Springfield Records* — "3 : 14 : 1646, John Steblins and Mary [worn off] were married.

there ftood a fmale Pole vppright in ye Chimy Corner) and then fhe gave a Start backward, and faid, Oh! he will fall vppon me: and at that Inftant fhe fell downe into her Fitt.

Rowland Stebbing being p^sfent, doth alfo teftifie the fame vppon Oath.

William Brooks teftifies vppon Oath, March 18, 1650, that the fame Day that Hugh Parfons was app^{r}hended, and about the fame Tyme of the Day that the Coneftable brought him alonge by the Dore of Goody Stebbing, fhe was firft taken wth her Fitts, and cryed, Ah! Witch! Ah! Witch! iuft as he was paffing by the Gate.

[9][1] Hugh Parfons at his Examination, March 1, 1650, being afked whether he thought there was not fome Witchcraft in the Diftemper of Mr. Moxons Children, faid, I queftion not but there is Witchcraft in it: but I wifh the Sadle may be fett vppon the right Horfe, being demanded who was the right Horfe, and whether he knew of Anybody elfe, he faid no, I am cleare for myfelf, neather do I fufpect any other. Being afked whether he had any Grounds to fufpect his Wife, he anfwered no, I do not know that euer I had any fuch Thought of her.

March 22, 1650. Jonathan Taylor[2] faith vppon Oath, that the fame Day that Mary Parfons went to be examined to Mr. Pynchons: Hugh Parfons came to me to Mericks Barne, and faid that he had often bin afraid that his Wife was a Witch: and her Examination was the Day before his. Jonathan Taylor alfo faith vppon Oath, that Hugh Parfons tould him that he hath fo farr fufpected his Wife to be a Witch,

---

[1] Page 8 of the original MS. is blank.

[2] There is a Record that Jonathan Taylor had by Wife Mary, a Daughter, born 1: 6: 1649, which was named Mary. He was doubtlefs married elfewhere, as no Record of his Marriage appears at Springfield.

that he would haue ferched her, and fhe refifted for fhe tould him it was an imodeft Thinge.

[10] March 13, 1650. William Branch[1] faith vppon Oath, that he hath often herd Hugh Parfons fay, when he is difpleafed wth Anybody, I do not queftion but I fhall be euen with him at one Tyme or other: I rember he faid fo of Goodman Bridgman, vppon the Difference that was between them ab^t a Tree: and I herd him fay he would fitt Jo Mathewes, fpeaking about the Bargaine of Brickes.

[11] Jonathan Taylor faith vppon Oath, March 21, 1650. That when I was at the Howfe of Hugh Parfons this Winter, and he tould me that he had bin at Mr. Pynchons to gett as much Whitleather as to make a Cappe for a Flayle, and he was willinge. But Symon[2] would not let him haue any: it had been as good faid he, he had, he fhall get Nothing by it. I will be euen wth him. Mary Parfons faid, Hufband why do you threaten the fellow fo, it is like he was bufy: he anfwered againe, if Goodman Cooly or any One elfe that he had liked had come he fhould haue had it. But Ile rember him.

Depofed before y^e Court 17: $\frac{4}{mo}$: 1651.

EDWARD RAWSON, *Secret*.

All the Teftimonies thus far taken vppon Oath before me WILLIAM PYNCHON.

Maij 20th, 1651.[3] The Depofition of Symon Bemon on Oath. This Deponent fayth, that about

---

[1] The fame probably who was made a Freeman, 1648; married, according to Springfield Records, 7: 7: 1643, Joanna Farnam, at "Winfore." He died 16 September, 1683. — *Ibid*.

[2] Simon Beamon, as will prefently appear. He was a Servant to Mr. Pynchon.

[3] The two following Teftimonies are inferted in the original MS. thus out of their Order, becaufe there happened to be blank Leaves, as it would feem.

ffebr^y laſt, Hugh Parſons came to him, in his Maſters [Mr. Pynchon's] Name, for a Peice of Whitleather, to make a Cap for a Flayle, and that he having his Horſes then in the Cart, and going out with them into the Woods, told him he could not now ſtay to giue it him, but another Tyme he would. Now the ſame day after, he beinge loaden wth a Peice of Tymber vnder ye Cart, and cominge Home the Horſes ſet a runninge ſodainly, as if they were ſkared, and yet he ſaw Nothing y^t ſhould ſkare them. And as he held back the Thilhorſe to ſtay them, he was beaten down wth the Cart, and if in his Fall he had not put off the Thilhorſe with a Kick of his Foote, the Cart Wheele had run over him; it went over Part of his Jackett, and cloſe to his Body, and one of the Wheels ran over a greate Stubb of Pine, 2 Foote and halfe high at leaſt, and yet y^e Cart did not overturne. I thought there was ſome Miſcheife in it from Hugh Parſons, for my Horſes had often gon that Rode, and never did y^e like before, nor ever ſince.

Depoſed before the Court 17 $\frac{4}{\text{mo}}$ 1651.

EDW: RAWSON, Secret^y.

[12] This Deponent alſoe ſayth vpon Oath, that about the End of laſt Sumer, he beinge at the Mill to fetch Home Meale, Hugh Parſons being there, deſired him to carry Home a Bag of Meale for him; but he refuſinge to do it, Hugh Parſons was offended at his Refuſall: and when he was gon about ſix Rod from the Mill, his Horſe beinge a gentle quiet Horſe, he fell downe from the Horſe and the Meale vpon him. He layd his Meale on the Horſe agayne, got vp and was well ſetled, and beinge gon about 2 or 3 Rod further, he fell downe agayne, and the Meale vpon him, and yet the Horſe never ſtarted to occaſion it. He layd vp his Sack agayne, the 3 Tyme, and got vp,

and when he was well fetled, and gon a Rod or two further, he fell doune agayne, and the fack vpon him, and yet y[e] Horfe ftoode quietly in his Place. And the 4th Tyme he laid it vp and came away.[1]

Teftefyed vpon Oath befo. me, HENRY SMITH.[2]

Depofed before the Courte, 17 $\frac{4}{mo}$, 1651.

EDWARD RAWSON, *Secrety*.

[What is on Pages 11 and 12, is in the Handwriting of Henry Smith, before whom the Depofition was given. The two laft Lines are Rawfon's.]

[13] William Branch faith vppon Oath, March 13, 1650. That about 2. y. fince when I liued in Towne, and when I went to Bed about two Howers w[th]in Night, and before I was a fleepe, there was a Light all ouer the Chamber, like Fier, and there came a Thing vppon me like a little Boy, w[th] a Face as red as Fyer, and put his Hand vnder my Chin, as I app[r]hended: and I felt fome Thinge like fcaldinge Water on my Back, and then I herd a Voice fayinge, it is done, it is done; then I waked my Wife and told her of it, and I haue been ill euer fince. I haue thought Hugh Parfons to be naught and haue bin troubled that he hath made fo many [ ] Arrandes to my Howfe for feueral Thinges, and yet I could not tell how to denie him what he defyred.

William Branch faith vppon Oath, that at Summer was twelve Monthes, I went to the long Meddow, and

---

[1] If the Fellow told the Truth about falling from his Horfe, he was doubtlefs too drunk to keep on. The feveral Falls muft have fobered him in fome Degree. He was careful not to tell how long he laid on the Ground before he finally fucceeded in "coming away."

[2] Mr. Smith was then in Bofton, a Member of the General Court. He was Mr. Pynchon's Son-in-law, having married his Daughter Anne. This Record by Smith was entered in Mr. Pynchon's MS. out of chronological Order, becaufe there happened to be a Blank fufficiently large.

Appendix. 257

as I was going before Hugh Parſons dore, I was taken with a ſtrange Stiffneſſe in my two Thighes, as if two Stakes had bin bound to my two Thighes: ſo that I was faint to thruſt myſelfe forwarde with great Difficulty: and this Stiffneſſe continued all that Day: after this I fell into ſuch a Diſtemper as burninge Heat in the Bottoms of my Feet that I neuer had the like before, and this Heat in ye Bottoms of my Feete continued neere 12 Monthes er I was well. I thought then it was ſome Worke of Witch Craft (from him) and ſo I think to this Day.

Theis laſt two Teſtimonies were taken vppon Oath before me   WILLIAM PYNCHON.

[14] Blank.
[15]^1
[16 to 22] Blank.

[1] Teſtimonies about Sara Millar and An Stebbings againſt Hugh Parſons. Taken vppon Oath before me   WILLIAM PYNCHON.

[2] Jonathan Taylor on Oath ſaith ſometime this Winter, on a Night, a Paire of good Mr. Mathews Pajles fell doune wth a Noyſe, and going out prſently to ſee the Occaſion thereof, could not pceaue any Thing; but going into his Howſe againe, it being very darke. Hugh Parſons was at his Backe, his Hand on his Doore aſſoone as his was of. he bidding him ſitt doune which he did. Parſons ſaying Goodman Collys Boy Nothing but beat my Calfe. his Maſter will take no Order with him but I will: anon after Goody Coolly came and inquired after her Boy whether this Deponent had ſeen him he telling her no: ſhe replyed I ſent him to Goodman Mathue a good Whiles ſince

---

^{1} On Page 15 of the original MS. was inſerted the Indictment, which has been given in a previous Page.

and cannot tell what is become of him, and defired him this Deponent to help her looke him which he did in all the Hay Mowes and out Howfes wth hooping and hallouing for him but could not find him nor heare of him: at laft they gaue ouer looking him, and y^s Deponent enquired of ye fajd Goody Cooly whether Hugh Parfons had not met him and tooke Order wth him, as he thretned him for beating his Calfe: and after they were parted a While the Boy came Home, and his Dame afking him where *₁he had bin, he fajd in a great Cellar and was carried headlong into it, Hugh Parfons going before him, and fell down [with mee] there, and afterwards he [willed] into it.*

[The above is all in the Hand of Secretary Rawfon, and was taken at Bofton after the Cafe was fent here. It ends abruptly, and no Ufe was probably made of it.]

No. 2.

DEPOSITIONS *and other Papers connected with the Proceedings againft Mrs. Elizabeth Morfe of Newbury, under the Charge of Witchcraft.*

Elizabeth Titcomb, aged about fifty.[2] After ye Burning of Apples at Enfigne Greenleaf, I was foone troubled at my Houfe with a Noyes knocking at ye Dore which did awake mee out of a found Sleepe: ye firft knocking I lay ftill harkening for to hear a Voice, and none I heard: I thought Somebody did want my

---

[1] The Words between thefe * * are written on the outer Margin of the Paper and then erafed (but wherefore does not appear), and I am unable to make them all out.

[2] William Titcomb married Elizabeth Stevens, March 3d, 1654. She was his fecond Wife.

help knocking a fecond Time; but I heard no Voyce: a third Time I heard knocking; then I went forth, and called to my Daughter Lydia: afked her if fhee did heare ye Noyes. Shee faid, Yes. Then I opened my Chamber Dore, and faide, Who are you? What is your bufines? But no Voyce. So I confidered y^t I had no Call to goe to ye Dore, and begg'd of God to give mee Reft: but I was much difturbed by the vyoulent Motion of a Creature which I did never know before nor fince.

Lydia Titcomb affirmeth the fame about the Noyes. The fame Peniel Titcome[1] affirmes.

[*The laſt Paragraph is in the Autograph of Mr. John Woodbridge, the Commiſſioner.*]

The Depofetion of Jonathan Woodman,[2] aged aboute thirty fiue Yeres, who teftifieth and faith, that, aboute feuen Yers agoe, beeing going Home in a darke Night from Infine Grenleffe apon the Grene at Wolchis[3] Seler, I met with a white Thing like a Cat, which did playe at my Legs, and I did offen cicke at it, haueng no Wepon in my Hand; at laft ftrocke it with my fut againft the Fenfe nerre Ifrall Webftars Houfe, and there it ftopt with a loud cry aftar the Manar of a Cat and I fee it no more. I furdar teftifie, that William Morfe of Neubury did owne that hee did fend for a Docktar for his Wife the fame Night and

---

[1] Son of William, mentioned in the laſt Note, by Joanna Bartlet. He was 29 Years old. Lydia *Titcome* was his Siſter. Her Age was 16.

[2] The fixth Child of Mr. Edward and Joanna Woodman of Newbury, born November 8, 1648, m. Hannah Hilton.

[3] Walſh, no doubt. This is the earlieſt Mention of the Name which I have met with. There is no Name of *Walſh* in Coffin's Liſt of the early Inhabitants of Newbury, nor has Savage the Name at all. The Name probably exiſted there till 1800, at leaſt. Michael Walch there compiled and publiſhed the *Mercantile Arithmetic*, firſt in 1801, a Work of great Popularity for more than a Quarter of a Century.

fame Time of Night that I wafe troubled with that Cat abouefe mentioned, whitch wafe fom Grounds of Sefpition, but there wafe Nothing in it, bee cafe har Hort in har Hed wafe don to or three Dayes before theye fent for the Docktar by Somthing falling out of the Chimly. He fordar fayd that fhee feme to macke letell of it tell that Night abouefe mentioned and then greue uery bad that hee wafe forft to fend for the Docktar.

Taken on Oath [by Mr. Woodbridge] Jan. 7th, 1679.

[To this ridiculous Teftimony Mr. Morfe faid, in his Petition of May 14th, 1681: "Jonathan Woodman feeing a Cat, and ftriking at it, and its vanifhing away; and I fending for Doctor Dole[1] to fee a Bruife my Wife had by the Fall of a Peece [Gun?] reaching downe fome Bacan in our Chimly, which was many Days before this Time, as Doctor Dole affirms it was no green Wound, though [I] neglected to fend for faid Dole till then."

The moft that can be faid in defence of that Teftimony is, that Woodman probably ftumbled upon a Skunk as he was croffing the Evening Ramble of that well known Animal. That an Attack was made on him by the Animal, whatever it was, was doubtlefs an Embellifhment of his Imagination.]

The Teftimony [of] Benniamin Richardfon aged a bought twenty on Yeares, teftifieth and faith, that as I came in the Morning from Cofon Tuckkers, a

---

[1] John Dole of Newbury, Son of Richard, who came to Newbury from Briftol, England, in 1639. John was born Auguft 10th, 1648, and hence was but about twenty-four Years of Age in 1672, when the Cat attacked Woodman. Dr. John Dole was the Father of Dr. Benjamin Dole of Hampton, who married Frances, Daughter of Capt. Samuel Sherburne of that Town. Dr. Benjamin died at Hampton, May 8th, 1707, and was buried in the old Burying-ground there.

Appendix. 261

bought three Wekes or a Month a goe, by the Cornor of good Man Moffes Houfe, I heard the Boy, John Stiles, cry out, and faid, the Houfe is a Fire, the Houfe is a Fire. Then Goodman Mos fee mee, made Sines and winckt to mee to com to fe where I could fpy any Thing. Then I went in and went up the Stairs, and then he barckt lick a Dog and yould lick [a] Cat; and then he grouled, and his Heare ftood up on End; and than he gumpt out of that Bed and went into a nother Bed, and ther was a Bord that leand againft the Cheft and flue from the Cheft and ftruck the Boy; and furdor I fee a fheap a friueled Hand to ftrik the Boy.[1]

Taken on Oath, Jan. 7: 1679.

The Teftemona of David Willer [Wheeler][2] aged abovt 54 Yeres or therabovt: teftefieth y^t I took Notis of feeverrall Paffagys: as forft of her akhenf^{ons} y^t fhe woold vfhally be diging and crobbing ye Ground with ye Eand of a Staff wich I never took Notis of anny Parfon y^t ackted in ye lieak Manner: forther, ye fayed David Willir heaving a Heeffer abovt 3 or 4 Yeer ovld, y^t came Home ovt of ye Woods on Day, was chawed vppon ye Back abovt ye Breath of a Hand; and abovt a Fortneatt after was chaw on^t ye other Siead by y^t abovt as mech moor: and ye fayed Heffer grew ill and wold fvmtims go into ye Riveer fo deep, vntill ye Watter tovch her Noos, and fhe ftvd ther vntill fvm of ovr Fammelee weer forfed to vaed to facht her ovt to fave her from dronding: and ye fame Heffer y^t is above menfhened, beeing miffing we covld nott fiend her fvm confeederabell Tieme: after wards wee

---

[1] This Benjamin Richardfon was Son of William by his Wife Elizabeth Wifeman, whom he married 23 Auguft, 1654. He was born 13 March, 1657. See *Coffin*.

[2] David Wheeler was born in Salifbury, England, 1625; went from Hampton to Newbury, 1645; married Sarah Wife, 11 May, 1650.—*Coffin*.

fovnd her in a ovt Hovſe yt had no other Paſſege anny other Way bvt a ſmall Gap we had cvtt for ſmall Caves: *and I was verely perſwaded that the Heifer was bewitched, and Goodwife Morſe was the Occaſion of it.* Taken on Oath, Jan. 7th, 1679.

[*The Addition in Italics is in the Hand of Mr. Woodbridge.*]

The Depoſition of Johua Richardſon,[1] aged a bought thirty Years: teſtifieth and ſaith, that a bought fiue Years a goe, then I had three Sheep to driue to Hamton: and when I came doune the Street I thought it beſt to cech my Sheep at good Man Morſſes Barne, becaſe it was neare my Canue that was to carry them our the riuer; and good Man Mors Cow Houſe Dore ſtood open next the Hie Way, and I loock iń and I ſaw Nothing there: ſo I droue my Sheep into the Cowhouſe, and as I was a ceching the Sheep, Gooddi Morſe came out, and was mighty with mee: and ſaid I had better aſke Leaue, and I went away with my Sheap: and when I came to Hamton, abought to Ours after, the Sheep weare all ſick, and did fome at the Mouths, and one of them died preſently; and they aſkt mee where I cecht the Sheep? and I tould them in Mors Cow Hous; and they ſaid they did beleue they wer bewicht, and ſo do I to.

Taken on Oath, Jan. 7th, 1679.

[*In the Autograph of the Deponent. The laſt Line by Woodbridge.*]

[To the Teſtimony of Joſhua Richardſon, Mr. Morſe replies (in his Petition before mentioned), as to his "looſing a Shepe, and his taking it forth off our Yeard, and my Wife ſhould ſay you might have aſked Leave, and whether overdriving it or what, now to bring it in 1 hope will be conſidered."

---

[1] A Joſhua Richardſon of Newbury married Mary Parker, 31 January, 1679. She died 7 March, 1685.—*Coffin.*

That Richardson caused the death of his Sheep by overdriving them on a hot Day, might have been a common-sense Explanation, if *Witchcraft* had not taken the Place of common Sense in the bewildered Brains of the People.]

The Testemony of Caleb Moody,[1] aged 42 Yearse, testphieth and sayeth, that I having lived nere to Elizabeth Mors about twenty Yeers, I haue lost seurall Catell in a usiall [*sic*] maner. About 16 Years a goe I had sume difrans with the seyd Mose; the next Morning one of my best Hogs lay deed in the Yrd, and no natrial Case, that I know of: at another Time the sayd Elisebeth Mors came to me leat of a Satrdye Nite and desird me to goe to Mr. Wodbg his Store to se after her Husbnd. I tould her I did not aprhd any Denger of hime. The next Morning I sent my eldest Sone to the House to inquier whether her Husbnd was come Home. The Lad came home and tould me that he was come Home, and that she the sayed Elizabeth Morse tould hime that I had ben as good I had gone to loke after her Husband. That uery Morning, as I was afterwards informed by John Ordwaye,[2] that as he was driuing out the Flock of Shep, that he then cept, one of my Sheepe laye done and dyed. At another Time I had a Cowe wase sudenly tacken in a uery stronge Maner, and tumled ovr Logs that layd in the Yord, and strived to turne reerd upon her Heade, and so continued a while, and

---

[1] He was son of William Moody, who came from Ipswich old England, to Newbury, in 1635. See *Founders of New England*, 70. His second Wife was Judith Bradbury, whom he married 9 Nov., 1665. He died 25 August, 1698, aged 61. On the List of Passengers his Name stands *Moudy*.

[2] The Father of this John Ordway, named James, came from Wales it is said, but at what Time he arrived in New England is not known. John married Mary Godfrey, December 5th, 1681, and had a large Family of Children. — *Coffin*. The Name may originally have been *Hardway*.

rofe vp agayne, and went awaye. After this I fawe the fame Cowe coming doune the Hill by Wm. Morfes Houfe, and I fawe the feyed Elizabeth Morfe ftand without the Doare, and my Cowe fall in to the like ftrange Condifion, as fhe did before, and tumbled into a Guter or Guly that was worne with the Runing of the Water: after fhe recoured and went awaye Home. At another Time, of a Sabath Daye Morning, one of my Cous, great with Calfe, was turnd in to the Stale with her Head under her, ftone dead; in fuch a Maner that I could not thinke it pofable for a Cow to pute herfelf in to fuch a Place, but conclud the Diuell by fume Inftrement did it; and feurall that faw it did faye they were of the fame Minde, or Wrds to that Porpofe. At an other Time, about thre or four Yers a goe, in the Sumer Time, I had a fouryeareold Hefer that was brout out of the Woods with a Calf about thre Wecks old, and I [put] theme into my Paftir, neere to the fayed Morfes Houfe, and let her goe there 2 or 3 Dayes with her Calf, to ufer to the Plaefe. Then I went to teacke awaye the Calf to kill it, the Heifer femed to tacke no Notis of the Calf when I fetchd it a waye, whitch maed me to maruill, ceafe fhe was uery fond of her Calf; after the Calf was kild I went to fe what wafe the Mater with the Heifer, and fhe was leyed doune in a fhedy Plafe among Thorne Bufhes, and would nether eat nor chew her Coad for fevrall Dayfe; and as I was trying to get er Hed vp I faw the feyed Elifbeth Mors within about 5 or 6 Rods of; fo I drove the Heifer a waye, but fhe would not feed; after words I went agyne to fee what would become of her, and fhe wafe layd doune agayne in the fame Plafe and I loked vp and faw the fayed Elizabeth Morfe nere the fame Plafe wher I had fene her before, and this I did, to the beft of my Memery three or four Times; the Heifer lay ner the

Appendix. 265

fame Plafe, and the fayed Elizabeth Mors was with in Sight. I do not rememer that I did fe her come or goe a waye, but faw her at onfe whitch did meack me uery mutch fufpect fhe had bewitched my Heifer; farther I do teftiphie that about a Munth or fiue Wecks a goe, W^m. Foning boroued my Meore to goe to Mill and being in my Pafter neere to the feyd Morfes Houfe, after Sonefeat, I herd W^m. Foning [Faning] at the feyed Mofes Barne talking with him about John Stiles, and I herd the fayd Foning threten to breack his Bonfe. The next Morning John Hall came over to my Houfe and tould me that W^m. Foning had cald at his Houfe before Daye and tould him that he was muth frited with a Cat in Capt. Peerfes Paftur.

Taken on Oath Jan. 7th, 1679. [*By Mr. Woodbridge.*]

[In the Handwriting of the Deponent.]

[To the fhocking Nonfenfe of Caleb Moody, brought up after a Lapfe of fome ten Years, Mr. Morfe makes the following mild Reply (in the before-mentioned Petition): "As to what befel him in and about his not feeing my Wife: that his Cow making no Hafte to hir Calfe, which wee are ignorant of, it being fo long fince; and [he] being in Church Communion with us, fhculd have fpoken of it like a Chriftian and y^n proceeded fo as wee might have given an Anfwer in lefs Time y^n tenn Yeares. Wee are ignorant y^t he had a Shepe fo dyed. And his Wife, known to be a Pretious Godly Woman, yt hath oftne fpoken to hir Hufband not to be fo uncharitable, and have and doe carry it like a Chriftian with a due Refpect in her Carridge towards my Wife all along."]

The Teftemony of W^m. Faning, aged about 36 Yeers, teftiphieth and fayeth, that about a Month or five Weeks agoe, liuing neere to Wiliam Morfes, in the

Ii

Euning, quickly after Sone feat, I faw John Stiles ftanding by Mr. Denifons Couehous and I afked him what was the beft News att their Houfe, and he tould mee that there was feuerall Hundreds of Diuels in the Eyer,[1] and they would be att their Houfe by and by, and they would be att my Hous a non: and that very Night ey [I] went to Sargent Moodeys Hous, which is my Neighbor, and borrowed his Mare to go to Mill; and I went to Mill with two Bufhels of Corn and got it ground; and when I came back againe, in John Hals Pafture, the Mare began to ftartell and fnort, and rared vp on End, fo that I could not gett her forward; and I loocked downe vpon the Mars Head I fpied a great whit Cat without a Tayl vpon my Breft and fhe had faft hold of my Neckcloth and Coat. I haueing a good Stick in my Hand, I ftroock her off. And againe the Cat was a coming up vpon my left Side, I toock my Stick in my left Hand and ftroock her down againe; then I alighted, and as foon as I alighted the Catt came between my Legs, fo that I could not well go forward; and watching my Opportunity I ftroock her a uery great Blow up againft a Tree, and after that I ftroock her another Blow which made her lay for dead, and I went prefently to John Hals Houfe, and he was abed. I caled to him and defiered him that he would go to futch a Tree and there I thought he would find a dead Catt, and I went ftraight way Home and told my Wife, and tould her what I had met with all.

Taken on Oath Jan. 7th, 1679. [*By Mr. Woodbridge.*]

[*The above, as far as the Mention of* "*Mr. Denifon Couehoufe,*" *is in the Hand of Caleb Moody.*]

---

[1] Perhaps now *eyre;* if fo, the Meaning of the Word is plain, viz: the Devils were *on their way*. But poffibly he meant *in the air*.

[Morfe's Anfwer to Fanning's Teftimony could not have been very fatisfactory to himfelf. It feems to have been dictated with as little Senfe as the Teftimony. It is thus reported in the Petition: "To William Fanning fhould fay my Boy faid the Devill was at his Howfe. Upon Fannings faying to the Boy ye Devill was at their Howfe, and he would have me chid ye Boy, which I tould faid Fanning ye Boy might be inftructed to know ye Devill was every where, though not at our Howfe, and fhould not in Time of Affliction upbraid him to our Griefe."

Perhaps Whifkey may not have been in Ufe in thofe Days, but Something quite as electrifying no doubt had affected the Imagination of Fanning. He had a Wife and feveral Children. His Wife was Elizabeth Allen, whom he married 24th of March, 1668.]

John Mighell,[1] aged about 44 Yeares, teftifieth, that about ten Years fince, I wente to William Moffes Houfe to worke, by the order of Jonathan Mofe, the Sone of William Mors. I went to hew Shingell, and at Night when I was going Home Gooddi Mors did ueri much urge me to ftay all Night, and help hir Sone the next Day; in fomutch that I was glad to aney Scufe; that I had tied a young Mare up in the Houfe and muft go Home to water hir. Then fhe faid, be fure to cume a gaine to Morow. So I went Home; but came thair no more, and fhe fent to me fauarall Times to cum to Work, and at the laft thaire was Word came to me, that fhe was ueri angeri with me, and fuddenly, after thair was a great Allteration in my Cattell; thair was one of my Coues that had a Calfe a bout a Fortnit ould, and at Night he was wet

---

[1] He is not mentioned by Coffin among the early Inhabitants of Newbury. He may have been a Son of Thomas of Rowley, and Brother of Samuel, who married Elizabeth, Daughter of Abraham Tappan of Newbury. The Name is often found fpelt *Mihil.*

when I put him up, and in the Morning I went to fetch him out to fuck, and the Haire and Skin was gone of his Back; and it was reed like a Burne, and would neuer heale but grue wors and worfe. At the Laft his Eyes came out of his Head, and then I thout it was Time to cnok him on the Head; and another of my Coues got a littel Pufh with an other Beaft, and the Dung rane out of hir Side; and a nother of my Coues ftud in the Medell of the Yard, when I went to ti them up anight, and fhe courd not go of the Place wheare fhe ftud, but I wafe glad to let hir ftand in the Middel of the Yard all Night, and my Mare was dround, and thus my Creatures were, that I had fcarfe ani Creature tha[t] was well; and Gooddi Mors being anggeri with me, and haueing bene talk of for a Wich, I was afeard that fhe had fum Hand in this.

Taken on Oath, Jan. 7th. 1679, [*by Mr. Woodbridge.*]

[To this Story of John Mighill, Mr. Morfe fays (in his Petition): "About yᵉ Lofs of his Catle, was yᵗ he came one Day to Worke and [I] would have had him come another Day to finifh it, becaufe yᵉ Raine came in fo upon us, and his not coming, [he] judges my Wife was angry and yrfore had fuch Lofs, which wee neuer knew of. This being twelve Yeares agoe did amaze us now to here of it."]

The Depofition of Robert Earle,[1] aged 45 Yeeres, or thereabouts, fayth that on Twefday Night laft, about to of the Cloke at Night goeing into the Camber where Elizabeth Morfe was fhut in, finding her fetting vpright in her Bed, fhe fayed to me that

---

[1] He was the Officer having Mrs. Morfe in Charge. At Bofton he was Jailor, or Prifonkeeper. He died in 1698, if Savage is right, at the Age of 64. There is extant a Genealogy of the Earl Family.

she was very glad that I was come in, for she was in great Troable, and that she thought she should dye for it now, for they were goeing to find out another Way for Blasphemye. And I went neere her Bedside, and I heard a strainge Kind of Noyse, which was like a Wheelpe sucking of the Dam, or, Kettins sucking, which made me to thinke whether any of the Catts had layd any of there Kittins vpon the Syde of the Bed, or wheather it might be some strainge Kind of Hissing within her. Further, I testifye, that Yesterday, when I went to fech her to ye Court, she sayd that now they say abroad I shall dye. I asking of her why she sayd soe, and whoe it was that sayd soe, she sayd, my Husband, and I haue beene talking to geither of it. And she sayed that I did know what they did say, if I would speake, and such as I that doe know such Things spoke of abroad. Then I remembering there was some did ask me what I thought would be don with her. I sayd I did not know but y^t she might dye for it, which made me have the more Suspition of her calling to mind w^t I had sayd abroad.

He further adds y^t on Wednesday Night last going into the Roome where ye s^d Elisabeth Morse was alike setting vp as before s^d, heard the like Noyes tho not so loud and y^s was neere about the same Time of Night.

[*The last Paragraph by Rawson. The other in a Hand much like that of Addington.*]

To Joseph Pyke Constable of Newbery.

In his Maj'^{tyes} Name you are requered to seaze on the Person of Elizabeth Morse, the Wife of Willjam Morse, and hir forthwith safely convey and deliuer hir to the Keeper of the Prison at Ipswich, by him safely to be kept till the Court of Assistants on its Adjournment to the 20th of May next who will give further Order: ſhe being preſented and left by the Grand Jury for Tryall, as to Witchcraft: and hereof you are not to faile. Dated in Boſton: from the 6th of March, 1679.

          By the Court   Edward Rawson, *Secrety.*
. . . ſent one W^{rt} of this Tenor
. . . . . vnd^{r}ſtand came not.

[The above all in Secretary Rawſon's Hand. Part of the Minute in the Margin torn off. The following Indorſement is on the Back of the above:—]

This Warrant receiued in Boſton Aprill 1th, 1680, and the Perſon within ſpeſſefied was deliuered to the Priſon Kepar in Ipſwich Aperill 2^d: 1680.
                    P^r me Joseph Pike[1]
                    Conſtable of Newbery.

To the Conſtable of Newery, Joſeph Pyke.
In his Majeſties Name you are requered, ſeaſonably to ſumon, and alike Require, Caleb Moody, William

---

[1] He was, according to Coffin, Grandſon of John Pike, who came to Newbury in 1635, and on Sept. 4th, 1691, was killed by the Indians at Haverhill. The diſtinguiſhed Maj. Robert Pike of Saliſbury was Son of that John. Coffin has very culpably neglected to tell us what Pike was the Anceſtor of Nicholas Pike of Newbury, who compiled the moſt extenſive American Arithmetick ever publiſhed in this Country, rivalling Malcolm (the Scotch Author) himſelf; a ſtout Octavo, dedicated to the Hon. James Bowdoin. It went through ſeveral Editions, under the Hands of different Editors, but there is no Edition ſo good as the firſt. Joſeph, the Conſtable, married Suſanna Kingsbury, 29 Jan., 1662, and among other Children had Joſeph, who married Hannah Smith, who, among other Children, had James, born March 1ſt, 1703. Theſe were the Parents of the great Mathematician, who died in 1819, aged 76. He was a Graduate of Harvard College, 1766, with ſeveral others afterwards diſtinguiſhed.

Chandler,[1] John Glading,[2] James Broune, Joanna Broune, Benjamin Richardſon, Wm. Card,[3] Joſeph Bayly, Zackery Dauis, Jonathan Hajnes, John Mihil, Joſhua Richardſon, Suſanna Gooduin, John Chaſe, John Ordeway, William Fanning, Jonathan Woodman, Benjamin Lowle,[4] Eliſabeth Titcomb, Peniel Tytcome, Lyddia Tytcom, Dauid Wheeler, Wm. Morſe wth John Styles, to make their and euery of their ſeuerall Appearances before the Court of Aſſiſtants on their Adjournment on the twentyeth Day of this Inſtant, May, at eight of the Clocke in the Morning, in Boſton; then and there to give in their Euidence againſt Eliſabeth Morſe, Wife to W^{m}. Morſe; ſhe being then to be on hir Trjall for Witchcraft, hauing ben preſented and indicted by the laſt Grand Jury in March laſt at the Court of Aſſiſtants: making your Returne to the Secretary at or before that Time, w^{th}out Fayle, at yor Perrill. Dated in Boſton the 4th Day of Inſtant, May, 1680.

By the Court   EDWARD RAWSON *Secty.*

[*All in the Hand of the Secretary.*]

Theas are to certeſie the honored Court of Aſſiſtants ſitting in Boſton on ad journment, Maye 20th 1680: that Calleb Moody, Wm. Chandlar, Jno. Gladin, James Browne, Hanah Browne, Beniamin

---

[1] Probably the Emigrant, he died March 5th, 1701, in his 85th Year. He was thrice married, and the Father of many Children. — See *Coffin.*

[2] John Gladding married Elizabeth Rogers, July 17th, 1666.

[3] Not found in Coffin's Liſt of the Inhabitants of Newbury, and Savage knows no more. Francis Card the Indian Captive may have been of the ſame Family.

[4] The Name was changed to *Lowell.* The Brothers John and Richard Lowle came from Briſtol, England, and ſettled in Newbury, 1639.

Richardſon, Will. Card, Joſeph Bayle, Zachariah Dauis, Jonathan Haynes, Jn°. Mighell, Joſhua Richardſon, Suſana Goodwin, John Chaſe, An Ordway, Will Fanning, Johnathan Woodman, Beniamen Lowle, Eliſabeth Titcomb, Penuell Titcomb, Liddea Titcomb, Daued Wheelar, Wm. Morſe with Jn^g. Stiles, wear all ſumoned to appear att y^e ſ^d honoured Court of Aſſiſtants on ye 20th of Inſtant, May, att eight of the Clock in ye Morning, according to this Warrant, dat: 17th May, 1680. By me
of Newbery.   JOSEPH PIKE, *Conſtable.*
For ye Secretary.

[*The above Return is on the Back of the Secretary's Warrant.*]

To the Conſtable of Charleſtoune.

In his Maj'^{tys} Name you are hereby requered to aſſemble the Fremen of yor Toune together, and ſignify to them that they are alike required to chooſe and ſend two able and diſcreet Perſons to ſerve on a Jury of Trjall at the Court of Aſſiſtants in Boſton on adjournment 20th Inſtant at eight of the Clocke in the Morning of a capitall Offendo^r, making yor Returne hereof to the Secretary at or before the Time: hereof not to faile. Dated in Boſton 13 of ſajd May, 1660.
By the Court   EDWARD RAWSON, *Secret.*

[*All in the Secretary's Hand.*]

[Endorſement.]

At a legall meeting of Fremen of Charleſtown, ther is choſen Mr. Nathan Heyman, and Mr. John Knite to ſerue on the Jury acording to Warent: P^r
         by me^e JOSEPH RYALL[1] *Conſtabel.*

---

[1] Savage has confounded the *Ryalls* with the *Royals*. The Name of this Family was never *Royal* we think. If it ſlid that way after the Time of *Joſeph Ryall*, it is no Excuſe for making a *Royaliſt of him.*

Appendix. 273

To the Conſtable of Boſton:—

In his Maj'ᵗʸes Name yow are required forthwith to aſſemble the Freemen of your Toune together and ſignify to them that they are hereby alike required to chooſe and ſend fiue able and deſcreet Perſons to the Court of Aſſiſtants on their Adjournment on the 20ᵗʰ of this Inſtant May, at eight of the Clock in the Morning to ſerue on a Jury for the Trjall of a capital Offendor: making yʳ Returne to the Secretary at or before that Time. Dated in Boſton the 13ᵗʰ Inſtant, May, 1680. Hereof not to faile.

By the Court. EDWARD RAWSON, *Secrety.*

[*Endorſed.*]

Boſton this 18ᵗʰ of May, 1680. Then ware the free Men of this Town aſſembled, in obedians to yowr Warrant, and did accordingly chuſe Mr. Richard Middlecott, Mr. Jeremiah Cuſhin, Mr. John Wait, Leftenant Richard Waye, and Mr. Thomas Harrod, for to ſerue as Jurimen. Thay are alſo warned for to attend yᵉ Servis upon the 20th of May at eight of yᵉ Clock in yᵉ Morning.

By me BOZOUN ALLEN,
Conſtable of Boſton.

To the Conſtable of Watertoune.

In his Maj'ᵗʸes Name you are required to aſſemble the Freemen of yᵉ Toune together and ſignify to them that they are alike required to chuſe and ſend two able and diſcreete Perſons to Boſton on the 20ᵗʰ of this Inſtant May, at eight of the Clock in the Morning to ſerue on a Jury of Triall at the Court of Aſſiſtants on their Adjornment of a capitall Offender: making yᵉ Returne hereof to the Secretary at or before that Time: hereof yow are not to faile. Dated in Boſton, 13ᵗʰ of ſajd May, 1680.

By yᵉ Court. EDWARD RAWSON, *Secrety.*

[*Endorſement, or Return.*]
The Freemen haue choſen John Stone and Rechard Child to ſarue upon the Ieury of Trials.
By me. JOHN MOSE, *Conſtable.*
17 : 3 : 1680.

To the Conſtable of Cambridge.
In his Maj^{ties} Name yow are hereby required forthwith to aſſemble the Freemen of yor Toune together and ſignifie to them that they are alike required to chooſe and ſend two able and deſcreet Perſons to Boſton, then and there, on the 20th Inſtant, May, at eight of the Clocke in the Morning to ſerve on a Jury at the Trjall of a capitall Offendor: making your Returne to the Secretary at or before that Time: hereof yow are not to faile. Dated in Boſton, the 13th of ſaid May, 1680.
By the Court. EDWARD RAWSON, *Secret.*

[*The Return thereon.*]
Bro. John Green of Cambridge, and Richard Robins are choſen to ſerue one the Jury of Trialls, according to the Warrant.
By the Cunſtabell, JONAS CLARKE.
One May the 20, 1680.

To the Conſtable of Dorcheſter.
In his Majties Name you are required forthwith to aſſemble the Freemen of ſaid Toune together and ſignify to them that they are alike required to chooſe and ſend two able and diſcreete Perſons to ſerue on a Jury of Trialls in Boſton at the Court of Aſſiſtants on their Adjournment, 20 Inſtant at eight of the Clocke in the Morning for the Triall of a capital Offendor: making yor Returne to the Secretary at or before that

Appendix. 275

Time: heereof yow are not to faile. Dated in Bofton, 13th fajd May, 1680.
By the Court, EDWARD RAWSON, *Secrety.*

[*The Return:*—]
Dor Chefter, 17: 3: 80. The free Men of the Tovne wear a fembled, and mad Choys of Jacob Hven and John Capen for this Cort for the Jvri of Trial.
As a teft   JAMES FOSTER, *Conft.*

The Teftimony of Efther Willfon[1] aged about 28. That fhe living with her Mother, Goodwife Chandler when fhe was ill, fhe would often cry out and complaine that G. Morfe was a Witch, and had bewitched her, and euery Time fhe came to fee her fhe was the Worfe for her. Though too meete were often forbidden, yett thay would not refraine coming. One coming to the Houfe afked why we did not nayle a Horfefhoe on the Threfhold, (for that was an Experiment to try Witches.) My Mother the next Morning, with her Staffe made a Shift to gett to the Doore, and nayled on a Horfefhooe, as well as fhe could. G. Morfe, while the Horfefhoe was on, would neuer be

---

[1] Coffin finds no Willfons at Newbury at this Time. Efther probably belonged to a neighboring Town. It is inferred that Wm. Chandler's firft Wife was Mary Wilfon or Willfon, who died, according to Coffin, in 1666. Hence Efther's Depofition relates to an Affair of at leaft fourteen Years' Standing. Morfe (in his Petition) refers to a Teftimony given by Wm. Chandler, but does not mention this of Efther Willfon. One was probably corroborative of the other. Morfe fays: "As for William Chandler's Teftimony aboute his Wife's long Sicknefs, and my Wifes vifiting hir, fhe through hir Weaknefs acted uncivilly, and y^t now to bring it againft my Wif, when, for fo many Yeares being in full Communion with us [&] never dealt with us aboute any fuch Thing, but had as loving Converfe with him as Chriftians ought, and knew no otherwife till now."

perswaded to come into the House; and though she were perswaded by the Deponent, and Daniel Rolfe, to goe in, she would not; and being demanded the Reason she would not tell me now, and sayd it was not her Mind to come in; but she would kneele downe by the Doore and talke and discourse, but not goe in, though she would come often Times in a Day, yett that was her practise. W^m. Moody coming to the the House, and vnderstanding that there was a Horseshoe nailed on the Doore, sayd a Piece of Witchery, and knockt it off and layd it by. Very shortly after, the same Day G. Morse came in, and thrust into the Palovr where my Mother lay before she was vp; and my Mother complained of her, and I earnestly desired her that she would be gon, and I could very hardly with my Importunity intreat her to do it. The Horseshooe was off about a Weeke and she would very often come in that Time. About a Weeke after, my Mother, to keep her out of the House, gott Daniel Rolfe to naile on the Shooe againe, wch continued so about 7 or 8 Dayes, and at that Time she would not come ouer the Threshold to come in, though often importuned to do it. Then W^m. Moody coming againe, tooke off the Horseshooe, and putt it in his Pockett, and carryed it away: then the sayd Goodwife Morse came as before, and would goe in as before. In a short Time after, I being at Home on a Sabbath Day, alone with my Mother, I had bin dressing her Head, and she cryed out on a Sudden, G. Morse, G. Morse is coming into the House. I sayd I could not see her, my Mother sayd I see her, there she is. Then I run to the Doore twice, but I could not see her; but my Mother cryed out, that wicked Woman would kill her, be the Death of her, she could not beare it, and fell into a grieuous Fitt, and I tooke her and carryed her in and layd her on a Bed: and hauing fo done I went out to fee if any Body were coming from Meeting, and ther (though I faw her not before) fhe rufhed in, and went into the Parlour to my Mother, and I ftepping out and feeing my Father coming lift vp my Hand to him to come and he made great Haft, and I called in fome of the Neighbours, and fo my Mother continued a confiderable Time before fhe recouered. In this Fitt, my Mother's Mouth was drawne awry, and fhe foamed at Mouth, and I wiped it of, but I was very much frighted to fee her fo till the Neighbours came in. This is all that at prefent fhe remembreth.

Taken on Oath, May 17th, 1680, before me
     Jo: Woodbridge, *Commiſſ^r*.
Read in Court, 20 May, 1680. E. Rawfon, Secr.

[*All the above in the Hand of Mr. Woodbridge, excepting the laſt Line.*]

The Teftimony of Elizabeth Titicomb, aged about 50 Years.

That fhee being lately with Sufanna Tappin, aged about 74 Years, the f^d Tappin related to her, that when Elizabeth Mors was in Examination for Witchcraft, and fhe being fummoned gaue in her Teftimony among others. When fhe went away fhe fayd Elizabeth Morfe came after her and tooke her about the Wrift, as if fhe would enquire what was the Euidence fhe gaue in ag^t her: who anfwered Nothing but what you fpake your felfe. The fayd Topan went Home, and in the Night fhe felt a cold Damp Hand clafping her about her Wrift, wch affrighted her very much, and putt her into a very great and dropping Sweat: and from that Time fhe continued ill, and an itching and pricking rofe vpon her Body, wch afterwards came to fuch a dry Scurfe, that fhe could fcrape it off as it were Scales from an Allewife; and that Side wch fhe was touched in was moft out of Frame; and fhe is fmitten in the lower Parts of her Body after the fame Manner that fhe had teftifyed agt the fayd Morfe what fhe heard her fpeake: and from that Time fhe hath continued very ill, but little from her Bed, and hath not bin able to goe abroad euer fince to the publike Meeting. Who alfo fayth that the very Night when fhe being defined to goe and enquire of the fayd Topan, what her Euidence was, fhe had a Beaft ftrangely hanged in a harrow and dead.

Taken on Oath, May 14th, 1680.

Jo: WOODBRIDGE, Commifr.

Sworn in Court the 20th May, 1680. E. R. Se^c.

[*All in Woodbridge's Hand except the laft Line.*]

Elizabeth Titcomb, formerly ferioufly telling G. Morfe of the Report that went of her as touching her Name for Witchcraft, and endeauouring to convince her of the Wickednefſe for it, fhe feemed to be much affected with it, and fell on weeping, and fayd fhe was as innocent as herfelfe, or the Child now unborn, or as God in Heaven.

Sworn, E. R., S.

Lydia Titcomb, aged about 17 Yeares, teftifyeth, that fhe heard the Difcourfe betweene her Mother and the fayd G. Morfe, and the Words wch her Mother hath expreffed; and alfo, that a little While after fhe and her Brother and Sifter, going home from the Pond where they fetcht water, there flew fomewhat out of the Buſhes, in her opinion like an Owle, and it came vp prefently to her, and was turned into the Shape of a Catt; and quickly after turned into the Shape of a Dog: fometimes would be all black, then haue a white

Appendix. 279

Ring about the Neck: fometimes would haue long Eares, fometimes fcarce any to be difcerned; fometimes a very long Taile, fometimes a very fhort one, fcarce difcernable, and in fuch Manner it followed vs fome Time, as if it would leap vpon our Backs, and frighted vs very much, and accompanyed vs till they came neere the Houfe: and the laft Time we faw it we left it playing about a Tree, and we went in and left it.

Taken on Oath, May 14th, 1680, before me
Jo: WOODBRIDGE, *Commiſſ^r*.
Sworn in Court, 20 May, 1680. E. R., S.

Sufan Topan[1] being examined about the Teftimony of Elizabeth Titcomb, before written, teftifyeth, that, for the Subftance, it is true; onely, there is a Miftake that G. Morfe tooke her by the Wrift, not at that Time, when fhe came Home from that Meeting, when the fayd Morfe was examined, but on a Sabbath Day after, when fhe came from the publike Meeting, wch fhe might eafily miftake her: and fhe fayth that the fayd Morfe came very haftily after her, as if fhe runne. And fhe cannot directly tell the Night when the cold Hand clafped her Wrift, but it was not the Night that fhe came Home from the Examination. In euery Thing elfe the Relation is exactly true.

Taken on Oath, May 17th, 1680, before me
Jo: WOODBRIDGE, *Con^s*.

[*All in Mr. Woodbridge's Hand, except the Lines figned E. R., S.*]

[1] Probably Daughter of the firft Abraham Toppan. — *Coffin*.

Thomas Nolton[1] fayth that when he brought down the Prifoner, Elizabeth Morfe, from Ipfwich, fhe faid fhe was accufed about Witchcraft, fhe faid fhe was as cleare of the Accufation as God in Heaven.

Sworn in Court pr Thomas Nolton, May 20, 1680.
EDW^D RAWSON, *Secry*.

[*All in Rawfon's Hand.*]

Thomas Knolten further teftifys, that as I brought Goody Moffe downe, fhe owned to me, that fhe ftroakt Goodwife Ordway Child over the Head, when it was fick, and the Child dyed.

Sworn in Court, 20th May, 1680.
E. RAWSON, *Secr*.

[*The Words*, "and the Child dyed," *in the above appear* to have been partially obliterated by the Paffage of the Finger on it before the Ink was dry.]

John Chafe. And as an Addition to my former Teftimony, I teftify and fay, that y^t very Day, to the beft of my Knowledge, yt Kaleb Powell came to take my Teftimony againft Goodwife Moffe yt I was taken with ye bloody Flux, and foe it held mee till I came to ye Court and charged her with itt, yt at ye very Inftant of Time itt left me, and I have not been troubled with it fince, and that my Wife has been forely troubled with fore Breafts, that fhe have loft them both, and one of them rotted away from her.

Sworn to in Court, 20th May, 1680.
EDW. RAWSON, *Sect^y*.

---

[1] This Surname is now more commonly written *Knowlton*. This Man was Jailor at Ipfwich, and died there (according to Savage) April 3d, 1692. A^s he did not write the Documents with his Name in them, it is not certain whether he fpelt his Name beginning with an N or K. We find one of the fame Name at Fort Maffachufetts in 1746.

Appendix. 281

[What the "former Teſtimony" of John Chaſe was does not appear, as it is not amongſt our Witch Papers. But in Morſe's Petition of May 14th, 1681, he thus anſwers or explains that Teſtimony; as "to John Chaſe ſaying y^t he ſaw my Wife in the Night coming in at a little Hole, and ye Like, when he himſelfe hath ſaid he did not know but he was in a dreame, and y^t unto ſeveral Perſons he hath ſo ſaid, though now as he teſtifies, when my Wife diſowns any ſuch Thing."]

The Teſtimony of Mrs. Jane Sewall,[1] aged about 54 Yeares. Who ſayth that ſome Yeares ſince Wm. Morſe being at my Houſe, began of his owne Accord to ſay that his Wife was accounted a Witch, but he did wonder that ſhe ſhould be both a healing and a deſtroying Witch, and gaue this Inſtance. Thomas Wells, his Wife being come to the Time of her Delivery, was not willing (by the Motion of his Siſter in whoſe Houſe ſhe was) to ſend for Goodwife Morſe, though ſhe were the next Neighbour, and continued a long Seaſon in ſtrong Labour and could not be delivered; but when they ſaw the Woman in ſuch a Condition, and without any hopefull Appearance of Delivery, determined to ſend for the ſayd G. Morſe, and ſo Tho. Wells went to her and deſired her to come; who, at firſt, made a Difficulty of it, as being unwilling, not being ſent for ſooner. Tho. Wells ſayd he would have come ſooner, but [his Wife's] Siſter would not let him; ſo at laſt ſhe went, and quickly after her coming the Woman was delivered. This, as ſhe remembreth, was the Subſtance [of the] Diſcourſe, though ſhe doth not remember his very Words: and ſhe ſuppoſeth, [that] Thomas Wells and his Wife

---

[1] Mrs. Sewall was Daughter of Stephen Dummer of Newbury.

living both at Bofton can giue more full Teftimony concerning this Thing.

Taken on Oath, May 18th, 1680. Before me,
                          Jo: WOODBRIDGE, *Comſr*.
Read in Court, 20 May, 1680.
                          E. RAWSON, *Secrety*.

Elizabeth Titcombe faith as to yt Pt of this Teftimony relating to ye fending for Elizabeth Morfe, fhe was prefent, and was one of thofe fecond fending for, and faw Goody Morfe when fhe came there, and fee a prefent fpeedy deliuery of the Woman.

Sworn in Court 20th May, 1680.
                          E. RAWSON, *Sec^y*.

[*In Woodbridge's Hand, excepting the Parts ſigned by Rawſon.*]

[*On the Back of the above Original is this Endorſement:* "This for the honoured Gouernour."]

The Teftimony of Jno. March,[1] aged 22 Years.

Teftifieth tha bout 6 Years fince I lived with Jno. Wells, he working then at Bofton, and with him

---

[1] John was a Son of Hugh March the Emigrant, and born at Newbury, June 10th, 1658. He was afterwards known as Major March. His Wife was Jemima True, whom he married March 1, 1679. Hugh emigrated in 1638, at the Age of 20, as given in the Lift of Paffengers in the Ship Confidence of London. See *Founders of New England*, 58. Coffin (*Hift. Newbury*, 309) does not raife John above the Rank of Major, but he is called Colonel in all the Hiftories. He was often upon Expeditions againft the Indians; had a Command in Sir William Phipf's difaftrous Canada Invafion, but the Time of his Death is not found. He was living in 1707, as on the 18th of May of that Year he failed with a large Armament of 23 Tranfports and 1000 Men to reduce Port Royal. The Attempt was a failure. *Penhailow, Belknap,* and *Book of the Indians.*

Appendix. 283

there. Hee fent me Home to Newbury about fome Bufines, and when I came Home the Wife of Jno. Wels tolde mee that fhee did not queftion but that as I fhould fee Something in the Chamber at Night and at Night I went to Bed and Daniell Greenleafe with mee; and after wee had beene at Bed a little While, and wee hearde agreat Noife in the Chamber. I looked up and faw feuerall Cats and Rats at Play together in the Chamber, running one after another; the Rats after the Cats, and I was very much amazed at it; and a little while after I flung feueral Things at them but could not ftrik them. The next Morning, before wee came out of the Chamber I heard Goody Mors and my Dame Wells a talking together without the Dore feuerall Words they had which was uery loude and I hearde my Dame Wels call Goody Mors Wich, and feuerall fuch Words, which I could not tell the Meaning of, before I came downe, and I came down my Dame Wels came in againe. She afked me if I faw fuch Things as are before expreffd. I afked her why fhee afked mee? fhe told mee that Goody Mors told her that I had feene Cats and Rats that Night. Then Goody Wels told me that fhee afked her how fhe knew it? She told her that fhee heard fo,[1] though neither I nor Daniel Greenleaf who only knew it, had not bin out of the Chamber to tell Anybody of it, nor feene any Body but onely ouerheard them talking.

The fayd Goodwife Wells hath profeffed before me feverall Times, that often going to G. Morfe her Houfe to fetch Water, fhee hath feene fome fmall Creatures, like Mice or Ratts run into the Houfe after her, and runn under her Coats.

Taken on Oath, May 12th 1680.

[1] From this Point to the End of the Depofition, is in the Autograph of Woodbridge. The previous Part is in a Hand not recognized.

This laft, Daniel Thurfton, and Rich. Woollworth haue heard the fayd Goodwife Wells affirme, as they teftify.

Sworn in Court May 20th 1680 for John March.

The Teftimony of John March is thus fummarily difpatched:—"He heard John Wells his Wife fay fhe faw Imp o' God into faid Morfs Howfe. She being profecuted would not owne it, and was adjudged to pay Damages, and now this is brought in."

The Depofisfhon of James Browne,[1] aged about 32 Years, teftyfyeth. yt about 15 Years agoe, I goein from my Fathers to Mr. Woodmans of an Arent, met with Goody Mofe and Gorge Whelere was under faille; Goody Mofe afckt me what uefals it was? I fayd Gorge Whellors. She replyed he goes out brafely; but Words to this Effect, that he fhoud not returne, for a Trick, fhe knewe: farder teftyfyeth that I was one Night at Salfbery, and the next Day was at Goody Mofes. She tould me of feferal of my miftdemeners; among the Reft of what I did the Nyght before, and I afckt her how fhe coulld tell of um? fhe faide eferey Body fed it was true. I replyed to her efery Body fes you arr a Wich: fhe faid to me again, our Safor Chrift was be lyed and foe is you and I. John Myrch teftyfyeth that he heard Goody Mofe owne before Mr. Woudbidg that fhe met with James Broune when Gorge Whellr was gone out. Johnathan Haines teftyphyeth y^t he heard Goody Mofe owne yt fhe did reproue James Browne for his Mefdemeners. *Y^e Addition of James Broune and Jonathan*

---

[1] Coffin does not tell us what James Browne this was, though he has feveral among his Newbury Lift. He is probably the one who married Hannah ——. His Parentage is about as eafily traced as that of *John Smith*. See Savage's *N. E. Gen. Dict.*, Article SMITH.

Heynes with former Oaths was by ym sworne vnto in Court, 20 *May*, 1680.

E. RAWSON, *Secy.*

[*The Part of the above in italic Type is in the Hand of Secretary Rawson. The previous Part is in a most difficult Chirography, and apparently by one of rare Ignorance of all Notions of Composition. Probably in the Autograph of the Deponent.*]

[More Importance seems to have been given to this Testimony than to any of the other, judging from the Length of the Reply to it in the Petition:—"To James Browne, y^t one Day George Wheeler going forth, my Wife should say for a Trifle she knew he should not come in againe, which my Wife knowes not of it, nor doth some of ye Owners ever remember such a Thing as to judge or charge it on hir, but now, but now is brought forth sixteen Yeares after when his Wife said to Goody Hale yt said Browne was mistaken. Hir Husband did come Home well that Voyage; and that James Browne should say to Robert Bedell, yt Powell, whom we sued, did put in these Words, and not himself in the Testimony, and y^t said Browne did oune to his Unkle, Mr. Nicholas Noyes yt he could not sware to such a Testimony; and did refuse to doe it before Mr. John Woodbridge, and Mr. Woodbridge did admire he had sworn to it. And for his seeing my Wife amongst Troopers. What Condition he might be in wee leave it to Consideration. Wee are Ignorant of such a Thing till now brought in so many Yeares agoe as he saith."]

The Testimony of Dauid Wheeler[1] of Newberry, aged fifty fiue Yeares or there abouts, testifieth and saith, that haueinge liued next Neighbour to Elizabeth Moss the Wife of W^m. Moss of Newberry aforesʳᵈ. He tooke Nottice of many strange Actions of her yᵉ said Eliz: Moss, more then euer hee sawe in any other Woman; Part whereof I haue giuen in my Euedence vnder Oath before Mr. Woodbridge, concerneing an Heifer whereunto I would farther add that all the Rest of yᵗ Breed of Cattle haue gennerally miscarrjed by strange Accedents euer since, till this present Time wᶜʰ is the Space of fifteene Yeares or thereabouts; as alsoe, that yᵉ sᵈ Eliz: Moss desired mee one Time to doe a smale Peece of Worke for her, wᶜʰ I neglected to doe soe soone as shee desired; and I goeinge many Dayes on fowleinge, att yᵗ Time, alwayes as to yᵉ Gennerality, came Home wᵗʰ lost Labour, wᶜʰ my Neighbour Moody tooke Notice of as well as my selfe, and hee told mee I would gett noe Geese vntill I had finished her Worke, wᶜʰ accordingly I speedily did; and afterwards I had Succefs as I vfed to haue formerly. Moreouer, feuerall other Accedents haue befallen mee wᶜʰ I belieue yt shee, the said Moss, through the Malice and Enuy of her Heart against mee might bee yᵉ Author of by Witchcraft, and farther saith not.

This Addition to his former Oath sworn to in Court 21 May, 1680.

E. RAWSON, *Sec.*

[In the Hand of Isaac Addington, or one similar, except the last Paragraph, which is in Rawson's Hand.]

[1] This Testimony of David Wheeler is not noticed by Morse. According to Coffin, he was born in Salisbury, England, in 1625, came to Hampton, thence to Newbury in 1645. He married Sarah Wife, May 11th, 1650, by whom he had feveral Children, whose Names and Dates of Birth may be found in the *Hist. of Newbury*, 321.

The Depoficon of Margett Mirack, aged about 56. This Deponent teftifieth y^t about a Letter y^t came from Pufcattaq^y, by Mr. Tho: Wiggens. Wee gott Mr. Wiggens to reade ye Letter, and he went his Way; and I p^{r}mifed to conceale ye Letter after it was read to my Hufband and myfelfe, and wee both did conceale it; neverthelefs, in few Daijes after Goode Mofs mett mee and clapt mee on ye Back, and fed, I comend you for fending fuch an Anfwerr to ye Letter. I p^{r}fently afkt her w^t Letter? Why, f^d fhee, hadft not thee fuch a Letter from fuch a Man at fuch a Time, and fent fuch and fuch an Anfwerr at fuch a Time? I came Home p^{r}fently and examined my Hufband about it. My Hufband f^d p^{r}fently, What? Is fhee a Witch, or a cunning Wooman? Wherevppon we examined our Family, and they f^d they knew Nothing of ye Letter. Afterwds I mett wth Goode Mofs and afkt her how fhee came to know it? and defired her to tell mee any one pfon y^t tould her, and I fhould be fatisfied. Shee afkt mee why I was foe inquifitiue, and told mee fhee could not tell. My Hufband teftifieth that I p^{r}fently tould him ye fame.

Sworne to in Court, 21 May, 1680.

EDW. RAWSON, *Sec.*

["To Goodwife Miricke about a Letter. My Wife telling her fomewhat of ye Letter, which fhe judges could not be and my Wife hearing of it, there was a Difcourfe, &c. aboute this love Letter, might fpeake Something about it by Guefs, and not by any fuch Way as fhe judged, and many haue fpoken, geffing at Things which might be." *Morfe's Petition &c.*]

James Ordwaijes Bill of Coft, from Munday Morning to Thurfday Night; my Wife being fumond by y^e

honnored Court to Bofton, and not being able of Body to goe nor ride of herfelfe, I was bound to affift my Wife and bring her to ye Court, which hath bin verry chargeable to mee; befides my Time to carry her Home againe; therfore I leaue it to ye Iudgement of ye honnored Court to giue mee w^t they fee good.

And my Wife, Attendance one day att Newbury before Mr. Woodbridge, and refeued Nothing but 1*s* at Mr. Turners for my felf and my Wife.[1]

Benia Lowles[2] Bill of Coft. 2 Days coming, and on Days Atendans of ye Cort. 2 Days going Hom,

---

[1] James Ordway's Wife's Teftimony is only to be inferred from Morfe's Petition: — "Hir Child being long ill, my Wife coming in and looking on it, pitting of it, did feare it would dy; and when it dyed Ifrael Webfter, our next Neighbour heard not a Word of it, nor fpoken of by others, nor any of y^t Family but hir Conceite, and now brought in."

A fimilar Cafe was that of "Widow Goodwin," who having a fick Child "gave forth y^t it was bewitched by my Wife, as fhe thought: wee hearing of it, dealt with hir about it, and fhe brake forth in Teares, craving Forgivnefs, and faid it was others put hir upon it, to fay as fhe did, but now urged by Powell to fay as fhe now faith."— *Morfe's Petition.*

[2] The *Lowles* of Newbury were the Anceftors of the *Lowells* of Bofton. The Name was written *Lowle* for feveral Generations after the Emigration, and appears to have been the original Spelling. Benjamin was Son of John Lowle who came to Newbury in 1639, with his Brother Richard. He married Ruth, Daughter of the firft Edward Woodman of Newbury, Oct., 1666. His Teftimony againft Mrs. Morfe has not been preferved, but from the Notice taken of it by Morfe it was doubtlefs as childifh as any of the Reft. Mr. Morfe remarks: — "To Benjamin Lowle about my Boy's [John Stiles] ketching a Pidgin; my Boy defired of me to fee to ketch a Pidgin by throwing a Stone, or ye like, and he brought a Pidgin, which I affirm was wounded, though alive." All we can gather from this is, that the young Rafcal Stiles fuccefsfully played off one of his Tricks upon Lowle, in which a Pigeon was concerned, and which went to fwell the Lift of fupernatural performances of Mrs. Morfe. See *ante,* Pages 141-2, 261.

on Day at Neuberey: and two and Threpens charg coming down. My Expences coming down. At Mr. Perkins fix Pens: and at Capt. Martialls,[1] fix Pence: and 2 Shilings 8 Pens of Mr. Turnor.

William Fannings Bill of Coft.
For Attendance at Newbury before M^r.
Woodbridge . . . . £0—2—6

---

[1] His given Name faid to be Thomas. Long a noted Ordinary or Tavern Keeper. Whatever may have been his given Name, he was, according to the Account given of him by John Dunton, an Officer in the Parliamentary Army in the Time of Charles I, and Cromwell. Dunton may have exaggerated fomewhat in his Notice of the Captain, a Failing from which he was not entirely free. But with a large Allowance for John's Propenfity in that Direction, enough is left to warrant the Belief of the main Facts of his Statement, which I extract entire from his famous *Life and Errors:*

"This Captain Marfhal is a hearty old Gentleman, formerly one of Oliver's Souldiers, upon which he very much values himfelf: He keeps an Inn upon the Road between Bofton and Marblehead: His Houfe was well furnifhed, and we had very good Accommodation. I inquired of the Captain what memorable Actions he had been in under Oliver, and I found I could not have pleafed him better; he was not long in refolving me of the Civil War at his Finger's Ends; and if we may believe him, Oliver did hardly Anything that was confiderable without his Affiftance; for his good Service at the fatal Battel of Nafeby (which gave fuch a Turn to the King's Affairs, that he could never after come to a pitched Battel,) he was made a Captain; from thence he went to Leicefter, and befieged that, then went to York, and afterwards to Marfton-Moor; and in fhort, rambled fo far in his Difcourfe, that if I would have ftayed as long as he would have talked, he would have quite fpoiled my Ramble to Plymouth; and therefore the Captain was forced to leave a great Part of his noble Exploits unrelated."

Some of our Cotemporaries, perhaps to appear wifer than others, fuggeft that Capt. Marfhall may have invented a Tale to amufe his Guefts. The Suggeftion appears to us very weak. Had Dunton been an American, born in New England, the Doubt might have fome Weight; whereas Dunton was more than an ordinary intelligent Englifhman juft from the Theatre of the Civil War, who would at once have detected any Attempt at an Abufe of that Sort. His Inn was probably in the Town of Reading.

For two Daijes coming . . . . £0—4—0
Attending at yᵉ Court one Day . . . . . 0—2—0
For two Daies going Home . . . . . . 0—4—0

James Brownes Expenſes for him ſelf and his Wife:—
For hiring a Horſe to bring downe his Wife £0—5—0
Expenſes at Rowley, my ſelfe, my Wife and
  my Horſe . . . . 0—1—0
Expences at Wennham, myſelfe, my Wife
  and Horſe . . . . 0—0—6
At Capt. Marſhalls . . . . 0—1—0
My Ferridge at Wem̄iſett . . . . . . 0—0—6
Pʳuiſſion and Lodging ſince we came to
  Boſton . . . . 0—2—0
Ferridge backe againe and Horſe Meate 3
  Nights . . . . 0—2—0
My ſelfe and my Wife ſumoned at New-
  bury . . . . 0—3—0
For Attendance vppon yᵉ Service *in toe
  Dayes comin, 2 Dayes Attendin in yᵉ Corte
  toe Dayes goin Hom* . . . . 1—4—0
*This is for comin from Nubery to wittnes a
  ginſt Goody Moſe.*

                                       £1-19—0

[*The part in italic Type is in the Hand of the Witneſs.*]

[*Endorſe (by Rawſon)*] Bills of Coſts for and againſt Elis. Morſe. Keepʳ of Ipſwich Bill, Dauis, Fanning, Knowlton and their Expenſe.

Dauid Whellors Bill of Coſt. On Days Atendans at Neuburey, and two Dayes coming down, and two

Appendix. 291

Days goeing Hom, and on Days Atendans hear at Bofton: I Spent on the Contreys Acoumpt, at Mr. Turnors,¹ fix Pens.

The Bill of Coft for Zacaryah Dauis.
For two Days attending before Mr. John
    Woodbridg . . . . £0—2—6
For two Days coming down . . . . . 0—4—0
For one Days Atendane att Bofton . . . 0—2—0
For two Dayes going Home . . . . . 0—4—0

For John Chafe Bill of Coft.
Two Dayes before Mr. John Woodbridge £0—2—6
For two Dayes coming down . . . . . 0—4—0
For one Dayes atending att Bofton . . 0—2—0
For two Dayes going Home . . . . . 0—4—0

Wᵐ. Chandlers Bill of Coft.
In pʳmis: for Attendance at Newbury be-
    fore Mr. John Woodbridge two Daijes £0—2—6
For two Daijes coming, a Day Attendance
    at Bofton . . . . 0—6—0
For two Daijes going Whome . . . . 0—4—0

I haue pᵈ moft of my Expences by yᵉ Way, in Mony out of my Pockett: I am aged, and came on Foot, wᶜʰ is verry hard for my aged Body to beare, therfore I hope this honnored Court will confider me for my Paines and hard Trauell.

---

¹ "Turners" was a popular Inn at that Time, and was known as the Blue Anchor Tavern. Within a Space of a few Years previous to 1681 it was kept by Robert and John Turner (Father and Son) and by George Monck. It was in what is now Wafhington Street, and on what is now Number 92, or on the Lot next foutherly of it.

Joseph Bayles Bill of Coſt.[1]
In pʳmis. 2 Daijes before Mr. Woodbridge £0—2—6
For two Daijes coming, 1 Day attending,
   and 2 Daijes going Home . . . . . 0—10—0
For my Expences coming, and att Boſton,
   Mony, ... 0—6—0
   Which I hope yᵉ honnored Court will confider of that I may haue thee Mony againe wᶜʰ I haue layd out of my owne Pockett.

   Boſton, 1680. This is to certify that by Order of oʳ Honʳᵈ Gouernour vnto Andrew Neale for the Entertainmᵗ and Dyet of fix of us that dwel at Nubury, as Teſtimonys agſt Elizabeth Moſs, ſhe being apʳhended vpon Suſpicion of Witch Craft, and being upon the Countryes Account, the faid Andrew Neale hath entertayned us with Dyet and Lodging, from the 19th of May to the 21ſt Day: our Names being
        John Glading,
        William Fanin,
        John Chafe,
        Zachary Davis,
        Benjamin Richardfon and
        William Card.
   Each of us 6 Meals, is 36 Meales, and our Lodging, and amounts to twenty Shillings as Money.

   [*Endorfed by Secʸ. Rawfon,*]—"Andrew Neales Account. A Warrant."

---

[1] Whatever Baylef's Teſtimony was, it does not appear to have been preſerved, and Morfe does not notice it. According to Coffin this Jofeph *Bailey* was Grandfon of the Emigrant John Bailey, who came from Chippenham, in Wiltſhire, England, to New England in 1635. Jofeph fettled in Arundel, Maine, about 1700; being driven thence in 1703 by the Indians, returned there in 1714. In October, 1723, he was killed by them, being then 75 Years old. He had a large Family of Children, a Record of which is given by Coffin.

Appendix. 293

We only know what John Glading fwore to by the Anfwer of Mr. Morfe in his Petition:—"To John Glading y^t faw Halfe of my Wife, about two a Clocke in the Daye Time; if fo, might [not he] then have fpoken, and not referved for fo long a Time; which fhe utterly denies it, nor know of any fuch Thing, where fhe fhould be at y^t Time as to clere her felf." Although a Dweller at *Nubury*, and mentioned by Coffin among the Witneffes, his Name is not found in the Lift of the Inhabitants by that Author.

Zachary Davif's Teftimony is given in Coffin's *Newbury*. It amounts to this. When faid Davis lived at Salifbury, he promifed from Time to Time to bring "a fmall Paffell of Winges" to Mrs. Morfe. He came over three or four Times without bringing the Wings, through Forgetfulnefs; and was yet reminded of his Promife by Mrs. Morfe every Time. "Soe fhe tel me fhe wonder my Memory fhould be foe bad; but when I came Home I went to the Barne, and there was three Cafes in a Pen. One of them fell a danceing and roreing, and was in fuch a Condition as I neuer faw on Cafe in before. But [it] being almoft Night the Cattle came Home and we put him to his Dam and he fucke and was well three or four Dayes. On of them was my Brothers. Then [he] came over to Nubery, but we did not think to fend the Winges. When he came Home I went to the Barne, this Cafe fel a danceing and roreing. So wee put him to the Cowe, but he would not fucke, but rane a roreing away, foe wee gate him againe with much Adoe, and put him into the Barne; and we heard him roer feuerall Times in the Night; and in the Morning I went to the Barne, and there he was feting upon his Taile like a Doge, and I neuer fee no Cafe fet after that Manner before; and fo he remained in thefe Fits while he died."

Morſe's Explanation is quite ſatisfactory and to the Point:—"To Zachariah Davis. To cenſure my Wife now for not bringing Quills about 16 Years agoe; y^t his Loſs of Calfes was for that, when his Father being in Communion with us, did profeſs it to us, yt, he judged it a Hand of God, and was farr from blaming us, but rather troubled [that] his Sonn ſhould ſo judge."

Beniamanrichiſin Bill of Coſt.
For Attendance at Neubry, before M^r. Woodbridge, ... £0—2—6
For too Dayes coming . . . . 0—4—0
Attending at ye Court one Day . . . . 0—2—0
For two Daies goin Home . . . . . 0—4—0

Caleb Moodys Bill of Coſt for atending at Nubery, my ſelf and Mrs. Gordinge, 2 Dayſe before Mr. Wodbridge, . . . £0—3—0
For Hoſs Hier in Monye . . . . . . 0—5—0
Expenſes at Rowly for Mrs. Gording My ſelf and Horſe . . . . 0—1—0
At Wenhome . . . . 0—0—6
At Capt. Morſhels . . . . 0—0—6
Ferige at Winaſimet . . . . 0—0—6
For Expenſes at Boſtone 3 Nits . . . . 0—3—0
For Time coming dovne, atending and going Home, 5 Dayſe . . . . . . 1—0—0
For my Hors at Wineſemet . . . . . 0—1—6
For Expenſes to carye uſe Whome . . . 0—2—0

£0—17—0

The Bill of Coft of Peniwell Titcumbs Euedens[1] againſt Elizebeth Morſe.

For atending at Nubery before Mr. Wodbridge, 1 Daye	£0—1—6
For 2 Dayſe coming doune	0—4—0
For 1 Daye tending the Cort	0—2—0
For 2 Days to goe Home	0—4—0
Reſeued of the Contrys Acovnt At Quarter Maſter Perkenſes	£0—0—6
At Capt. Marſhals	0—0—6
Expenſes at Mr. *Lorens?*	0—2—8

The Bill of Coft of John Mortch, Witneſs againſt Elizebth Morſe:—

On Daye at Nubery befor Mr. Wodbredge	£0—1—6
For fiue Dayſe coming doune and atending one to goe Home	0-10—0

21st 3mo 1680.

The Bill of John Glading.

A Day for atending before Mr. Woodbridge	£0—2—0
For to Days couming downe	0—4—0
A Day at Boſton	0—2—0
To Days to goe Whom	0—4—0

Joſhua Richardſon Bill of Coſt.

For Attendance at Home before M^r. Jno. Woodbridge to Dayes	£0—2—6

[1] As no ſeparate Evidence is found of Penuel Titcomb, it was no Doubt for that of his Mother and Siſter that theſe Charges were made.

For 2 Daijes coming, a Day attending ye Court, and 2 Daijes going . . . . . 0—10—0
For Expences vppon ye Rode and my Ferridge . . . . 0—2—10

All that I spent on ye Countys a Count as I cam doun wos six Pens, at quar Mr Pirkins. At Capt. Masshals six Pens.

[*The part in Italics in the Hand of the Witness, probably.*]

William Card Bill of Cost.
For Attendance at Nebury, before M^r. Woodbridge . . . . £0—2—6
For two Dayes comming . . . . . . 0—4—0
Attending at ye Court one Day . . . . 0—2—0
For two Daies goin Home . . . . . 0—4—0

[No Intimation of what William Card's Testimony was is found.]

Thus is concluded all the Documents concerning the Trial of Mrs. Elizabeth Morse in the Editor's Possession; showing the Origin of the lamentable Affair from its Commencement to the Bills of Costs of the Witnesses. To characterize the Proceedings, further than has been done in the Progress of printing the Documents occasioned by them, would be a superfluous Labor, and they are therefore submitted without further Remark.

FINIS.

ERRATA.—Page 65, Note, make 1661, 1651. Page 95, line 12, for Godwin, read Godman.

INDEX.

Names are spelt according to their present Manner, generally, in this Index. To have followed that of the Documents used in the Work would have much increased it, as the Names of the same Person are often spelt several Ways; often beginning with a different Letter.

ADAMS, N., Annals of Portsmouth, 106.
Addison, Joseph, xxviii.
Addington, Isaac, 148, 286.
Age of Reason, alas for the, xlviii.
Albany, Witchcraft in, 208.
Allen, Bouzoun, Constable, 273.
Andover, Witchcraft in, 87, 113, 206.
Antagonism, a Warfare between Reason and Superstition, xviii; what it is, xix.
Apparitions, xxiv, xlii, 132.
Aquendero, Indian Chief, 208.
Ashcom, Charles, 172.
Ashley, Mary, 234, 239, 242; Robert, ib.
Ashwood, John, Captain, 89.
Atheists, Unbelievers in Witchcraft, xxix.
Atherton, Humphrey, 98.
Atwater, Mrs., 89, 90, 95; Mr. David, 92.

BACK-BAY, Boston Churches in, xiv.
Bacon, Francis, believed in Witchcraft, xxviii.
Bacon, Leonard, Discourses of, xxxii.

Bailey, Joseph, 271-2; Family of, 292.
Baldwin, Goodwife, 82.
Ballard, Joseph, 206.
Banks, John, an early Lawyer, 78.
Bard of Lynn (Lewis) xliii-vi.
Barlow, Goodwife, 83.
Bartholomew, William, 75.
Bartlett, Joseph, 139; Mary, 134; Samuel, 140.
Barton, Bernard, Extract from, xxiii; Eliza, 106; Elizabeth, 133.
Basset, Goodwife, Trial of, 73-4, 85.
Baxter, Richard, on Witchcraft, xi, xii.
Beale, William, bewitched, 205.
Beaman, Robert, 174; Simon, 220, 254-5.
Bedell, Robert, 285.
Bellamont, Richard, (Earl) 208-10.
Bellingham, Richard, 98, 107.
Bentley, William, on Witchcraft, 98.
Benton, Andrew, 123; G., ib.
Besse, Joseph, Sufferings of the Quakers, 107, 119.
Bible, Witches explained out of, xl.

298   Index.

Bishop, Bridget, executed, 191; George, 107, 108, 119; Mrs., 89.
Blacke, John, Juror, 139.
Blackstone, William (Sir), xxviii.
Blue Anchor Tavern, Boston, 291.
Bodorthe, Blanche, 224-7, 239; Rice, 220.
Body of Liberties, 56.
Booth, Elizabeth, 189, 204; James, 51.
Boston, Churches in a Quagmire, xiv; Witchcraft in, 58-61, 98, 107, 180-5; bloody Town of, 119; an Army of Devils in, 61.
Boutle, Henry, a Witness, 93.
Bradbury, Judith, 263.
Bradshaw, Sarah, 125.
Bradstreet, John, a Magician, 74-5.
Bradstreet, Simon, 87, 98, 113-14, 140, 145, 147, 170.
Branch, William, 254, 256-7.
Brasbridge, Rachel, 155.
Brewster, Eliz., 80; Mary, 81, 85, 95.
Bridges, Robert, of Boston, 98.
Bridgman, Goodman, 254.
Brinley, John, on Witchcraft, xv.
Brooks, William, a Witness, 253.
Broughton, Brian (Sir), xv.
Browne, William, Assistant, 145; James, 271, 284-5, 290.
Brundish, Bethia, a Witness, 83.
Bryan, Alex^r., a Lawyer, 78.
Buckley, Gershom, 86; Peter, 145.
Buff —— (Barefoote W.?), 153.
Burnham, Thomas, a Witness, 223.
Burnings for Witchcraft, 124-5, 215.
Burroughs, B., 210; George, executed, 191.
Burt, Abigail, 224; Jonathan, 237-8.
Burton, Robert, on Witchcraft, xxviii.
Butler, S., References to and Extracts from his Hudibras, xxxvii, 68, 123-4, 160.

CABEL, Sarah, 83.
Calef, Robert, xv, 181.
Capen, John, Juror, 145, 275.
Card, William, 271, 292, 296.
Carrier, Martha, executed, 192.
Carrington, John, 233.
Case, Thomas, bewitches Quakers, 158.
Chandler, William, 271, 275, 291.
Chapman, Henry, 210-11.
Charles Second, xxxi.
Chase, John, 271-2, 280-1, 291-2.
Chauncy, C., his Enthusiasticus, 159.
Child, Richard, Juror, 145, 274.
Christeson, Wenlock, 119.
Churchill, Sarah, in a Witch Circle, 189.
Clarke, John, Constable, 274; William, Juror, 169.
Clausen, Elizabeth, immersed, 187.
Clinton, Lawrence, 200; Rachel, ib.
Cloyse, Sarah, 194.
Coffin, J., cited, 143, 145, 148-9.
Cole, Ann, 120-2; Eunice, 100-3; William, 100.
Collins, Zacheus, of Lynn, 205.
Colman, Thomas, molested, 102.
Colton, George, a Witness, 229, 236-9.
Colve, Anthony, Captain, 134.
Cooke, Aaron, a Juror, 169.
Coolin, Annakey, 172.
Cooly, Benj., a Witness, 238-41, 254; Mrs., 257.
Cooper, Thomas, 222-3, 244; Goodman, 252.
Cornish, John, 210-11.
Corwin, Jonathan (Judge), 190.

Index. 299

Cory, Giles, preſſed to Death, 192-4; Martha, hanged, 194.
Cotton, John, Laws of, 97.
Coulter, Goodwife, 152.
Coutch, Robert, 107.
Cranch, Andrew, John, &c., 151.
Cudworth, Ralph, a Believer, xxviii.
Cullender, Roſe, executed, 124.
Cullick, John, 63.
Cuſhin, Jeremiah, Juror, 145, 273.

DALTON, SAMUEL, Councillor, 151-2.
Dane, Francis, 115-16; John, *ib.*; Nathan, 115.
Danforth, Mrs., a Witch, lii; Thomas, 145, 170.
Daſten, Goodwife, accuſed, 205.
Davenport, John, 77, 78, 89.
Davis, Zacheriah, 271-2, 291-2.
Davy, Humphrey, Councillor, 145.
Day, Phebe, 200; Timothy, *ib.*
Dean, John Ward, cited, 115.
Deane, S., Hiſt. Scituate, 117.
Decanniſſora, Onondaga Chief, 209.
Defoe, Daniel, cited, xxvi, 180.
Demagogue, a contemptible one, xxv.
Demoniacs, tortured by the Devil, xli.
Denham, Elizabeth, a Witneſs, 151.
Deniſon, Daniel, 98, 136, 145.
Derbond, Henry, Juror, 151.
Deſborough, Mercy, tried, 186; Nicholas, moleſted, 166; Thomas, 186.
Devil, may do Miſchief without a Witch or Wizard, xvi; Origin of the, xxi; cauſes Earthquakes, Thunder and Lightning, &c., xxii; his Agency overlooked by Writers, xxxii; explained out of the New Teſtament, xxxvi, xl; appears to M. Luther, xxxvii; tortures Demoniacs, xli; Leagues with, limited, li; Converſe with, forbid by Law, 56; an Army of Devils in Boſton, 61; he performs menial Service for a Woman, 62; ſcares Hogs, 63; appears at Springfield, 67; one fined and whipt for having Familiarity with, 74; among the Women at New Haven, 75; hovering in the Air, 88; Subjects for, *ib.*; of the Indians, 90; at Hampton, 100; an Attempt to cheat him, 108; in C. Southwick, 109; makes a Woman ſpeak Dutch, 120; Hudibras on, 123; gives a Woman ten Shillings, for which ſhe is burnt to Death, 124; at Groton, 131-2; Blaſphemes, 132; Indians forbid to worſhip, 137; at Newbury, 143; inſtigates Arguments, 148; Contracts with a Hampton Man, 156; ſadly ſwindled, 157; viſits Plymouth, 158; bites a Woman, 160-1; throws down Log Fence, 162; throws Stones, 163; ſteals Axes, 164; at Hartford throwing Stones and Corn Cobs, 166; on the Side of Juſtice, 167; in Mary Webſter, 168; triumphs with C. Mather, 179; deſerts a Woman, 184; cannot aſſume the Shape of an innocent Perſon, 201-2; performs Baptiſm, 207; cannot be ſummoned, 208; in South Carolina, 215; at Springfield, 244; meets his Witches, 245; in the Hogs, 263; at Newbury, 266-7.
Dictionaries, none early, xxvii.
Dike, Richard, 201; Rebeckah, *ib.*
Dinſon, Rachel, Widow, 200.
Dole, John, 260; Benjamin, *ib.*

Dorchester, Anthony, 230-2, 236-8, 241.
Downing, Mehitable, released, 200.
Drake, Abraham, 102 ; Juror, 151.
Drake, Robert, of Hampton, 102.
Drake, S G., Witchcraft Delusion, xii, xxvi, lii ; Founders of New England, 61, 116, 282 ; History of Boston, 61, 98, 131.
Drystreet, Henry, 171.
Ducking to determine Witchcraft, 122, 180, 186, 211-15.
Dudley, Joseph, Councillor, 145.
Dummer, Stephen, 281.
Dunen, Jonathan, 158.
Dunton, John, Extract from, 289.
Duny, Ann, burnt for a Witch, 124.
Dwight, Timothy, cited, xxxi.

EARLE, ROBERT, Deposition, 268-9.
Earthquakes, caused by the Devil, xxii.
Easthampton, Witchcraft in, 110.
Easty, Mary, executed, 194.
Eaton, Theophilus, 95.
Edwards, Alexander, 229-30.
Elkins, Gershom, Juror, 151.
Elwell, Samuel, Wife imprisoned, 201.
Endicott, John, 98, 109-10.
English, Philip, Indictment of, 203 ; imprisoned, 204.
Erasmus, Desiderius, cited, xxxvi.
Evans, Mrs., 106 ; Benjamin, 152.
Evil, Origin of, xxiv.
Evils, when not Evils, xxi.

FAIRFIELD, Witchcraft in, 79, 83-4.
Fanning, William, 265-7, 271-2, 289, 292.
Felt, Joseph B., Hist. of Ipswich, 74.

Fenn, Benjamin, Magistrate, 95.
Fernald, Renald, Magistrate, 104.
Filmer, Robert, Sir, on Witchcraft, xv, 208.
Fortune-telling, Witchcraft, xlii.
Foster, John, Juror, 139 ; James, Constable, 275.
Fowler, William, Magistrate, 83.
Fuller, John, Wife accused, 150-6.

GARLICKE, Mrs., accused, 110-12 ; Joseph, 111.
Gardner, Lion, 111-12.
Gedney, Bartholomew, 145.
George the First (King), 125.
Ghosts, akin to Witches, xxiv ; Progenitors of, xlii ; seen near the Metropolis, xlii ; in the Metropolis, xliii ; at Fort Warren, xliv.
Glading, John, 271, 292-3, 295.
Glover, Mrs , executed at Boston, 181-5.
Godfrey, John. 87 ; Children bewitched, 150-4, 113-16.
Godman, Elizabeth, 88, 90-5.
Good, Sarah, accused, 190 ; executed, 196.
Gookin, Daniel, 98, 136, 145.
Goodwin, John, Case of his Children, 180-5 ; Susanna, 271-2, 288.
Goodyear, Stephen, 89, 91, 97.
Goodinge, Mrs., a Witness, 294.
Gould, Mrs., an Accuser, 82-3 ; Hannah F., cited, 149-50.
Green, John, Juror, 145, 274.
Greenleafe, Daniel, 259, 283.
Greensmith, Mrs., executed, 121 ; Nathaniel, 119, 121, 123.

HADLEY, Witchcraft in, 174-8.
Haines, Jonathan, 271-2, 285.

Index. 301

Hale, Matthew (Sir), xi-xiii, xxviii, 124.
Hall, Cornelius, 82 ; Mary, 126-7; Ralph, 126 ; Rebeckah, 82.
Hall, John, 265 6.
Ham, old, Negro, 107.
Hampton, Witchcraft in, 99, 103, 150.
Hancock, George, 210-11.
Harper, John, 212.
Harrifon, Katherine, a Witch, 129.
Harrod, Thomas, Juror, 273.
Harwood, Thomas, Juror, 145.
Hafkins, Thomas, Juror, 138.
Haftings, Thomas, Juror, 140.
Hathorne, John, Judge, 190.
Haunted Houfe, one vifited, xlii.
Hayman, Nathan, Juror, 145, 272.
Haynes, Edmund, 219 ; John, 73 ; Jofeph, 121.
Herman, Goodman, 221.
Hibbins, Anne, 98 ; executed, 99.
Hill, Luke, molefted, 210-11.
Hilton, Hannah, 259.
Hinman, R. R., cited, 74.
Hollifter, Geo. H., cited, 86.
Holmes, William, Juror, 117.
Hooke, William, 89, 91-3, 96.
Hooker, Samuel, Magiftrate, 121.
Hooper, Madam, Fortune-teller, xlix-lii.
Hopkins, Matthew, 60, 123-4.
Hortado, Antonio, 159-60.
Howe, Elizabeth, executed, 196.
Howland, John, Juror, 139.
Hudibras, extracted. See BUTLER, S.
Hudfon, Alice, burnt for a Witch, 124.
Huen, Jacob, Juror, 145, 275.
Hull, John, Affiftant, 145.
Hutchinfon, Edward, 69 ; Francis, 123-4 ; Thomas, xxxiii, 99, 119, 133, 190.

IGNORANCE, the Parent of Superftition, xvi, xxx.
Indians, God of the, 79, 80, 82 ; Devil of the, 90 ; a Child of, 112 ; Witchcraft, 136, 208-10 ; none at the Vineyard, 139 ; in Advance of the Englifh, 140 ; fome at Albany, 209 ; forbid to powow, 137.
Ingham, Mary, accufed, 137.
Innocent, viii, Pope, xxix.

JACKSON, A., on counterfeit Money, xviii ; Abraham, 139.
Jacobs, George, 189; executed, 196 ; Margaret, ib.
James the Firft, his Demonology, xxvi ; recommended throwing accufed Perfons into the Water, 123.
Johnfon, Elizabeth, accufed, 205 ; Mary, confeffed Familiarity with the Devil, 62 ; executed, ib.; Samuel, a believer in Witchcraft, xxviii ; Thomas, 89, 97.
Jones, Griffin, 232, 251 ; Margaret, executed, 58-61 ; Miftres, 79, 80, 85 ; Mary, 128 ; Mr., 60-1, 82.
Judd, Sylvefter, cited, 65, 127, 129-30, 134, 136.

KINGSBURY, SUSANNA, marriage of, 270.
Knap, Elizabeth, bewitched, 131.
Knapp, Mrs., Trial and Execution, 77-86 ; Samuel L., Extract from, xlviii.
Knight, John, Juror, 145, 272.
Knowlton, Thomas, Jailor, 144, 280, 290.

LACY, EDWARD, Accufation againft, 165.
Lamberton, Elizabeth, 89, 91.

Lankton, George, 219; Hannah, 220-1, 248-9.
Lardner, Nathaniel, xxxvi, xl.
Larremore, Goodwife, 89, 90.
Laws againſt Witchcraft, xxvi, 55-7, 97; againſt Powowing, 137.
Leet, William, 89, 95.
Leonard, Sarah, a Witneſs, 239.
Leverett, John, Governor, 136.
Levet, Aratus, 151; Thomas, *ib.*
Levit, Hazen, a Witneſs, 155.
Lewis, Alonzo, Extract from, xliii-vi; Mercy, 189, 205.
Littleton, Witchcraft in, 216.
Lockwood, Deborah, 82; Mrs., 80; Suſan, 82.
Lowle, Benjamin, 271-2; Family, *ib.*, 288.
Ludlow, Roger, 77, 82, 86.
Lumbard, John, 221, 243, 250.
Luther, Martin, Encounter with the Devil, xxxvii.
Lux, Chriſtopher, 151.
Lyon, Richard, 84.
Lynn, Witchcraft in, 205.

MAGIC, Book of, 75.
March, John, 282; Family, *ib.*, 284, 295.
Marſhall, Abiſhag, 151; Thomas, 289-90, 295-9.
Marſhfield, Mrs., 71, 226, 244; Samuel, 225, 250-2; Sarah, 250-1; Thomas, 222.
Marſton, Thomas, Juror, 151; William, *ib.*
Martin, Suſannah, proſecuted, 128-9; executed, 196.
Maſon, John, at Saybrook, 112.
Mather, Cotton, on Witchcraft, xi, xiii, xxii; on Witchcraft in Europe, xxxiii; Extract from, 57, 61; on "an Army of Devils," *ib.*; on Moleſtations, 75-6; equal-

led, 143; "Triumph with the Devil," 179; Diſcovers the Devil in an old Woman, 184; ſhuffles out in a Miſt, 201.
Mather, Increaſe, on Witchcraft, xi; Extracts from, xxxvii, 76, 122, 132, 165-6, 186.
Mathews, John, a Witneſs, 228, 244, 254; Pentcoſt, killed, 228.
Matſon, Margaret, a Witch, 171-2; Neels, 173.
Merrick, 231; Thomas, 244; Mrs., 245-6.
Middlecott, Richard, a Juror, 145, 273.
Mighell, John, Evidence, 267-8, 271-2.
Miles, Mary, 89, 95.
Millennium, Calculators of, eſtimated, xxxv; Humbug, xxxvi.
Miller, Thomas, a Witneſs, 222, 251; Sarah, bewitched, 252; William, xxxv.
Mirack, Margaret, a Witneſs, 287.
Miracles, diminiſh in Number, xxiii; all things Miracles, xxiv.
Moody, Caleb, 263, 265, 271, 294; Joſhua, a Witneſs, 165; William, 276.
Morgan, Miles, 251; Prudence, 251-2.
Morſe, Abner, reference to, 148; Elizabeth, proſecuted, 144; impriſoned and ſentenced to be hung, 145; John, 274; William, moleſted, 141; a Proſecutor, 143; Petition of, 147; his Reſidence, 149; Trial, &c., 258-296.
Moſely, Edward, Col., 210-11.
Moulton, Jonathan, Gen., makes a League with the Devil, 156; ſwindles him out of a vaſt Sum of Money, 156-7.
Moxon, George, Rev., Children

Index. 303

bewitched, 65, 71, 228; a Witness, 228, 235, 250, 253.
Mun, Abigail, a Witness, 224, 232; Goodman, 223.
Myftery, how folved, xxii; Love of, xxiii; all things Myfteries, xxiv, xxxix.

NEALE, ANDREW, Innkeeper, 292.
Necromancers, contract with the Devil, xvi.
Neelfon, Anthony, 173.
Newhall and Lewis, Hiftory of Lynn, xlvii.
New Haven, Witchcraft in, xxvi, 75, 77.
Newman, Francis, 89, 95.
Newton, Ifaac (Sir), fuperftitious, xxviii.
Nicolls, Richard (Governor), 125.
Nolton. — See KNOWLTON.
Northampton, Witchcraft in, 134.
Nourfe, Rebecca, 194; executed, 197.
Noyes, Nicholas, 195; "Firebrands of Hell," 196; Election Sermon, 198, 285.

ODEL, Goodwife, 80, 81, 84.
Oliver, Mary, executed, 64.
Ordway, Ann, 272; James, *ib.*, 263, 287; John, 263, 271.
Original Sin, xxiv.
Ofborn, Ruth, 180; Sarah, 190.
Oyfter Bay, Witchcraft in, 117.

PANTON, RICHARD, 131.
Parat, Francis, a Witnefs, 75.
Paris, Samuel, Rev., 190.
Parker, Alice, hanged, 197-8; John, 198; Mary, hanged, *ib.*
Parfons, Hugh, accufed of Witchcraft, 66; indicted, 68; profecuted for Libel, 71-2; Examination of, 119; bewitched a Pudding, *ib.*, 222; whets Saws in the Night, 223; threatening Speeches, 224; makes a Light in a Woman's Chamber, 225; tortures her in Bed, 226; appears as a Dog, 227; bewitched Moxon's Children, 228; a Brick-maker, *ib.*; caufes a Girl to have Fits, *ib.*; dries up a Cow, 229-30; fpirits away a Neat's Tongue, 230-32; abducts a Knife without Hands, 233; bewitched his Child, 235; dreamed of a Fight with the Devil, 240; accufed by his Wife, 239-43; bewitched a Trowel, 243; a Beer Barrel, 246; fends Snakes to one, 247; another Pudding bewitched, 249; bewitched Sarah Miller, 252; Goody Stebbing, 253; frightens Horfes, 255; bewitches Bags of Meal, 255; alfo William Branch, 256.
Parfons, John, accufed, 136, 140.
Parfons, Jofeph, 134; Mary his Wife profecuted, 134; pleads her own Caufe, 135-6.
Parfons, Mary, Wife of Hugh Parfons, 66-68; accufes her Hufband of Witchcraft, 222; Reafon why, 233-5, 239-40, 243, 251.
Partrigg, Samuel, Clerk, 169.
Payne, George, of Great Ifland, 151; Robert, Juror, 204.
Pearfon, George, 151.
Pell, Thomas, 79, 80, 84, 85.
Pendleton, Bryan, 104.
Penn, William, Judge, 171, 172.
Pepper, Francis, a Witnefs, 242, 251.
Perkins, Abraham, Juror, 151; John, 289, 295-6; William, Authority on Witchcraft, xi.

Index.

Pharao, old, Negro Slave, 205.
Phips, William, Sir, discharges Prisoners, 191.
Philadelphia, Witchcraft in, 173.
Philip, King, his War, 137.
Pike, Joseph, Constable, 269-70; Family, *ib.*, 272.
Pitcher, Mary, History of, xlv-viii.
Plymouth Colony, infested, 56, 158.
Pope, Alexander, Extract, xxiii.
Pope, Seth, Juror, 139.
Portsmouth, Witchcraft in, 103.
Powell, Caleb, 142, 143, 280, 285.
Powowing, Law made against, 137.
Pratt, Benijah, Juror, 139.
Prescott, Mrs., a Witch, 152.
Pritchard, Joanna, 221; Roger, 249.
Prime's Hist. Long Island, 110-12.
Procter, John, 189; executed, 198.
Prophets in all Periods, xxxv.
Pudeater, Ann, executed, 198.
Pudding, one bewitched, 219-22; another, 248-9.
Puddington, Agnes, John, Witnesses, 106.
Puritans, much abused, xxxi; unjustly reproached, *ib.*; by a Western Bishop, xxxiv.
Putnam, Ann, Thomas, 189.
Pynchon, John, 70, 145, 169.
Pynchon, William, 65, 76; his Record of Proceedings against Hugh Parsons, 219-258.

QUAKER POET, in Error, xlii, xliii.
Quakers accused of Witchcraft, 107-10; a Crime to be a Quaker, 118, 158.

RAWSON, Edward, 88, 98, 103, 109, 146, 232, 254-56.
Randall, Mary, 185; William, 186.
Redman, John, a Witness, 103.

Reed, Doctor, 152; Willmot, executed, 198-9.
Rhode Island, Witchcraft in, 217.
Richards, John, 145, 203, 211.
Richardson, Benjamin, Testimony, 26, 271-2, 292, 294; Joshua, 262, 271-2.
Richmond, John, a Juror, 139.
Robins, Richard, Juror, 145, 274.
Roby, Goodman, 103; Henry, Juror, 151-2.
Rogers, Ann, died of Witchcraft, 126.
Rolfe, Daniel, 278.
Ross, David, Judge, 125; Mary, possessed, 158.
Rowe, Elizabeth, 106; Nicholas, 106; Phebe, 200; Hugh, 201.
Rowley, Witchcraft in, 74.
Russell, James, a Juror, 145.
Ryall, Joseph, Constable, 272.

SAINT Dunstan Church, xiv.
Salem, unduly reproached, ix, xxx; Witchcraft in, 187-208.
Salter, William, Prison-keeper, 101.
Saltonstall, Nathaniel, 145; Richard, *ib.*
Sanborn, John, Juror, 151.
Saunderling, James, 172.
Savage, James, Perversity, 76; cited, 111, 151, 167; "the Devil and Cotton Mather," 179; Opinion of the Judges, 208, 272, 285.
Savage, Thomas, Councillor, 145.
Saybrook, Witchcraft in, 112.
Scituate, Witchcraft in, 116, 137.
Scott, Margaret, executed, 199.
Searl, Joanna, 224; John, 229.
Seger, Elizabeth, Trial, 127.
Sewell, Besse, 245, 249; Jane, 281; Thomas, 221.
Sewall's History of the Quakers, 118.

Index. 305

Sheldon, Susannah, 189.
Sherburn, Henry, 104 ; Samuel, 260.
Sherwood, Mrs., 79, 84 ; Grace, Proceedings againſt for Witchcraft, 210-15.
Simcook, John, 172.
Smith, Henry, 242, 243, 256.
Smith, John, a Juror, 151 ; Mrs., 240.
Smith, Nathaniel, a Witneſs, 152.
Smith, Philip, bewitched, 169, 174, 176-7 ; William, 211.
Snow, Mark, a Juror, 139.
Soames, Abigail, impriſoned, 201.
Southampton, Witchcraft in, 165.
South Carolina, Witchcraft in, 215.
Southwick, Caſſandra, 108-10.
Spafford, H. G., Gazetteer, cited, 127.
Spencer, Edmund, extract, lii.
Spirit Rappings, xxxviii ; a Colony of S. Rappers, xxxix, xlii, xlviii.
Spiritualiſm, Divination, xli.
Sprat, Henry, a Juror, 211.
Springfield, Witchcraft in, 64-72, 185.
Squire, Goodwife, a Witneſs, 84.
Staplies, Thomas, his Wife accuſed, 77-85.
Stebbings, John, 140, 245, 252-3.
Stiles, John, 141 ; Miſcreant, 142, 261, 271, 288.
Stone, John, Juror, 145 ; Samuel, 63, 120.
Stoughton, William, 145, 208.
Stratford, Witchcraft in, 72, 74.
Superſtition, debaſing, ix ; Emblems of, xv, xvii ; at War with Reaſon, xviii ; Fetters to Mankind, xxiii ; a Millennium Humbug, xxxvi.
Sylveſter, Dinah, 117.
Symonds, Samuel, 98.

TABLE TURNING, a branch of Witchcraft, xlii.
Talbot, Gerud, 139.
Talcott, Captain, 123.
Tappin, Suſanna, 277.
Taylor, Anthony, 151 ; Jonathan, 70, 232, 240, 245, 248, 253-4, 257.
Thompſon, B. F., Hiſtory of Long Iſland, 111, 117 ; John, 84.
Thorrowgood, Major, 211.
Thorpe, Goodman, 89.
Thurſton, Daniel, a Witneſs, 284.
Titcomb, Elizabeth, 271, 277-9 ; Lydia, 278 ; Penuil, 272, 292.
Towle, Mrs., 151 ; Iſabella, 156.
Tilton, Peter, 169, 170.
Time, Indian Squaw Servant, 92.
Titcomb, Elizabeth, Witneſs, 258 ; Peniel, 259.
Tituba, Indian Servant impriſoned, 190.
Tomſon, Attorney General, 211.
Travelly, Thomas, 165.
Trimmings, Oliver, 105 ; Suſannah, 104.
Trumbull's Col. Records, 111, 112.
Turpin, Thomas, 107.
Turell, Ebenezer, 216-17.
Turnor, John, Innkeeper, 288-9.
Tyler, Job, 87-8, 113-14.
Tyng, Edward, 145.

UPHAM, C. W., cited, 74, 198, 200.

WADSWORTH, JOHN, 138.
Wait, John, Juror, 145, 273.
Walford, Thomas, 103 ; Mrs., 103-7.
Walch, Machael, 259.
Walcut, John, 189 ; Mary, 182, 204.

Oo

Index.

Waldron, Richard, 101.
Walton, George, 162-5.
Ward, Andrew, 79, 85.
Wardwell, Samuel, executed, 199.
Warren, Mary, afflicted, 189.
Warrener, William, 224.
Watson's Annals of New York, 126-7.
Waye, Richard, Juror, 145, 273.
Webster, Israel, 288.
Webster, Mary, 168-71, 174.
Wells, John, 282-4; Thomas, 281.
Westchester, Witchcraft in, 133.
Western Bishop, Sneers of one, xxxiv.
Wheeler, David, Testimony, 261, 272, 286; George, 284.
Whiting, John, 121, 122.
Whitlocke, Goodwife, 83.
Whitnels, Jeremy, 89, 90.
Whittier, John G., 107-10, 118, 158.
Wiggin, Thomas, 98, 287.
Wigglesworth, Michael, 203.
Willard, John, executed, 199; Samuel, 131-2; Simon, 98.
Wildes, Sarah, executed, 199.
Williams, Abigail, 189.
Willis. See WYLLYS.
Willson, Esther, a Witness, 275.
Winslow, Josiah, 137; Nathaniel, 129.

Winthrop, John, 57, 59.
Wife, Sarah, marriage of, 286.
Wiseman, Elizabeth, 261.
Witch Books, xi-xvi, 174, 189.
Witch Circles, 189.
Witchcraft, Cases of, in N. Eng., similar to those in Old Eng., vi, viii; the World never free from, xxx; among Indians, 136-7, 208.
Witch-finders, 60.
Witch Teats discovered, 80, 214.
Wonders of the Invisible World, 128.
Wood, George, bewitched, 126; Silas, Hist. of L. I., 110.
Woodbridge, John, Commissioner, 144, 259.
Woodhouse, Horatio, 211.
Woodman, Edward, 288; Jonathan, Deposition, 259-60, 271-2.
Woodworth, Mehittable, 137-8.
Woolworth, Richard, a Witness, 284.
Wright, Hannah, 119; Mary, 117-19t Samuel, 225.
Wyllys, George, 112-13; Samuel, 112, 123.

YANKEES, flurred by a Western Bishop, xxxiv.
Yates's Smith's New York, 127.